Linking Human Rights and the Environment

Romina Picolotti AND Jorge Daniel Taillant EDITORS

Linking HUMAN RIGHTS and the ENVIRONMENT

THE UNIVERSITY OF ARIZONA PRESS • TUCSON, ARIZONA

The University of Arizona Press

www.uapress.arizona.edu

First paperback printing 2010
ISBN 978-0-8165-2934-6 (pbk. : alk. paper)

Library of Congress Cataloging-in-Publication Data

Linking human rights and the environment / Romina Picolotti and Jorge Daniel Taillant, editors.
p. cm.
Includes bibliographical references.
ISBN 0-8165-2261-8 (cloth : acid-free paper)
1. Environmental law. 2. Human rights. I. Title: Linking human rights and the environment.
II. Picolotti, Romina, 1970– III. Taillant, Jorge Daniel, 1968–
K3585.L56 2003
341.7'62—dc21 2002151872

Manufactured in the United States of America on acid-free, archival-quality paper.

15 14 13 12 11 10 7 6 5 4 3 2

To Ulises

Contents

Foreword

A book is more than a verbal structure or series of verbal structures; it is the dialogue it establishes with its reader and the intonation it imposes upon his voice and the changing and durable images it leaves in his memory. A book is not an isolated being: it is a relationship, an axis of innumerable relationships.

—JORGE LUIS BORGES

Books have the ability to reach beyond their pages into the lives—and the work—of those who read them. *Linking Human Rights and the Environment* is not simply an archive of history or a collection of thoughts in the increasingly overlapping areas of human rights and environmental protection, it is a catalyst for inspiring ideas and action. This book offers the reader a fulcrum upon which to balance and build relationships between human rights and environment, between people and institutions, and among those who strive to achieve human rights and environmental justice.

As the fields of human rights and environment expand and intertwine, so does the work of the people who champion those rights. To respond effectively to the growing cases of human rights violations resulting from environmental degradation, people must know their rights, understand the evolving legal framework, and be able to defend themselves and their environment. Such work depends on dialogue and collaboration to advance. It also relies on our growing awareness of the links between the issues and on the rapprochement of the actors who work in each area to construct solutions.

In recent years, international environmental law scholars and activists have looked increasingly to the law of human rights as a model for the progressive development of international environmental law, as well as for an independent legal strategy for protecting the environment. This approach and others that exemplify the evolution of environmental advocacy through human rights mechanisms are the subject of the chapters you are soon to read.

Linking Human Rights and the Environment is the result of the efforts of the Center for Human Rights and Environment (CEDHA). Since its inception, the Center has served as a catalyst to seek understanding and to respond to international environmental and human rights crises. It has also strove to further its goals of sustainable development and global justice through research, information dissemination, and innovation in these overlapping fields. In doing so, CEDHA has been instrumental in compiling the experience and knowledge of an international community of colleagues and establishing relationships among those working in the two fields to develop creative answers to the question: Is there a human right to a healthy environment? Romina Picolotti and Jorge Daniel Taillant, as well as being accomplished advocates in the fields of international human rights and environment, are the founders and directors of CEDHA. With CEDHA they have promoted environmental rights and have strengthened the advocacy network on a global level. Their efforts, exemplified in the publication of this book, offer constructive and effective solutions and serve a critical function in the advancement of global development. This book is an important and a valuable collection to help others see the vision being created by CEDHA and its founders.

Durwood Zaelke
President and Founder
Center for International Environmental Law
Washington, D.C.—Geneva, Switzerland

Acknowledgments

Every publication is a birth of sorts. *Linking Human Rights and the Environment* is no exception. The idea was born right alongside the Center for Human Rights and Environment (CEDHA), in what was almost a two-year endeavor.

We are deeply indebted to our funders, of course, who grease the wheels so that they may spin freely and so that we may keep busy at our desks and find advocacy inroads to change the awkward system in which we live. But of much greater importance than our funders' financial support is their belief in an idea that began on the back of an envelope on a train to Geneva, where we etched the first sketches of CEDHA. We would like to thank two persons in particular for their unwavering support. Durwood Zaelke of the Center for International Environmental law dreamed with us of the unimaginable on cool breezy afternoons on his veranda in Washington, D.C. We sipped lemonade and met an endless number of friends, colleagues, and other high-flying folk, many of whom were to help us along the way. And David Lorey of the Hewlett Foundation expressed belief over a moonlit lake in Parque Síquiman, with icy-cold fernandos, that these two intrepid souls could make CEDHA fly. Thanks both of you.

This book would not have been possible without the collaboration of the contributing authors, who waded through the editing and reediting. Special thanks to James Anaya who introduced us to University of Arizona Press and saw in the volume the same exciting material we did when we set out to put it together. Finally, we thank Tirza Hollenhorst, who all the way from California and then while working for CEDHA's Responsible Business Program, and while converting our Argentine staff to vegetarian cuisine (no small task), assisted us with final editing. And for all of the unmentioned but certainly not undervalued helping hands, thanks.

Romina Picolotti and Daniel Taillant, Editors

Introduction

This we know: the earth does not belong to man: man belongs to the earth . . . All things are connected like the blood which unites one family . . . Whatever befalls the earth, befalls the sons of the earth. Man did not weave the web of life: he is merely a strand in it. Whatever he does to the web he does to himself.

—CHIEF SEATTLE

Today more than ever, society has come to recognize that the anthropogenic destruction of our planet's sustainable biodiversity negatively impacts humankind, placing *human life* at great risk. The cause-and-effect relationship that exists between environmental collapse and the subsequent risk to our existence can no longer be ignored.

World Resources' Annual Report 2000–2001, which focuses on people and ecosystems, points out that people of all nations—rich and poor—are experiencing the effects of ecosystem decline in one form or another; water shortages, soil erosion, fish kills, landslides on deforested slopes, and fires in disturbed forests are but a few manifestations of environmental degradation that have a direct impact on human beings.[1] The World Commission on the Environment and Development (the Brundtland Commission) provides further statistics that portray the severity of the problem: since 1970 the planet Earth has lost about 200 million hectares of forest and 11.4 million hectares of rain forest annually. One-fifth of the land devoted to agricultural production is now desert.

Concerning the human consequences of environmental degradation, the World Bank stated that more than 850 million persons live in regions affected by desertification. The rain forest is depleted at a rate equivalent to a football field per second. More than two million deaths and billions of cases of disease can be attributed to pollution. Nearly half a billion persons, mainly women and children in poor rural areas, live in severely polluted environments; 500 million annual premature deaths can be attributed to the high levels of pollution in cities. It is estimated that the deterioration of the ozone layer will lead to more than 300,000 additional cases of skin cancer in the world and 1.7 million cases of cataracts.[2]

The magnitude and severity of the problem are overwhelming, and the impact on human rights is alarming. The links between environmental degradation and human living conditions are of even greater relevance when one considers that the victims of environmental degradation tend to belong to the more vulnerable sectors of society (racial and ethnic minorities or the poor), who regularly share a disproportionate burden of environmental contamination. Examples include municipal waste sites and industrial toxic dumps that are placed systematically in sectors where certain populations, who are less able to defend themselves against such exposure, live. This phenomenon is what some have labeled "environmental discrimination" or "environmental racism."[3] Former U.S. President William Clinton noted in 1992 that it is no accident that in those countries where the environment has been most devastated, human suffering is the most severe.[4] Those who are able to defend themselves against such exposure would not tolerate such suffering.

Most of our basic human rights are affected by environmental degradation. *The right to health* is affected by environmental contamination of natural resources such as water, air, and sound (noise pollution). *The right to property* is often directly violated by commercial intrusion into indigenous lands. Property values collapse with industrialization and pollution of residential neighborhoods. *The right to equality* is of great concern to certain sectors of society (minority and certain ethnic groups, for example) who suffer a disproportionate burden of environmental contamination. *The right to participate* is a basic premise of democratic societies, highlighted not only by the Universal Declaration on Human Rights, but also by more recent commitments made under Agenda 21 at the 1992 World Summit on Sustainable Development. This right is understood to be the individuals' right to participate in decisions (investment decisions, urban planning decisions, commercial policy decisions) that directly or indirectly affect their habitat. Undoubtedly, few communities participate in the decisions that bring about severe environmental contamination in their areas and result in deterioration of health. Yet local and international organizations, governments, and civil society in general tend to isolate human rights issues into a limited sphere and treat environmental degradation as an entirely unrelated issue.

Human rights institutions, tribunals, judges, attorneys, and human rights civil society groups who bring human rights cases to the courts have tended to place certain human rights issues on their agendas. This is perhaps largely influenced by recent history in which dozens of military regimes around the world systematically violated civil and political human rights. Hence civil society groups and legal redress began to focus on guaranteeing these civil and political rights. It was in fact only in recent years that the instruments to guarantee human rights, such as the existing human rights tribunals in the Inter-American System and in Europe, developed. Their agendas were largely dominated by civil and political rights cases.

Environmental advocacy has also taken on a narrow scope, focusing principally on natural resource preservation. We tend to think of environmentalists as being concerned with air, forests, and water. The impacts of environmental degradation on human rights are generally not on the environmental agenda, including the agendas of development organizations, or nongovernmental or governmental agencies.

In practice, specifically in how we formulate policy and in the recognition of human rights and environmental protection, we have failed to take into account how environmental degradation affects humans, and more specifically, how it affects the full enjoyment of human rights. In fact, the environment and our relationship to it are generally not considered to be a human rights issue. We treat the environment and human rights through separate frameworks and approaches, as if they were somehow unrelated, failing to address the natural, symbiotic relationship that exists between the two. Environmentalists and human rights advocates simply do not communicate with one another, believing they have very different agendas. One is about people, and the other about nature.

This division is mirrored in national and intergovernmental agencies. Human rights public servants focus on civil and political issues. The environment, on the other hand, is usually dealt with as an infrastructure issue or, as in many Latin American countries, is latched onto a sector such as agriculture, forestry, or mining. Academia also generally addresses the environment from a strictly natural-resource approach. It was only recently that an advanced law degree program devoted a course specifically to the links between human rights and environment.[5] So when people are denied their human rights due to environmental contamination, or when we are not allowed to participate in decision making on environmentally sensitive public or private works, such problems, even if they find their way to court, are not viewed as "human rights" issues. Instead they are addressed through mechanisms that do not have a human rights framework or basis as a guide. They are hence likely to be treated with a lower set of standards and priority than would be human rights concerns.

As a society, we must understand that everything and anything that influences our environment directly influences our human condition, and a violation of our environment is a violation of our human rights. Worldwide, more than fifty-one million people die annually. Nearly a third of these deaths are due to parasitic and infectious diseases, which constitute the main cause of world mortality rates. In its 1997 report on global resources, *Bridging the Gap,* the World Bank recognized that the resurgence of infectious diseases is directly associated with climate changes caused by agricultural and economic development, or due to changes in the patterns of land use.[6] The Intergovernmental Panel on Climate Change states that global warming will provoke immeasurable consequences in the future patterns of infectious diseases, since minimal alterations in temperature have significant effects on the vectors that transmit them.[7]

These indisputable statistics make the need to address the link between human rights and environment urgent. We must understand this relationship clearly and develop the necessary mechanisms, laws, and protection to guarantee socially and environmentally sustainable development.

Linking Human Rights and the Environment gathers a variety of contributions from human rights and environmental experts, who have given thought to the links between the environment and human rights, and especially between the environment and human rights law. Our aim is to provide the reader with an assortment of issues and approaches to address these links, and more specifically, to address the growing interrelationship between human rights law and the environment. While much is still to be debated and defined, we hope that this publication will serve as a useful reference to guide the growing discussion about the relationships between these two inseparable and interdependent areas of law.

Linking Human Rights and the Environment is not intended to be an exhaustive reference edition. It does, however, cover a series of issues that generally come up when addressing the areas where human rights law and the environment overlap. The book is intended to serve to generate debate and discussion, and to provide some guiding references to deepen the human rights and environment debate. The Shelton and Kiss pieces review the international law that frames our discussion. Picolotti and Saladin examine participation in view of commitments made in Agenda 21 and in an era where global trends are greatly influencing public policy and the development paradigm. Alvarez and Shaw look at two particular rights, the right to water and women's rights, that have much to do with the environment and human rights. Dommen and Taillant look at human rights systems and practical ways in which environmental issues can be approached through human rights instruments. Wiersema looks at the acute relationship that exists between indigenous peoples and the environment. Anaya traces the Mayagna indigenous community's efforts to gain recognition of traditional lands. Finally, we've chosen to reproduce an *amicus curiae* (legal brief) that makes legal arguments for linking human rights to the environment, just as it was filed before international human rights tribunals. As the manuscript for this edition went to press, the Inter-American Court on Human Rights handed down a precedent-setting decision on this case; we've offered some excerpts of the sentence. The brief is especially important to the discussion as it is a contemporary example as to how the relationship between environment and human rights can be presented before judicial bodies in leading cases.

The publication of this volume comes at a moment when the links between human rights and environment are becoming key issues on the international development agenda. The debate revives an initiative of the mid-1990s at which time the United Nations created the post of Special Rapporteur on Human Rights and Environment. From that initiative, in collaboration with several civil society organizations, the Ksentini Report (as the Rapporteur's report is commonly referred to) became a critical document that lays out a framework to consider the links between human rights and environment. The United Nations Environmental Program (UNEP) and the United Nations High Commission on Human Rights (UNHCHR) are now debating how to revive this initiative and address this link from a collaborative and institutional perspective. A similar initiative is also under way in the Inter-American System at the Organization of American States where Member States are resolved to study the link between human rights and environment. Intergovernmental agencies, governments, and many civil society organizations are also exploring ways to address this link through their program agendas. We hope this work will contribute to this important process.

Romina Picolotti and Jorge Daniel Taillant
January 2003

NOTES

1. UNEP et al, *World Resources 2000–2001: People and Ecosystems: The Fraying Web of Life* (Washington, D.C., 2001), viii.

2. For further information, see UNDP, *World Development Report, World Bank, and Human Development Report,* 1993.

3. See Jorge Daniel Taillant, *Environmental Discrimination: Issues and Themes* (CEDHA, 2000), at www.cedha.org.ar

4. Quoted in Michael Kane, 18, The Yale Journal of International Law.

5. The American University LLM program offers a seminar on human rights and environment. Course materials, curricula, and syllabus can be found at www.cedha.org.ar

6. World Health Organization, *The World Health Report on Global Resources* (Geneva, 1995), 18–20; World Bank, *World Resources: A Guide to the Global Environment 1996–1997,* 181–82. For more information, see Mary E. Wilson, *Anticipated New Diseases,* Current Issues in Public Health, 1 (1995), 90–94; J. Lesderberg, R. E. Shope, and S. Oaks, *Emerging Infections: Microbial Threats to Health in the United States* (Washington, D.C.: Institute of Medicine, Educational National Academy Press, 1992), 47.

7. International Panel on Climate Change, "The Social Costs of Climatic Change: Greenhouse Damage and the Benefits of Control," chap 6 in *Second Assessment Report, Working Group 3* (Geneva: World Meteorological Organization/ UNEP, 1995), 9.

Linking Human Rights and the Environment

1

The Environmental Jurisprudence of International Human Rights Tribunals

Dinah Shelton

INTERNATIONAL LAW FOR THE promotion and protection of human rights and international environmental law reflect two fundamental values and aims of modern international society.[1] The primary objective of human rights law is to allow individual self-actualization by protecting each person from abuse of power by State agents, and by ensuring that basic needs can be fulfilled. States also must exercise due diligence to prevent human rights violations by nonstate actors. Environmental law, in turn, seeks to protect and preserve the basic living and nonliving resources and ecological processes on which all life depends. A human rights approach to environmental protection partly integrates the two subject areas by seeking to ensure that the natural world does not deteriorate to the point where internationally guaranteed rights such as the rights to life, health, property, a family and private life, culture, and safe drinking water are seriously impaired. Environmental protection is thus instrumental, not an end in itself.[2]

Linking environmental harm to international human rights law allows global and regional human rights complaint procedures to be invoked against those States that violate human rights through poor environmental protection. There are advantages to this approach compared to efforts to incorporate a right to environment in human rights treaties.[3] First, it "avoids the need to define such notions as a satisfactory or decent environment, falls well within the competence of existing human rights bodies, and involves little or no potential for conflict with environmental institutions."[4] Second, it allows victims of harm to bring complaints. Given the general absence of petition procedures in environmental treaties and international institutions, those who have suffered harm generally cannot choose between bringing an international human rights case or an international environmental case because almost no forum exists for the latter.[5] In nearly all cases, human rights tribunals provide the only international procedures currently available to challenge government action or inaction respecting environmental protection.

United Nations human rights organs began annually considering environmental issues in the late 1980s, when African countries expressed concern about transboundary movements of hazardous and toxic wastes. In 1988, the United Nations Sub-Commission on Prevention of Discrimination and Protection of Minorities considered this specific question under its agenda item on human rights, and scientific and technological developments. It adopted resolution 1988/26, drafted and cosponsored primarily by its African members. The resolution referred to the right of all peoples to life and the right of future generations to enjoy their environmental heritage. It noted that the movement and dumping of toxic and dangerous products endanger basic human rights, such as the right to life, the right to live in a sound and healthy environment, and consequently the right to health. To help remedy problems with toxic dumping, the resolution called for both a ban on the export of toxic and dangerous wastes and a global convention on that subject. In March 1989, the Commission approved the Sub-Commission text.[6] Two months later the Basel Convention on the Control of Transboundary Movements of Hazardous Wastes and Their Disposal was adopted,[7] but African States expressed disappointment at what they viewed to be a weak agreement. Consequently, the topic remained on the human rights agenda and gradually expanded to include other dangerous products as well as wastes.

At its fifty-first session in 1995, a divided Commission appointed a Special Rapporteur to study the adverse effects of the illicit movement and dumping of toxic and dangerous products and wastes on the enjoyment of human rights.[8] As part of her mandate, the Special Rapporteur was given explicit authority to receive and examine communications and do fact-finding on illicit traffic and dumping, allowing the development of a complaint procedure on the subject. The Rapporteur could recommend measures to States Parties and had to provide an annual list of the countries and transnational corporations engaged in illicit dumping, as well as a census of persons killed, maimed, or otherwise injured due to the practice. In contrast to other international human rights procedures, this one produced a relatively large proportion of complaints or communications from States between 1995 and 2000.[9]

Permanent international tribunals also have considered cases where environmental harm is alleged to infringe on human rights. The human rights invoked include the rights to life, association, expression, information, political participation, personal liberty, equality, and legal redress, all contained in international legal instruments. Economic and social rights, including the right to health, the right to decent living conditions and the right to a decent working environment, are also implicated. International organs and tribunals have expanded or reinterpreted many of these guarantees in light of environmental concerns. The following discussion reviews the jurisprudence of international human rights tribunals as they have addressed environmental matters. The conclusion suggests the utility of such cases to prevent or remedy environmental harm, but also indicates the limits to this approach.

Procedural Rights

Principle 10 of the Rio Declaration on Human Rights and the Environment calls on States to provide information to the public on the state of the environment, allow those who are potentially affected to participate in decision making concerning the environment, and afford remedies for environmental harm. These procedural rights also are found in human rights instruments and have been the subject of several complaints to various tribunals.

Information

Human rights texts, like many international environmental agreements, generally contain a right to freedom of information or a corresponding State duty to inform.[10] Article 10 of the European Convention on Human Rights and Fundamental Freedoms guarantees "the freedom to receive information."[11] This provision, however, has been interpreted restrictively.[12] In the case of *Leander v. Sweden,* the applicant alleged violation of Article 10 after he was denied access to a file that was used to deny him employment. The Court unanimously stated: "the right to receive information basically prohibits a Government from restricting a person from receiving information that others wish or may be willing to impart to him. Article 10 does not, in circumstances such as those of the present case, confer on the individual a right to access to a register containing information on his personal position, nor does it embody an obligation on the Government to impart such information to the individual."[13] This strict interpretation of Article 10 was applied to environmental information in *Anna Maria Guerra and 39 others against Italy.*[14] The applicants complained of pollution resulting from operation of the chemical factory "ENICHEM Agricoltura," situated near the town of Manfredonia, the risk of major accidents at the plant, and the absence of regulation by the public authorities. Invoking Article 10 of the European Convention on Human Rights, the applicants asserted in particular the government's failure to inform the public of the risks and the measures to be taken in case of a major accident, prescribed by the domestic law transposing the EC "Seveso" directive.[15]

The former European Commission on Human Rights admitted the complaint insofar as it alleged a violation of the right to information.[16] It did not accept the claim of pollution damage, even though most of the facts were uncontested. The Commission found that the government had classified the factory as a "high risk" facility in applying the criteria established by the EC directive and Italian law, and that there had been accidents at the factory, including an explosion that sent more than 150 persons to the hospital. A technical commission named by the city of Manfredonia found that according to the factory's own study, the treatment of emissions was inadequate and the environmental impact study incomplete.

During the operations of the chemical factory, the government instigated several inquiries. In addition, the residents of Manfredonia instituted civil actions. The Commission nonetheless found that the law was inadequately enforced, giving the company almost complete impunity to pollute. In addition to its failure to hold the company responsible for polluting, the government took no action between the adoption of the Seveso law and the cessation of chemical production by the factory in 1994 to inform the population of the situation or to make a contingency plan operational.

The decision centered on the interpretation of State duties under Article 10. The applicants insisted that they sought information from the government that was not otherwise available to them. The government in turn claimed that the law protected industrial secrets, prohibiting authorities from divulging such information in their possession. The essential question before the Commission was whether the right to information for the public who was directly affected imposed on the government a positive duty to inform.

By a large majority, the Commission concluded that Article 10 imposes on States the positive duty to collect, collate, and disseminate information that would otherwise not be directly accessible to the public or brought to the public's attention. In arriving at its conclusion, the Commission relied upon "the present state of European law" *(l'état actuel du droit européen)*, which it said confirmed that public information represents one of the essential instruments for protecting the well-being and health of the populace in situations of environmental danger. The Commission referred specifically to the Chernobyl resolution, adopted by the Parliamentary Assembly of the Council of Europe, which it said recognized, at least in Europe, a fundamental right to information concerning activities that are dangerous for the environment or human well-being.

The case was referred to a Grand Chamber of the European Court of Human Rights, which issued its judgment 19 February 1998. The Court reversed the Commission on its expanded reading of Article 10, but unanimously found a violation of Article 8, the right to family, home, and private life.[17] The Court reaffirmed its earlier case law holding that Article 10 generally only prohibits a government from interfering with a person's freedom to receive information that others are willing to impart. According to the Court, "[t]hat freedom cannot be construed as imposing on a State, in circumstances such as those of the present case, positive obligations to collect and disseminate information of its own motion."[18] Eight of the twenty judges suggested in separate opinions that positive obligations to collect and disseminate information might exist in some circumstances.

In another case, the European Court held that the State may not extend defamation laws to restrict dissemination of environmental information of public interest. In the case of *Bladet Tromsø and Stensaas v. Norway,*[19] a Grand Chamber of the European Court held 13 to 4 that Norway had violated the rights of a newspaper and its editor by fining them both for defamation after they published extracts of a report by a governmental seal hunting inspector.[20] The report claimed among other things that seals had been flayed alive and that there were other violations of seal hunting regulations. The names of the crew were deleted from the publication but they successfully sued for defamation. The European Court held that the judgment was an unjustified interference with Article 10 of the Convention. The Court found that the reporting should have been considered in the wider context of the newspaper's coverage of the controversial seal hunting issue, a matter of public interest. Its reporting conveyed an overall picture of balanced reporting. The Court also was influenced by the fact that the report was an official one that the Ministry of Fisheries had not questioned or disavowed. In the view of the Court the press should normally be entitled, when contributing to public debate on matters of legitimate concern, to rely on the contents of official reports without having to undertake independent research. Otherwise its public-watchdog role could be undermined.

Participation

The right to information is a prerequisite to effective participation in decisions affecting individuals and groups. Human rights instruments, like environmental texts, generally guarantee a right to participate in government.[21] This right produces a set of relationships between human rights, environment, and political democracy.[22] Most important to environmental rights is the notion of a right to ongoing and active participation in governance and the institutions of society,[23] involving the empowerment of individuals and groups with respect to decisions that condition life in the State.[24] Human rights provisions do not specify how persons are to take part in the conduct of public affairs. For environmental protection, environmental law fills the gap by mandating and detailing participatory environmental impact procedures and other means of public participation.[25]

Effective exercise of the right to participate in decision making can preclude later complaints about the merits of the decisions taken, according to the UN Human Rights Committee. The case of *Apirana Mahuika et al v. New Zealand* (CCPR/C/70/D/547/1993) posed the problem of balancing indigenous rights to natural resources with governmental efforts to conserve natural resources.[26] The communication, filed by the Maori Legal Service on behalf of eighteen petitioners, claimed violations of the rights of self-determination, right to a remedy, freedom of association, freedom of conscience, nondiscrimination, and minority rights. The communication challenged New Zealand's efforts to regulate commercial and noncommercial fishing in light of the dramatic growth of the fishing industry in the past three decades.

The Treaty of Waitangi, legally unenforceable without specific legislation, guarantees to Maori "the full exclusive and undisturbed possession of their lands, forests, fisheries and other properties which they may collectively or individually possess so long as it is their wish and desire to retain the same in their possession." Since the 1980s, the government has sought to determine Maori fishing claims. After extensive negotiations, on 23 September 1992, representatives of the government and the Maori executed a deed of settlement to regulate all fisheries issues between the parties. In all, 110 signatories signed the deed.

The authors of the communication represented tribes and subtribes that objected to the settlement. They first brought their claims to the courts of New Zealand, then to the Waitangi Tribunal. All concluded that the settlement was valid except for some aspects that could be rectified in anticipated legislation. Having exhausted local remedies, the petitioners filed their complaint with the Human Rights Committee pursuant to the first Optional Protocol to the Covenant on Civil and Political Rights.

According to the petitioners, the contents of the Settlement were not always adequately disclosed or explained and thus informed decision making was seriously inhibited. They also argued that the negotiators did not represent individual tribes and subtribes. They claimed that the Settlement denies them their right to freely determine their political status and interferes with their right to freely pursue their economic, social, and cultural development, in violation of the right of self-determination contained in the Covenant on Civil and Political Rights. They also alleged threats to their way of life and the culture of the tribes in violation of Article 27 of the Covenant.[27]

The government accepted that the enjoyment of Maori culture encompasses the right to engage in fishing activities. It acknowledged its obligations to ensure recognition of the right. In its view, the Settlement expresses both the right and the obligation. It noted that minority rights contained in Article 27 are not unlimited but may be subject to reasonable and objective justification, balancing the concerns of the Maori and the need to introduce measures to ensure the sustainability of the fishing resources. The system of fishing quotas that was introduced reflects the need for effective measures to conserve the depleted inshore fishery, carrying out the government's "duty to all New Zealanders to conserve and manage the resource for future generations." Its regime was "based on the reasonable and objective needs of overall sustainable management."

The Committee considered first whether minority rights under Article 27 of the Covenant had been violated by the Settlement, noting the agreement of both sides that the Maori constitute a minority and that use and control of fisheries are essential elements of their culture. The question was whether the acts of the government amounted to a denial of that culture. The Committee reiterated that a State's freedom to encourage development or allow economic activity must comport with the obligations undertaken in Article 27. The latter "requires that a member of a minority shall not be denied his right to enjoy his own culture. . . . However, measures that have a certain limited impact on the way of life of persons belonging to a minority will not necessarily amount to a denial of the right under Article

27." Further, in the case of indigenous peoples, the State may need to take protective measures and measures to ensure the effective participation of members of minority communities in decisions that affect them. In regard to the latter point, the Committee emphasized that "the acceptability of measures that affect or interfere with the culturally significant economic activities of a minority depends on whether the members of the minority in question have had the opportunity to participate in the decision-making process in relation to these measures and whether they will continue to benefit from their traditional economy." The complicated process of consultation undertaken by the government was held to comply with this requirement, because the government paid special attention to the cultural and religious significance of fishing for the Maori.

In resolving the conflict between various members of the minority group, the Committee indicated that it would consider whether the limitation in issue is in the interests of all members of the minority and whether there is a reasonable and objective justification for its application to those who object. The Committee found it to be a matter of concern that the Settlement and its process contributed to divisions among the Maori, but the Committee concluded that the government had taken the necessary steps to ensure compatibility of the Settlement with Article 27. The Committee thus found no breach of the Covenant guarantees.

Remedy

Universal and regional human rights instruments expressly guarantee the right to a remedy when a right is violated.[28] The United Nations Human Rights Committee has identified the kinds of remedies required, depending on the type of violation and the victim's condition. The Committee has indicated that the State having committed human rights violations must undertake to investigate the facts, take appropriate action, including bringing those found responsible to justice, and must provide appropriate redress to the victims. Several treaties also expressly refer to the right to legal protection for attacks on privacy, family, home, or correspondence, significant provisions because many human rights cases involve assertions that environmental harm is a violation of the right to respect for privacy and the home.[29]

In some instances, the issue of redress has been raised by human rights organs in General Comments. The third General Comment of the Committee on Economic, Social and Cultural Rights concerns the nature of State obligations pursuant to Article 2(1) of the Covenant on Economic,

Social and Cultural Rights. The Committee determines that appropriate measures to implement the Covenant might include judicial remedies for rights deemed justifiable. It specifically points to the nondiscrimination requirement of the treaty and cross-references the right to a remedy in the Covenant on Civil and Political Rights. A number of other rights are also cited as "capable of immediate application by judicial and other organs," but no mention is made of environmental harm.[30]

The American Convention entitles everyone to effective recourse for protection against acts that violate the fundamental rights recognized by the Constitution "or laws of the state or by the Convention," even where such acts are committed by persons acting in the course of their official duties (Article 25).[31] The States Parties are to ensure that the competent authorities enforce remedies that are granted. The Inter-American Court has commented on the obligation of States to make available effective internal remedies, stating, "Under the Convention, States Parties have an obligation to provide effective judicial remedies to victims of human rights violations (Article 25), remedies that must be substantiated in accordance with the rules of due process of law (Article 8(1)), all in keeping with the general obligation of such States to guarantee the free and full exercise of the rights recognized by the Convention to all persons subject to their jurisdiction (Article 1)."[32] The Court concluded that the obligation to ensure rights generally requires that remedies include due diligent efforts by the State to prevent, investigate, and punish any violation of the rights recognized by the Convention.[33]

In the European system, Article 6,[34] which provides judicial guarantees of a fair trial, has been construed as including a right to a tribunal for the determination of rights and duties.[35] Applicability of Article 6 depends upon the existence of a dispute concerning a right recognized in the law of the State concerned, including those created by licenses, authorizations, and permits that affect the use of property or commercial activities.[36] In *Oerlemans v. Netherlands,* Article 6 was deemed to apply to a case where a Dutch citizen could not challenge a ministerial order designating his land as a protected site.[37]

In *Zander v. Sweden,* Article 6 of the European Convention provided the basis for a complaint that the applicants had been denied a remedy for threatened environmental harm.[38] The applicants owned property next to a waste treatment and storage area. Local well water showed contamination by cyanide from the dumpsite. The municipality prohibited use of the water and furnished temporary water supplies. Subsequently, the permissible level of cyanide was raised and the city supply was halted. When the company maintaining the dump site sought a renewed and expanded permit, the applicants argued that the threat to their water supply would be sufficiently high that the company should be obliged to provide free drinking water if pollution occurred. The board granted the permit, but denied the applicants' request. The applicants sought but could not obtain judicial review of the decision. The European Court held that Article 6 applied and was violated. The applicability of Article 6 was based on the Court's finding that the applicants "could arguably maintain that they were entitled under Swedish law to protection against the water in their well being polluted as a result of VAFAB's activities on the dump."[39] According to the Court, "As regards the character of the right at issue, the Commission notes that the right related to the environmental conditions of the applicants' property and that existence of environmental inconveniences or risks might well be a factor which affects the value of a property. Consequently the right at issue must be considered to be a civil right to which Article 6, para 1 of the Convention applies."[40]

Some environmental threats have been deemed too remote to give rise to a claim within the purview of Article 6 (1). In *Balmer-Schafroth and Others v. Switzerland*, applicants argued that they were entitled to a hearing over the government's decision to renew an operating permit for a nuclear power plant.[41] The European Court found that the applicants had not established a direct link between the operating conditions of the power station and their right to protection of their physical integrity, because they failed to show that the operation of the power station exposed them personally to a danger that was serious, specific, and, above all, imminent. The applicants failed to establish the dangers and the remedies with a degree of probability that made the outcome of the proceedings "directly decisive" for the right they invoked. Seven judges dissented, objecting that the Court had failed to specify why the connection that the applicants were trying to make was "too tenuous." In their view, Article 6 should have applied to allow the applicants to establish before a tribunal the degree of danger they were facing rather than requiring them to prove at the outset the existence of a risk and its consequences. A likelihood of risk and damage should be sufficient, invoking the precautionary principle:

> The majority appear to have ignored the whole trend of international institutions and public international law towards protecting persons and heritage, as evident in European Union and Council of Europe instruments on the environment, the Rio Agreements, UNESCO instruments, the development of the precautionary principle and the principle of conservation of the common heritage. United Nations Resolution No. 840 of 3 November 1985 on the

> abuse of power was adopted as part of the same concern. Where the protection of persons in the context of the environment and installations posing a threat to human safety is concerned, all States must adhere to those principles.

A different case asserting risk of harm from nuclear radiation arose in the United Nations Human Rights Committee, which found the case inadmissible on the ground that the claimants did not qualify as "victims" of a violation. The communication concerned France's nuclear tests among the atolls of Mururoa and Fangataufa in the South Pacific.[42] Although the case did not allege denial of the right to a remedy, it is considered here along with the prior case because the Committee, like the European Court, seemed concerned with the remoteness of the harm.[43] Applicants claimed that the tests represented a threat to their right to life and their right not to be subjected to arbitrary interference with their privacy and family life. They attempted to place the burden of proof on the government, contending that French authorities had been unable to show that the tests would not endanger the health of the people living in the South Pacific or the environment by further damaging the geological structure of the atolls. The Committee held that the applicants had not substantiated their claim that the tests had violated or threatened violation with the rights invoked. As for their contention that the tests increased the likelihood of catastrophic accident, "the Committee notes that this contention is highly controversial even in concerned scientific circles; it is not possible for the Committee to ascertain its validity or correctness." Thus, as in the prior case, the lack of scientific certainty coupled with the burden of proof on the applicants limited the claimant's ability to obtain relief through human rights proceedings.

The right to a remedy extends to compensation for pollution. In the European case *Zimmerman and Steiner v. Switzerland,* the Court found Article 6 applicable to a complaint about the length of proceedings for compensation for injury caused by noise and air pollution from a nearby airport.[44] Article 6 does not, however, encompass a right to judicial review of legislative enactments. In *Braunerheilm v. Sweden,* the Commission denied a claim that Article 6 was violated when the applicant could not challenge in court a new law that granted fishing licenses to the general public in waters where the applicant previously had exclusive rights.[45]

Violations of Substantive Human Rights

Despite the lack of explicit reference to environmental rights in most human rights instruments, global and regional tribunals—the United

Nations Human Rights Committee, the Inter-American Commission on Human Rights, the European Commission and Court of Human Rights, the European Court of Justice, and the African Commission on Human Rights—have developed a jurisprudence that recognizes and enforces rights linked to environmental protection. The substantive rights that have been invoked are principally those of the right to life, the right to respect for one's private life and home, the right to health, the right to culture, and the right to the peaceful enjoyment of one's possessions.

The United Nations Human Rights Committee has indicated that State obligations to protect the right to life can include positive measures designed to reduce infant mortality and protect against malnutrition and epidemics.[46] In the context of the periodic reporting procedure of the International Covenant on Economic, Social and Cultural Rights, States sometimes report on environmental issues as they affect guaranteed rights. In 1986, Tunisia reported to the Commission on Economic, Social and Cultural Rights, in the context of Article 11 on the right to an adequate standard of living, on measures taken to prevent degradation of natural resources, particularly erosion, and about measures to prevent contamination of food.[47] Similarly, the Ukraine reported in 1995 on the environmental situation consequent to the explosion at Chernobyl in regard to the right to life.

Committee members sometimes request specific information about environmental harm that threatens human rights. Poland, for example, was asked to provide information in 1989 about measures to combat pollution, especially in upper Silesia.[48] Members of the Committee on the Elimination of Racial Discrimination and the Committee on the Rights of the Child have also posed questions of States Parties concerning environmental matters related to the guarantees of the treaties they monitor.

Pursuant to the Optional Protocol, the Human Rights Committee has received several complaints concerning environmental damage as a violation of one or more civil and political rights. First, a group of Canadian citizens alleged that the storage of radioactive waste near their homes threatened the right to life of present and future generations. The Committee found that the case raised "serious issues with regard to the obligation of States Parties to protect human life," but declared the case inadmissible due to failure to exhaust local remedies.[49] The Committee has also received complaints, discussed below, concerning violation of the rights of indigenous groups and minorities to protection of their traditional cultures.

On the regional level, Human Rights Commissions in Europe, the

Americas, and Africa have dealt with alleged violations of human rights linked to environmental harm. In the Inter-American system, claims linked to environmental harm have generally asserted that the right to life is threatened, or that the rights of indigenous groups have been violated. The cases submitted to the African system have generally invoked the right to health, protected by Article 16 of the African Charter, rather than the right to environment contained in the same document. In *Communications 25/89, 47/90, 56/91 and 100/93 against Zaire* the Commission held that failure by the Government to provide basic services such as safe drinking water constituted a violation of Article 16.[50]

In Europe, most of the victims have invoked either the right to information, discussed above, or the right to privacy and family life (Article 8). Article 8(1) of the European Convention on Human Rights and Fundamental Freedoms provides that "everyone has the right to respect for his privacy, his home and his correspondence." The second paragraph of the Article sets forth the permissible grounds for limiting the exercise of the right.[51] A related provision, Article 1 of Protocol 1, ensures that "every natural or legal person is entitled to the peaceful enjoyment of his possessions." The European Commission accepts that pollution or other environmental harm may result in a breach of Article 1 of Protocol 1, but only when such harm results in a substantial reduction in the value of the property and when that reduction is not compensated by the State. The Commission has added that the right to peaceful enjoyment of possessions "does not, in principle, guarantee the right to the peaceful enjoyment of possessions in a pleasant environment."[52]

Decisions of the European Commission on Human Rights indicate that environmental harm attributable to State action or inaction that has significant injurious effect on a person's home or private and family life constitutes a breach of Article 8(1). The harm may be excused, however, under Article 8(2) if it results from an authorized activity of economic benefit to the community in general, as long as there is no disproportionate burden on any particular individual; that is, the measures must have a legitimate aim, be lawfully enacted, and be proportional. States enjoy a margin of appreciation in determining the legitimacy of the aim pursued. The Court, in recent decisions, seems to balance more overtly the competing interests of the individual and the community than does the Commission, while it does afford the State a certain margin of appreciation.

Most of the European privacy and home cases involve noise pollution. In *Arrondelle v. United Kingdom,* the applicant complained of noise from Gatwick Airport and a nearby motorway.[53] The application was declared admissible and eventually settled with the payment of 7500 pounds. *Baggs v. United Kingdom,* a similar case, was also resolved by friendly settlement.[54] The settlement of the cases left unresolved numerous issues, some of which were addressed in *Powell and Raynor v. United Kingdom* at the Court.[55] The Court found that aircraft noise from Heathrow Airport constituted a violation of Article 8, but was justified under Article 8(2) as "necessary in a democratic society" for the economic well-being of the country. Noise was acceptable under the principle of proportionality, if it did not "create an unreasonable burden for the person concerned," a test that could be met by the State if the individual had "the possibility of moving elsewhere without substantial difficulties and losses." The European Commission and the Court often accept that the economic well-being of the country will excuse a certain amount of environmental harm, following the Powell and Raynor case.[56] In contrast, in the Vearncombe case, the Commission found that the level and frequency of the noise did not reach the point where a violation of Article 8 could be made out and therefore the application was inadmissible.[57]

In *G and E v. Norway,* two Sami alleged a violation of Article 8 due to a proposed hydroelectric project that would flood part of their traditional reindeer grazing grounds.[58] The Commission accepted that traditional practices could constitute "private and family life" within the meaning of Article 8. It questioned, however, whether the amount of land to be flooded was enough to constitute an "interference" and found that, in any case, the project was justified as necessary for the economic well-being of the country. The application was therefore inadmissible.

The major decision of the Court on environmental harm as a breach of the right to private life and the home is *Lopez-Ostra v. Spain.*[59] The applicant and her daughter suffered serious health problems from the fumes of a tannery waste treatment plant that operated alongside the apartment building where they lived. The plant opened in July 1988 without a required license and without having followed the procedure for obtaining such a license. The plant malfunctioned when it began operations, releasing gas fumes and contamination, which immediately caused health problems and nuisance to people living in the district. The town council evacuated the local residents and rehoused them free of charge in the town center during the summer. In spite of this, the authorities allowed the plant to resume partial operation. In October the applicant and her family returned to their flat where there were continuing problems. The applicant finally sold her house and moved in 1992.

The *Lopez-Ostra v. Spain* decision is significant for several reasons. First, the Court did not require the applicant to exhaust administrative remedies to challenge operation of the plant under the environmental protection laws, but only to explore remedies applicable to enforcement of basic rights. Mrs. Lopez-Ostra exhausted the latter remedies when the Supreme Court of Spain denied her appeal on a suit for infringement of her fundamental rights and her complaint with the Constitutional Court was dismissed as manifestly ill founded. Two sisters-in-law of Mrs. López-Ostra, who lived in the same building as her, followed the procedures concerning environmental law. They brought administrative proceedings alleging that the plant was operating unlawfully. On 18 September 1991 the local court, noting a continuing nuisance and that the plant did not have the licenses required by law, ordered that it should be closed until they were obtained. However, enforcement of this order was stayed following an appeal. The case was still pending in the Supreme Court in 1995 when the European Court issued its judgment. The two sisters-in-law also lodged a complaint, as a result of which a local judge instituted criminal proceedings against the plant for an environmental health offence. The two complainants joined the proceedings as civil parties.

The European Human Rights Court noted that severe environmental pollution may affect individuals' well-being and prevent them from enjoying their homes in such a way as to affect their private and family life adversely, without, however, seriously endangering their health. It found that the determination of whether this violation had occurred in *Lopez-Ostra v. Spain* should be tested by striking a fair balance between the interest of the town's economic well-being and the applicant's effective enjoyment of her right to respect for her home and her private and family life. In doing this, the Court applied its "margin of appreciation" doctrine, allowing the State a "certain" discretion in determining the appropriate balance, but finding in this case that the margin of appreciation had been exceeded. It awarded Mrs. Lopez-Ostra 4,000,000 pesetas, plus costs and attorneys' fees.

In *Maria Guerra v. Italy,* in regard to Article 8, the Court reaffirmed that it can impose positive obligations on States to ensure respect for private or family life. Citing the Lopez-Ostra case, the Court reiterated that "severe environmental pollution may affect individuals' well-being and prevent them from enjoying their homes in such a way as to affect their private and family life."[60] Noting that the individuals waited throughout the operation of fertilizer production at the company for essential information "that would have enabled them to assess the risks they and their families might run if they continued to life at Manfredonia, a town particularly exposed to danger in the event of an accident at the factory" the Court found a violation of Article 8.

The Court's decision is strained, resulting from the Court's reluctance to overturn its prior case law interpreting Article 10. The basis of the complaint was the government's failure to provide environmental information, not pollution like that found in the Lopez-Ostra case. The Court also declined to consider whether the right to life guaranteed by Article 2 had been violated, considering it unnecessary in light of its decision on Article 8. The decision seems unwarranted, given that deaths from cancer had occurred in the factory, which would have a clear bearing on damages. In regard to the latter, the Court found that applicants had not proved pecuniary damages but were entitled to ITL 10,000,000 each for nonpecuniary damage. The applicants also sought a clean-up order, which the Court declined to give on the ground that it lacks the power to issue orders.

It must be recognized that existing human rights guarantees are primarily useful when the environmental harm consists of pollution. Issues of resource management and nature conservation or biological diversity are more difficult to bring under the human rights rubric without a right to a safe and ecologically balanced environment. A 1974 opinion of the European Commission on Human Rights indicates the attitude of some human rights bodies and the limits of the human rights approach. In an application challenging the refusal to allow an Icelandic resident to have a dog as a violation of the right of privacy and family life guaranteed by Article 8 of the European Convention on Human Rights, the Commission stated:

> The Commission cannot however accept that the protection afforded by Article 8 of the Convention extends to relationships of the individual with his entire immediate surroundings, in so far as they do not involve human relationships and notwithstanding the desire of the individual to keep such relationships within the private sphere. No doubt the dog has had close ties with man since time immemorial. However, given the above considerations this alone is not sufficient to bring the keeping of a dog into the sphere of the private life of the owner.[61]

Several recent cases in the European human rights system mark renewed efforts to address issues of nature protection through human rights. All of the cases were brought against France and concerned a French law imposing an obligation on certain owners of small areas of land to belong to the local hunting association and to permit hunting on their property. The applicants oppose hunting and complained that the French law violated their right to peaceful enjoyment of their possessions, their right to freedom of association, and the right to freedom of conscience. They also maintained that the obligations are discriminatory. They relied on Article 1 of Protocol 1 and Articles 9 and 11 of the Convention, separately and in conjunction with Article 14 of the Convention.

The Commission issued its report on the first of the cases, *Marie-Jeanne Chassagnou, Rene Petit and Simone Lasgrezas v. France,* on 30 October 1997.[62] It found a violation of all the rights except freedom of conscience, which it decided it need not address because of the other findings. The report was submitted to the Committee of Ministers. The second two cases, *Leon Dumont and others v. France* and *Josephine Montion v. France,* involve identical issues and were submitted by the Commission to the Court in March 1998. In a judgment of 29 April 1999, the European Court of Human Rights agreed with the Commission that the applicants' rights to freedom of association and peaceful enjoyment of property had been violated, as well as the requirement of nondiscrimination.[63] Like the Commission, the Court declined to address the issue of freedom of conscience, although a separate opinion argued that the case should have included consideration of environmental or ecological beliefs within the scope of Convention Article 9. In fact, the issue seems to have influenced the Court to some extent. In other cases, as described below, the Court has applied the doctrine of margin of appreciation to afford considerable deference to governmental decisions when property rights, in particular, have been limited for environmental purposes in the public interest. In this case, in contrast, the Court was unwilling to accept French arguments that the public interest and the environment were being protected through measures designed to manage and conserve the stocks of wild fauna hunted by humans. There was some evidence in the case that the French Loi Verdeille was actually implementing policies that were more environmentally sound than those advocated by the landowners, but the Court declined to defer to the government, perhaps because of the nature of the claim and the sensitivity of the hunting issue.

In other cases, the Court has rejected claims that rights have been violated when the government has acted for environmental reasons. In most of these cases, the Court has found that environmental protection is a legitimate aim and that the restrictions are reasonable. Thus, in *Mateos e Silva, Ltd. and Others v. Portugal,* the Portuguese government sought to create a nature reserve out of land on the Algarve coast, including parcels owned by the applicants.[64] The Court found that the applicants' rights had been violated because their case against the decision had been pending in local courts for more than thirteen years. On the right to property, the Court accepted that measures pursued through town and country planning for the purposes of protecting the environment serve a legitimate public purpose justifying restrictions on property rights, but found that in this case the restriction was not "necessary" because the government had never implemented the proposed plan for the nature reserve. In contrast to this case, the decision in *Pine Valley Developments Ltd. and Others v. Ireland* upheld the government's interference with property rights in order to protect the environment.[65] The Court found that there was an interference with the right to peaceful enjoyment of possessions when permission was denied to build an industrial warehouse and office development in a zoned green belt, but the interference was for a legitimate government aim—protection of the environment—and the actions were proportionate to the ends.[66]

Indigenous Peoples

Environmental law recognizes the importance of indigenous peoples and local communities, particularly their traditional knowledge about environmentally sustainable practices. In turn, human rights treaties and instruments concerned with indigenous populations contain specific environmental protections. ILO Indigenous and Tribal Peoples Convention (number 169, Article 4), for example, contains environmental rights for the indigenous, requiring States Parties to take special measures to safeguard the environment of indigenous peoples. In particular, governments must provide for environmental impact studies of planned development activities and take measures, in cooperation with the peoples concerned, to protect and preserve the environment of the territories they inhabit.

The provisions of the Covenant on Civil and Political Rights, in particular the guarantee of minority rights, have been invoked to protect indigenous land and culture from environmental degradation. The United Nations Human Rights Committee has interpreted Article 27 of the Covenant on Civil and Political Rights in a broad manner:[67]

> With regard to the exercise of the cultural rights protected under Article 27, the Committee observes that culture manifests itself in many forms, including a particular way of life associated with the use of land resources, especially in the case of indigenous peoples. That right may include such traditional activities as fishing or hunting and the right to live in reserves protected by law. The enjoyment of those rights may require positive legal measures of protection and measures to ensure the effective participation of members of minority communities in decisions which affect them.... The protection of these

rights is directed towards ensuring the survival and continued development of the cultural, religious and social identity of the minorities concerned, thus enriching the fabric of society as a whole.[68]

Article 27 protects the cultural life rather than physical life of indigenous peoples, even though the survival of the group, *qua* group, may be at stake. In a rare case decided on the merits, the Committee decided that Article 27 was not violated by the extent of stone quarrying permitted by Finland in traditional lands of the Sami.[69] The applicants, forty-eight Sami reindeer breeders, challenged the decision of the Central Forestry Board to permit the quarry. The Committee observed that a State may wish to encourage development or economic activity, but found that the scope of its freedom to do so must be tested by reference to the obligations of the State under Article 27. The Committee explicitly rejected the European doctrine of margin of appreciation, holding that measures whose impact amount to a denial of the right to culture will not be compatible with the Covenant, although those which simply have a "certain limited impact on the way of life of persons belonging to a minority" will not necessary violate the treaty. The Committee also referred to its General Comment on Article 27, according to which measures must be taken "to ensure the effective participation of members of minority communities in decisions which affect them."

The Committee concluded that the amount of quarrying that had taken place did not constitute a denial of the applicants' right to culture. It noted that they were consulted and their views taken into account in the government's decision. Moreover, the Committee determined that measures were taken to minimize the impact on reindeer herding activity and on the environment. In regard to future activities the Committee stated, "if mining activities in the Angeli area were to be approved on a large scale and significantly expanded," then it might constitute a violation of Article 27. According to the Committee, "[t]he State party is under a duty to bear this in mind when either extending existing contracts or granting new ones."[70]

In *Bernard Ominayak and the Lubicon Band v. Canada,* applicants alleged that the government of the province of Alberta had deprived the band of their means of subsistence and their right to self-determination by selling oil and gas concessions on their lands.[71] The Committee characterized the claim as one of minority rights under Article 27 and found that historic inequities and more recent developments, including the oil and gas exploitation, were threatening the way of life and culture of the band and thus were in violation of Article 27.

In the Inter-American system, the Commission established a link between environmental quality and the right to life in response to a petition brought on behalf of the Yanomami Indians of Brazil. The petition alleged that the government violated the American Declaration of the Rights and Duties of Man by constructing a highway through Yanomami territory and authorizing the exploitation of the territory's resources.[72] These actions led to the influx of nonindigenous people who brought contagious diseases that remained untreated due to lack of medical care. The Commission found that the government had violated the Yanomami rights to life, liberty, and personal security guaranteed by Article 1 of the Declaration, as well as the right of residence and movement (Article 8) and the right to the preservation of health and well-being (Article 11).[73]

Apart from deciding the individual complaints brought to it and discussed above, the Inter-American Commission on Human Rights has the authority to study the human rights situation generally or in regard to specific issues with a Member State of the OAS. In two recently published studies, the Commission devoted particular attention to environmental rights of indigenous in Ecuador[74] and Brazil.[75]

In regard to Ecuador, the Commission noted that it had been examining the human rights situation in the Oriente for several years, in response to claims that oil exploitation activities were contaminating the water, air, and soil, thereby causing the people of the region to become sick and to have a greatly increased risk of serious illness.[76] It found, after an on-site visit, that both the government and inhabitants agreed that the environment was contaminated, with inhabitants exposed to toxic by-products of oil exploitation in their drinking and bathing water, in the air, and in the soil. The inhabitants were unanimous in claiming that oil operations, especially the disposal of toxic wastes, jeopardized their lives and health. Many suffered skin diseases, rashes, chronic infections, and gastrointestinal problems. In addition, many claimed that pollution of local waters contaminated fish and drove away wildlife, which threatened food supplies.

The Commission in its discussion of relevant human rights law emphasized the right to life and physical security. It stated that "[t]he realization of the right to life, and to physical security and integrity is necessarily related to and in some ways dependent upon one's physical environment. Accordingly, where environmental contamination and degradation pose a persistent threat to human life and health, the foregoing rights are implicated."[77]

In this regard, States Parties may be required to take positive measures to safeguard the fundamental and nonderogable rights to life and physical integrity, in particular to prevent the risk of severe environmental pollution that could threaten human life and health, or to respond when persons have suffered injury.

The Commission also directly addressed concerns for economic development, noting that the Convention does not prevent nor discourage it, but rather requires that it take place under conditions of respect for the rights of affected individuals. Thus, while the right to development implies that each State may exploit its natural resources, "the absence of regulation, inappropriate regulation, or a lack of supervision in the application of extant norms may create serious problems with respect to the environment which translate into violations of human rights protected by the American Convention."[78]

The Commission concluded that "[c]onditions of severe environmental pollution, which may cause serious physical illness, impairment and suffering on the part of the local populace, are inconsistent with the right to be respected as a human being. . . . The quest to guard against environmental conditions which threaten human health requires that individuals have access to: information, participation in relevant decision-making processes, and judicial recourse."[79]

This holding can clearly be applied outside the context of indigenous peoples and sets general standards for environmental rights in the Inter-American system. The Commission elaborated on these rights, stating that the right to seek, receive, and impart information and ideas of all kinds is protected by Article 13 of the American Convention. According to the Commission, information that domestic law requires be submitted as part of environmental impact assessment procedures must be "readily accessible" to potentially affected individuals. Public participation is viewed as linked to Article 23 of the American Convention, which provides that every citizen shall enjoy the right "to take part in the conduct of public affairs, directly or through freely chosen representatives." Finally, the right of access to judicial remedies is called "the fundamental guarantor of rights at the national level." The Commission quotes Article 25 of the American Convention that provides everyone "the right to simple and prompt recourse, or any other effective recourse, to a competent court or tribunal for protection against acts that violate his fundamental rights recognized by the constitution or laws of the state concerned or by th[e] Convention."

The Commission called on the government to implement legislation enacted to strengthen protection against pollution, to clean up activities by private licensee companies, and to take further action to remedy existing contamination and prevent future recurrences. In particular, it recommended that the State take measures to improve systems to disseminate information about environmental issues, and to enhance the transparency of and opportunities for public input into processes affecting the inhabitants of development sectors.

The report on Brazil also included a chapter on indigenous rights. Among the problems discussed are those of environmental destruction leading to severe health and cultural consequences. In particular, cultural and physical integrity is said to be under constant threat and attack from invading prospectors and the environmental pollution they create. State protection against the invasions is called "irregular and feeble," leading to constant danger and environmental deterioration.

Conclusion

Without the link of property, conscience, or association, it is difficult to see human rights tribunals moving more broadly into nature protection, given the current human rights catalog. Neither scenic areas, including flora and fauna, nor ecological balance are viewed as rights to which humans are entitled, without an explicit recognition of the right to a specific environment. No doubt debate will continue over whether such a recognition serves to enhance environmental protection or simply to further the anthropocentric, utilitarian view that all the world exists to further human well-being.

If a right to environment becomes widely accepted as part of the human rights catalog, there remains the problem of balancing it with other human rights. The General Assembly has declared repeatedly the indivisibility, interdependence, interrelatedness, and universality of all human rights.[80] In December 1997 it reiterated its conviction of this reality and emphasized that transparent and accountable governance in all sectors of society, as well as effective participation by civil society, is an essential part of the necessary foundations for the realization of sustainable development.[81] Yet, the possibility of collision or conflict between rights cannot be avoided. For example, among the human rights guaranteed by international law is the right of each family to decide on the number and spacing of their children. Demographic pressures have been recognized as a threat to environmental quality and economic development, however, leading to demands that national birthrates be lowered to achieve sustainable development.[82] The possibility that some human rights may be limited to achieve the right to environment is seen in the Constitution of Ecuador in which Article 19 establishes "the right to live in an environment free from contamination." The Constitution invests the State with responsibility for ensuring the enjoyment of this right and "for establishing by law such restrictions on other rights and freedoms as are necessary to protect the environment." As noted by the Inter-American Commission on Human Rights, the Constitution thus establishes a hierarchy according to which environmental protection may have priority over other entitlements.[83]

Recently, the concept of environmental justice has come to play an important role in international environmental law and policy as a means of integrating human rights and environmental law, even as the content and scope of the term remains under discussion. It is increasingly recognized that favorable natural conditions are essential to the fulfillment of human desires and goals. Preservation of these conditions is a basic need of individuals and societies. Environmental justice encompasses preserving environmental quality, sustaining the ecological well-being of present and future generations, and reconciling competing interests. There is also an element of distributional justice, as it has become clear that the poor and marginalized of societies, including the global society, disproportionately suffer from environmental harm.

Environmental justice emphasizes the environment as a social good rather than a commodity or purely economic asset. The focus is on the proper allocation of social benefits and burdens, both in the present and in the future. Thus, it requires the equitable distribution of environmental amenities and environmental risks, the redress and sanctioning of environmental abuses, the restoration and conservation of nature and the fair allocation of resource benefits. The "polluter-pays" principle itself is based on the concept of environmental justice, as it encompasses the notion that those who engage in and profit from activities that damage the environment should be liable for the harm caused. On the most fundamental level, environmental justice can be seen as a term that encompasses the twin aims of environmental protection and international protection of human rights.

NOTES

1. See Alexandre Kiss, "The Right to the Conservation of the Environment," this volume.

2. Judge Weeramantry of the International Court of Justice reflects this view:

"The protection of the environment is . . . a vital part of contemporary human rights doctrine, for it is a *sine qua non* for numerous human rights such as the right to health and the right to life itself. It is scarcely necessary to elaborate on this, as damage to the environment can impair and undermine all the human rights spoken of in the Universal Declaration and other human rights instruments." Case Concerning the Gabcikovo-Nagymaros Project *(Hungary v. Slovakia)*, 1997 ICJ Rep 7 (25 September; sep op., Judge Weeramantry), 4.

3. Efforts to catalog the internationally guaranteed human rights had been largely completed when environmental issues became matters of international concern. The relatively recent United Nations Convention on the Rights of the Child is the only United Nations human rights treaty to refer to aspects of environmental protection, linking it to the right to health (General Assembly, Document A/RES/44/49, Supplement 49, prepared in pursuit of resolution 44/25, and United Nations GAOR, Document 166, 1989, reprinted at 28 ILM 1448, 1989). It specifies in Article 24 that:

1. States Parties recognize the right of the child to the enjoyment of the highest attainable standard of health and to facilities for the treatment of illness and rehabilitation of health. . . .
2. States Parties shall pursue full implementation of this right and, in particular, shall take appropriate measures:

   . . .

   (c) To combat disease and malnutrition . . . through inter alia the application of readily available technology and through the provision of adequate nutritious foods *and clean drinking water, taking into consideration the dangers and risks of environmental pollution; [emphasis added]*

   . . .

   (e) to ensure that all segments of society, in particular parents and children, are informed, have access to education and are supported in the use of, basic knowledge of child health and nutrition, . . . hygiene and *environmental sanitation* and the prevention of accidents. *[emphasis added]*

4. Alan Boyle, "The Role of International Human Rights Law in the Protection of the Environment," in Alan Boyle and Michael Anderson, eds., *Human Rights Approaches to Environmental Protection* (1996): 43–69.

5. As discussed by Professor Kiss, supra note 1, the North American Agreement on Environmental Cooperation (14 September 1993) grants individuals limited recourse to complain about a State's failure to enforce its environmental law. In addition, the Aarhus Convention of 25 June 1998 foresees the possibility of developing a procedure of communications from members of the public.

6. United Nations ESCOR, Forty-fourth session, Document C/CN.4/1989/86, Supplement 2, prepared in pursuance of Resolution 1989/42, 1989, 111.

7. Basel Convention on the Control of Transboundary Movements of Hazardous Wastes and Their Disposal. United Nations, document UNEP/WG.190/4, 1989, reprinted at 28 ILM 657.

8. United Nations, Fifty-first session, Resolution 1995/81. The vote was 32 to 15, with six abstentions. The division was geographic, with all developing coun-

tries of the south voting in favor of the proposal and all northern States expressing opposition. France, on behalf of the European Union, argued that the question could be dealt with much more effectively through instruments such as the Basel Convention on the Control of Transboundary Movements of Hazardous Wastes and Their Disposal. Consequently, the study "would lead to needless duplication of international mechanisms and to dissipation or wastage of resources."

9. In the 1998 report, for example, the government of Paraguay informed the Special Rapporteur that it was investigating a serious case of illicit movement and dumping of toxic wastes that may have occurred in its territory. The government asked the Special Rapporteur for assistance in the investigation. Similarly, the government of Thailand informed the Special Rapporteur of a 1991 fire in warehouses in the port of Bangkok, which caused loss of life and property in the surrounding areas. In her 2000 report, three State-initiated cases are discussed: Cambodia against Taiwan; Panama against the United States; and Paraguay against a private company, Delta Pine E/CN.4/2000/50, 20 March 2000.

10. The right to information is included in United Nations, General Assembly, Document A/810, Article 19, *Universal Declaration of Human Rights,* prepared in response to UN General Assembly Resolution 217A, 1948; United Nations, General Assembly, Article 19(2), *International Covenant on Civil and Political Rights* (ICCPR), prepared in response to Resolution 2200, 21, annex, 1966; reprinted in 6 ILM 368 (1967); OAS, Ninth International Conference of the American States, Article 10, *American Declaration of the Rights and Duties of Man,* prepared in response to Resolution 30, 1948, Bogota; OAS, Official Records, OEA/Ser.L/V/I.4, revised 1965; OASTS, Article 13, number 36, The American Convention on Human Rights, 1978, OAS Official Record OEA/Ser.L/II.23, Document 21, revised 1969, San Jose, 6; OAU, Article 9, *The African Charter on Human and Peoples Rights,* OAU Document CAB/LEG/67/3, revision 5, 1981, Banjul, reprinted in 21 ILM 59, 1982.

11. European Convention for the Protection of Human Rights and Fundamental Freedoms (Rome, 4 November 1950), 213 UNTS 221; ETS 5, UKTS 71 (1953), CMD 8969.

12. See Stefan Weber, *Environmental Information and the European Convention on Human Rights,* 12 Hum. Rts. L. J. 177 (1991).

13. *Leander v. Sweden,* ECHR series A, number 117, para 74 (1987). See also *Gaskin v. United Kingdom,* ECHR series A, number 160, 1987, which states that the government did not breach convention in failing to allow access to a personal file of a former foster child.

14. *Guerra et al v. Italy,* 1998-1 ECHR 14967/89, Judgment of 19 February 1998.

15. EEC Directive on Major Accident Hazards of Certain Industrial Activities, 82/501/EEC, 1982 OJ 230, amended by 87/216/EEC, 19 March 1987. The European Community's Seveso law required disclosure of the production process; the substances present and their quantities; possible risks for employees, workers, the population, and the environment; security measures and rules to follow in case of accident. Other laws supplemented the right to environmental information.

16. The European Commission on Human Rights ceased to function with the entry into force of protocol 11 to the European Convention, which created a permanent European Court of Human Rights. Protocol 11 to the European Convention for the Protection of Human Rights and Fundamental Freedoms, adopted 11 May 1994, entered into force 1 November 1998, ETS 155, reprinted in 33 ILM 960 (1994). The new court was inaugurated on 1 November 1998.

17. *Lopez-Ostra v. Spain,* ECHR (1994), series A, number 303C.

18. Supra note 14, at para 53.

19. The case is *Bladet Tromso and Stensaas v. Norway,* Judgment of 20 May 1999.

20. The government had decided, on the basis of Norwegian law, not to publish the report because it contained allegations of statutory offenses.

21. Universal Declaration of Human Rights, Article 21; International Covenant on Civil and Political Rights, Article 25; European Convention on Human Rights, Protocol I, Article 3; American Declaration of the Rights and Duties of Man, Article 20, 24; American Convention on Human Rights, Article 23; African Charter of Human and Peoples' Rights, Article 13, supra note 10.

22. Some argue that democratic governance is itself an emerging right. See Thomas Franck, *The Emerging Right to Democratic Governance,* 86 AJIL 46 (1992); Gregory Fox, *The Right to Political Participation in International Law,* 17 Yale L. J. Int'l L., 539 (1992); Henry Steiner, *Political Participation as a Human Right,* 78 Harv. Hum. Rts. Y'bk 78 (1988).

23. See Henry Steiner and P. Alston, *International Human Rights in Context* (Oxford University Press, 1996): 659.

24. Brad Roth, *Democratic Progress: A Normative Theoretical Perspective,* 9 Ethics and Int'l Aff., 55 (1995).

25. See Alexandre Kiss, chap 2, this volume.

26. United Nations. Human Rights Committee, Communication No. 547/1992, *Apirana Mahuika et al v. New Zealand,* CCPR/C/70/D/547/1993, 16 November 2000.

27. Article 27 provides: "In those States in which ethnic, religious or linguistic minorities exist, persons belonging to such minorities shall not be denied the right, in community with the other members of their group, to enjoy their own culture, to profess and practice their own religion, or to use their own language." ICCPR, supra note 10.

28. See, for example, 1998-1 Universal Declaration of Human Rights, Article 8; International Covenant on Civil and Political Rights, Article 2(3); American Declaration of the Rights and Duties of Man, Article 27; African Charter, Article 7 ("[E]very individual shall have the right to have his cause heard, including the right to an appeal to competent national organs against acts violating his fundamental rights as recognized and guaranteed by conventions, laws, regulations and customs in force"); African Charter Article 21(2) ("the right to adequate compensation in regard to the spoliation of resources of a dispossessed people") and African Charter Article 26 ("guaranteeing the independence of the courts and the establishment and improvement of appropriate national institu-

tions entrusted with the promotion and protection of rights and freedoms guaranteed by the Charter). The ILO Convention concerning Indigenous and Tribal Peoples in Independent Countries, ILO 169, 27 June 1989, in force 5 September 1991, 28 ILM 1382 (1989), Article 15(2), refers to "fair compensation for damages"; Article 16(4) refers to "compensation in money"; and Article 16(5) refers to full compensation for "any loss or injury."

29. See Universal Declaration of Human Rights, Article 12; International Covenant on Civil and Political Rights, Article 17; Convention on the Rights of the Child, Article 16; American Declaration of the Rights and Duties of Man, Article 5; American Convention on Human Rights, Article 11(3); European Convention on Human Rights, Article 8; African Charter on Human and Peoples Rights, Article 5.

30. United Nations, *Compilation of General Comments and General Recommendations Adopted by Human Rights Treaty Bodies,* HRI/GEN/1/Rev. 4, 7 February 2000. The Committee also has referred to environmental issues in its General Comments on the Right to Adequate Food and the Right to Adequate Housing. In the first, General Comment 12, E/C.12/1999/5, the Committee interpreted the phrase "free from adverse substances" in Article 11 of the Covenant to mean that the State must adopt food safety and other protective measures to prevent contamination through "bad environmental hygiene." The Comment on housing, General Comment 4 of 13 December 1991, states that "housing should not be built on polluted sites nor in proximity to pollution sources that threaten the right to health of the inhabitants."

31. American Convention on Human Rights, Article 25.

32. *Velasquez Rodriguez Case (Preliminary Exceptions)* IACtHR (1987), series C, number 1, para 91.

33. *Velasquez Rodriguez Case (Merits),* IACtHR (1988), series C, number 4, para 166. Report No. 30/97, *Gustavo Carranza v. Argentina,* IACHR, *Annual Report of the Inter-American Commission on Human Rights 1997,* OEA/Ser.L/V/II.98, 7 December 1998, 266–67. The Inter-American Commission has further elaborated on the duty to provide a remedy. It views Article 8 as requiring due process during procedures to determine rights, including determination of the matter in question by a competent, independent, and impartial judicial body. It views Article 25 as encompassing the right to "effective" judicial protection, not mere access to a judicial body.

34. Article 6, para 1, states: "In the determination of his civil rights and obligations or of any criminal charge against him, everyone is entitled to a fair and public hearing within a reasonable time by an independent and impartial tribunal established by law."

35. *Golder v. United Kingdom,* ECHR (1975), series A, number 18; *Klass v. Germany,* ECHR (1978), series A, number 28.

36. *Benthem v. Netherlands,* ECHR (1985), series A, number 97.

37. *Oerlemans v. Netherlands,* ECHR (1991), series A, number 219.

38. *Zander v. Sweden,* ECHR (1993), series A, number 279B.

39. Ibid., para 24.

40. Ibid., para 45 (commission opinion).

41. *Balmer-Schafroth et al v. Switzerland,* 1997-IV ECHR, Judgment of 26 August 1997.

42. Communication 645/1995, U CCPR/C/57/D/645/1995, 30 July 1996.

43. The applicants also coauthored a complaint on the same case and submitted it to the European Commission on Human Rights, where it was registered as case 28204/95. The case was declared inadmissible on 4 December 1995.

44. *Zimmerman and Steiner v. Switzerland,* ECHR (1983), series A, number 66.

45. *Braunerheilm v. Sweden,* App. No. 11764/85 (9 March 1989). See Maguelonne Dejeant-Pons, *Le Droit de l'homme a l'environnement, droit fondamental au niveau europeen dans le cadre du Conseil de l'Europe, et la Convention europeenne de sauvegarde des droit de l'homme et des libertes fondamentales,* 4 Revue Jur. de L'environnement (1994).

46. See the General Comment on Article 6 of the Civil and Political Covenant, issued by the United Nations Human Rights Committee, in *Compilation of General Comments and General Recommendations adopted by Human Rights Treaty Bodies,* UN Doc. HRI/GEN/1/Rev.3 (1997) 6–7 [hereinafter *Compilation*].

47. E/1986/3/Addendum 9.

48. E/1989/4/Addendum 12.

49. *EHP v. Canada,* Communication 67/1980, Two Selected Decisions of the Human Rights Committee (1990), 20.

50. The finding followed the consolidation of the four listed communications that asserted torture, killings, arbitrary detention, unfair trials, restrictions on the right to association and peaceful assembly, suppression of freedom of the press, denial of the right to education and of the right to health. In regard to the last the commission said, "Article 16 of the African Charter states that every individual shall have the right to enjoy the best attainable state of physical and mental health, and that States Parties should take the necessary measures to protect the health of their people. The failure of the Government to provide basic services such as safe drinking water and electricity and the shortage of medicine as alleged in communication 100/93 constitutes a violation of Article 16." (AHG/207(22), Annex VIII, 8.)

51. Paragraph 2 provides, "There shall be no interference by a public authority with the exercise of this right except such as is in accordance with the law and is necessary in a democratic society in the interests of national security, public safety or the economic well-being of the country, for the prevention of disorder or crime, for the protection of health and morals, or for the protection of the rights and freedoms of others."

52. *Rayner v. United Kingdom* 47 DR 5, 14 (1986).

53. *Arrondelle v. United Kingdom* 19 DR 186 (1980); 26 DR 5 (1982).

54. *Baggs v. United Kingdom* 44 DR 13 (1985); 52 DR 29 (1987).

55. *Powell and Rayner v. United Kingdom,* ECHR (1990), series A, number 172.

56. *Vearncombe et al v. United Kingdom and Federal Republic of Germany,* 59 DR 186 (1989).

57. See also *S. v. France,* 65 DR 250 (1990). The application was deemed in-

admissible. The court ruled that the nuisance due to a nuclear power station built three hundred meters from the applicant's house constituted a breach of Article 8(1) but was justified under Article 8(2) because the economic well-being of the country made it necessary in a democratic society, and there was no unreasonable burden placed on the applicant because compensation was paid.

58. *Joined Applications 9278/81 and 9415/81,* 35 DR 30 (1984).

59. *Lopez-Ostra v. Spain,* ECHR (1994), series A, number 303C.

60. Ibid., para 60.

61. *Application 68/25/74,* 5 DR 86.

62. *Marie-Jeanne Chassagnou, Rene Petit, and Simone Lasgrezas v. France,* http://www.dhcommhr.coe.fr/fr/25088R31.F.html

63. *Chassagnou et al v. France,* 1999-III ECHR, Judgment of 29 April 1999.

64. *Mateos y Silva Ltd. et al v. Portugal,* 1996-IV ECHR, Judgment of 16 September 1996.

65. *Pine Valley Developments Ltd. et al v. Ireland,* ECHR series A, number 222 (1991). The court did find a violation of Article 14 taken in conjunction with the right to peaceful enjoyment of possessions.

66. See also *Buckley v. The United Kingdom,* 1996-IV ECHR, Judgment of 25 September 1996, in which a gypsy woman was fined for having a caravan on her land under a law that required gypsy caravans to be located in specially designated areas to "protect the natural beauty of the environment." A claim that this infringed Article 8 was rejected because the law was held to pursue a legitimate State interest and was not disproportionate.

67. Covenant on Civil and Political Rights, Article 27, provides that members of minority groups "shall not be denied the right, in community with other members of their group, to enjoy their own culture, to profess and practice their own religion, or to use their own language."

68. General Comment 23, paras 7, 9 in *Compilation* supra note 30 at 117. See *Kitok v. Sweden,* Comm. 197/1985, *II Official Records of the Human Rights Committee 1987/88,* United Nations, Document CCPR/7/Addendum 1, at 442. The Swedish 1971 Reindeer Husbandry Act held not to violate rights of an individual Sami as a reasonable and objective measure necessary for the continued viability and welfare of the minority as a whole.

69. Communication 511/1992, *Ilmari Länsman et al v. Finland,* Human Rights Committee, Final Decisions, 74, CCPR/C/57/1 (1996).

70. Other cases involving Sami reindeer breeders include Communication 431/1990, *O. S. et al v. Finland,* decision of 23 March 1994, and Communication 671/1995, *Jouni E. Länsmann et al v. Finland,* decision of 30 October 1996.

71. United Nations, Document CCPR/C/38/D/167/1984, Communication 167/1984, *Decisions of the Human Rights Committee* (1990).

72. Pan American Union, Final Act of the Ninth Conference of American States, Resolution 30 (1948) 38, reprinted in OAS, *Basic Documents Pertaining to Human Rights in the Inter-American System* (1996).

73. Inter-American CHR Case 7615 (Brazil), *1984–1985 Annual Report 24,* OEA/Ser.L/V/II.66, Document 10, Revision 1 (1985).

74. Inter–Am.C. H. R., *Report on the Situation of Human Rights in Ecuador,*

OEA/Ser.L/V/II.96, Document 10, Revision 1 (1997)[hereinafter Report on Ecuador].

75. Inter–Am.C. H. R., *Report on the Situation of Human Rights in Brazil,* OEA/Ser.L/V/II.97, doc. 29, rev. 1 (1997).

76. Report on Ecuador, supra note 74. The commission first became aware of problems in this region of the country when a petition was filed on behalf of the indigenous Huaorani people in 1990. The commission decided that the situation was not restricted to the Huaorani and thus should be treated within the framework of the general country report.

77. Report on Ecuador, ibid., 88.

78. Ibid., 89.

79. Ibid., 92, 93.

80. See United Nations, General Assembly, Document A/CONF.157/24, Part 1, *The Vienna Declaration and Program of Action,* adopted by the World Conference on Human Rights, 1993.

81. United Nations, General Assembly, Resolution 52/136, Document A/52/644/Add.2, 1997.

82. See United Nations Publication E.95.XIII.18, *Report of the International Conference on Population and Development,* 5–13 September 1994, Cairo.

83. Inter-American Commission on Human Rights, Report on Ecuador, supra note 74, 87.

2

The Right to the Conservation of the Environment

Alexandre Kiss

AT THE END OF THE 1960S, environmental concerns had emerged to become a major international issue, but there was little developed international law on the topic. Growing environmental awareness led the United Nations to consider the interdependence of environmental protection and human rights, both recognized as fundamental values of humankind. The 1972 Stockholm Conference on the Human Environment made an important step in this direction by proclaiming in Principle 1 of the Declaration on the Human Environment that "Man has the fundamental right to freedom, equality and adequate conditions of life, in an environment of a quality that permits a life of dignity and well-being, and he bears a solemn responsibility to protect and improve the environment for present and future generations." This formulation clearly links human rights and environmental protection. It sees human rights as a fundamental goal and environmental protection as an essential means to achieve the "adequate conditions" for a "life of dignity and well-being" that are guaranteed.

Almost twenty years later, in Resolution 45/94, the United Nations General Assembly recalled the language of Stockholm, stating that it "Recognizes that all individuals are entitled to live in an environment adequate for their health and well-being; and calls upon Member States and intergovernmental and non-governmental organizations to enhance their efforts towards ensuring a better and healthier environment."[1]

In the meantime the African Charter on Human and Peoples Rights, adopted in Nairobi on 27 June 1981, proclaimed that "All peoples shall have the right to a general satisfactory environment favorable to their development."[2]

A more complete formulation, inserted in the Additional Protocol to the American Convention on Human Rights in the Area of Economic,

Social and Cultural Rights, adopted in San Salvador on 17 November 1988, takes into account the right of individuals as well as the duty of States in this field:

1 Everyone shall have the right to live in a healthy environment and to have access to basic public services.
2 The States Parties shall promote the protection, preservation and improvement of the environment.[3]

For years, the question was discussed whether such declarations and provisions amount to the creation of a "right to environment" and if so, what the exact meaning of such a right is. The objections concerned the difficulty to reach general consensus on the definition of the environment. Moreover, it was contested that even if such consensus could be established, the question remained: How would jurisdictions be able to protect rights that have such a general scope, and who could claim for the respect of such a right?

The answer that the authors of the declaration suggested was to consider the right to environment as some generally recognized fundamental rights that cannot be guaranteed by legal means other than by imposing sanctions against their violation. The most fundamental of all human rights, such as the right to life and the right not to be submitted to torture or cruel and degrading treatment, fall in this category. It was submitted that their real guarantee is the existence of procedures that ensure their protection. Similarly, the right to environment should be understood as a right protected by specific procedures and should be formulated not as the right to a general environmental quality but as the right to the protection of the environment. This means that individuals and their groups should dispose of available procedures that do not include such protection.

An important condition must be imposed when adopting such an approach. The environment must be protected as far as possible by preventive measures; often environmental degradation cannot be repaired or the cost of repair is too high to make compensating measures acceptable. As a consequence, the right to the protection of the environment should incorporate preventive procedures in addition to procedures tending to ensure adequate remedies for the violation of such a right. Individuals should be able to obtain prior information on projects and actions that may damage their environment and should also be given the opportunity to participate in making the decisions that concern the adoption and implementation of such plans and actions.

Principle 10 of the Declaration on Environment and Development, adopted by the 1992 Conference of Rio de Janeiro, can be considered as a worldwide recognition of such formulation of the right to environment. It provides that individuals shall have appropriate access to information concerning the environment that is held by public authorities, including information on hazardous materials and activities in their communities, and the opportunity to participate in decision-making processes. States shall facilitate and encourage public awareness and participation by making information widely available. Effective access to judicial and administrative proceedings, including regress and remedy, shall be provided. Even before the Rio Conference, various aspects of the right to the protection of the environment had been confirmed.

The Right to Environmental Information

A "right to information" can mean, narrowly, freedom to seek information, or, more broadly, a right to access to information, or even a right to receive it. Corresponding duties of the State can be limited to abstention from interfering with public efforts to obtain information from the State or from private entities, or expanded to require the State to obtain and disseminate all relevant information concerning both public and private projects that might affect the environment. If the government's duty is limited to abstention from interfering with the ability of individuals or associations to seek information from those willing to share it, then little may actually be obtained. A governmental obligation to release information about its own projects can increase public knowledge, but fails to provide access to the numerous private-sector activities that can affect the environment. Information about the latter may be obtained by the government through licensing or environmental impact requirements. Imposing upon the State a duty to disseminate this information in addition to details of its own projects provides the public with the broadest basis for informed decision making.

As noted above, Rio Principle 10 calls for States to provide environmental information. Similarly, chapter 23 of Agenda 21, on strengthening the role of major groups, proclaims that individuals, groups, and organizations should have access to information relevant to the environment and development held by national authorities, including information on products and activities that have or are likely to have a significant impact on the environment, and information on environmental protection matters.

Informational rights are widely found in environmental treaties. The Framework Convention on Climate Change, Article 6, provides that its Parties "shall promote and facilitate at the national and, as appropriate, subregional and regional levels, and in accordance with national laws and regulations, and within their respective capacities, public access to information and public participation."

In contrast to the Climate Change Convention, the Convention on Biological Diversity does not oblige States Parties to provide public information. It refers in its Preamble to the general lack of information and knowledge regarding biological diversity. Article 14 provides that each contracting Party, "as far as possible and as appropriate," shall introduce "appropriate" environmental impact assessment procedures and "where appropriate" allow for public participation in such procedures.

Other recent multilateral treaties contain broader guarantees of public information, including the Helsinki Convention on the Protection and Use of Transboundary Watercourses and International Lakes (Article 16), the Espoo Convention on Environmental Impact Assessment in a Transboundary Context (Article 3(8)), and the Paris Convention on the North-East Atlantic (Article 9). The last mentioned is typical in requiring the contracting Parties to ensure that their competent authorities make available relevant information to any natural or legal person, in response to any reasonable request, without the person having to prove an interest, without unreasonable charges and within two months of the request.

The Rotterdam Convention on the Prior Informed Consent Procedure for Certain Hazardous Chemicals and Pesticides in International Trade (11 September 1998) imposes a direct duty on States Parties to make information available to the public (Article 15).[4] Paragraph 2 requires each State Party to ensure "to the extent practicable" that the public has "appropriate" access to information on chemical handling and accident management and on alternatives that are safer for human health or the environment than the chemicals listed in Annex 3 to the Convention.

Other treaties require States Parties to inform the public of specific environmental hazards. The International Atomic Energy Agency Joint Convention on the Safety of Spent Fuel Management and on the Safety of Radioactive Waste Management is based to a large extent on the principles contained in the IAEA document "The Principles of Radioactive Waste Management."[5] The Preamble of the treaty recognizes the importance of informing the public on issues regarding the safety of spent fuel and radioactive waste management. This is reinforced in Articles 6 and 13, on siting of proposed facilities, which require each State Party to take the appropriate steps to ensure that procedures are established and implemented to make information available to members of the public on the safety of any proposed spent fuel management facility or radioactive waste management facility.

On a regional level, within the European Community, the right to information generally means that the individual has the right to be informed about the environmental compatibility of products, manufacturing processes and their effects on the environment, and industrial installations.[6] Specific directives vary regarding public rights to information. Some air pollution directives, for example, provide that information shall be made available to the public concerned in accordance with the national legal procedures.

Two general directives address rights of information. First, the duty to provide information in connection with mandatory environmental assessment projects is made explicit in Council Directive 85/337 Concerning the Assessment of the Effects of Certain Public and Private Projects on the Environment.[7] Second, on 7 June 1990 the Community adopted a Directive on Freedom of Access to Information on the Environment.[8] The directive includes virtually all environmental data, covering information held by public authorities that relates to the state of the environment, activities or measures adversely affecting or likely to affect the environment, and activities or measures designed to protect the environment (Article 2(a)). "Public authorities" is defined to include all administrations with responsibilities relating to the environment (Article 2(b)), but Article 6 extends the directive's application to all bodies that have responsibilities for the environment that derive from public authorities. Thus, the Directive applies to anyone delegated environmental functions, except judicial and legislative bodies acting "in a judicial or legislative capacity." Access to information is available to any "natural or legal person" without distinction according to nationality and without the necessity to prove an interest (Article 3(1)), thus allowing individuals in another member State or even those from outside the Community to have access to information. The State must respond within two months to any request for information and must give reasons for any refusal to supply the requested information. A judicial or administrative review of the decision must be provided in accordance with the relevant national legal system.

While the scope of the directive is broad, the exceptions are as well. Member States may refuse a request for information when it affects the confidentiality of proceedings of public authorities, international relations, and national defense; public security; matters that are or have been in litigation or under inquiry, or that are the subject of preliminary investigation proceedings; commercial and industrial confidentiality, including intellectual property; and the confidentiality of personal data and files. Member States may also refuse material supplied by a third party without that party being under a legal obligation to do so, material the disclosure of which would make it more likely that the environment would be damaged; material that involves a supply of unfinished documents, or dated or internal communications. Finally they may refuse any request that is manifestly unreasonable or formulated in too general a manner. The scope of the right of access to information as well as the grounds for refusal should be subject to review by the European Court of Justice in a properly brought case.

Other organizations have issued nonbinding declarations that proclaim a right to environmental information. The World Health Organization's European Charter on the Environment and Health states that "every individual is entitled to information and consultation on the state of the environment."[9] The States participating in the Helsinki process have confirmed the right of individuals, groups, and organizations to obtain, publish, and distribute information on environmental issues.[10] The Bangkok Declaration, adopted 16 October 1990, affirms similar rights in Asia and the Pacific[11] while the *Arab Declaration on Environment and Development and Future Perspectives* of September 1991 speaks of the right of individuals and nongovernmental organizations to acquire information about environmental issues relevant to them.[12]

Public Participation in Environmental Decision Making

The process by which rules emerge, the ways that proposed rules become norms and norms become law, is highly important to the legitimacy of the law, and legitimacy in turn affects compliance. To a large extent, legitimacy is a matter of participation; the governed must have and perceive that they have a voice in governance through representation, deliberation, or some other form of action.

The major role the public plays in environmental protection is participation in decision making, especially in environmental impact or other permitting procedures. Public participation is based on the right of those who may be affected, including foreign citizens and residents, to have a say in the determination of their environmental future.

The right to participate has two components: the right to be heard and the right to affect decisions. Principle 23 of the 1982 World Charter for

Nature provides for these rights most explicitly: "All persons, in accordance with their national legislation, shall have the opportunity to participate, individually or with others, in the formulation of decisions of direct concern to their environment, and shall have access to means of redress when their environment has suffered damage or degradation."

The preparation of the Rio Conference was an important step in encouraging the participation of nongovernmental organizations and the representatives of economic interests. The Global Forum of Rio, a meeting of nongovernmental organizations parallel to the official conference, represented world public opinion in favor of conserving the world's ecosystem. The Rio Declaration reflects and confirms the importance of this opinion.

The Rio Declaration, Principle 10, recognizes a right to public participation, but in addition to Principle 10, the Declaration also includes provisions for the participation of various components of the population: women (Principle 20), youth (Principle 21), and indigenous peoples and local communities (Principle 22). The democratization of the international negotiating process reflected in the Declaration is a fundamental contribution of the Rio Conference.

Public participation also is emphasized in Agenda 21. The Preamble to chapter 23 states:

> One of the fundamental prerequisites for the achievement of sustainable development is broad public participation in decision making. Furthermore, in the more specific context of environment and development, the need for new forms of participation has emerged. This includes the need of individuals, groups, and organizations to participate in environmental impact assessment procedures and to know about and participate in decisions, particularly those that potentially affect the communities in which they live and work. Individuals, groups and organizations should have access to information relevant to environment and development held by national authorities, including information on products and activities that have or are likely to have a significant impact on the environment, and information on environmental protection measures.

Most recent multilateral and many bilateral agreements contain references to or guarantees of public participation. The Climate Change Convention, Article 4l(i), obliges Parties to promote public awareness and to "encourage the widest participation in this process including that of nongovernmental organizations." The Convention on Biological Diversity allows for public participation in environmental impact assessment procedures in Article 14(1)(a). Outside the UNCED context, the 1991 Espoo Convention on Environmental Impact Assessment in a Transboundary Context requires States Parties to notify the public and to provide an opportunity for public participation in relevant environmental impact assessment procedures regarding proposed activities in any area likely to be affected by transboundary environmental harm. In a final decision on the proposed activities, the State must take due account of the environmental impact assessment, including the opinions of the individuals in the affected area. The Desertification Convention goes furthest in calling for public participation, embedding the issue throughout the agreement. Article 3(a and c) begins by recognizing that there is a need to associate civil society with the actions of the State. The treaty calls for an integrated commitment of all actors—national governments, scientific institutions, local communities and authorities, and nongovernmental organizations, as well as international partners, both bilateral and multilateral.[13]

There are exceptions to the general trend toward including rights of public participation in multilateral environmental agreements. The United Nations Convention on the Law of the Non-Navigational Uses of International Watercourses (New York, 21 May 1997) and recent regional agreements for water management provide for interstate cooperation, but do not include provisions for the public to participate in decisions regarding the uses and management of international watercourses.[14]

The North American Agreement on Environmental Cooperation (NAAEC) (14 September 1993), also known as the NAFTA Side Agreement, contains institutional arrangements for public participation. It creates a permanent trilateral body, the Commission for Environmental Cooperation, composed of a Council, a Secretariat and a Joint Public Advisory Committee (Article 8). The Joint Public Advisory Committee includes fifteen members from the public and five from each member country, and advises the Council as well as provides technical, scientific, or other information to the Secretariat. The Committee also may advise on the annual program and budget as well as reports that are issued. It meets annually, along with the regular meetings of the Council. NAAEC is also the first environmental agreement to establish a procedure that allows individuals, environmental organizations, and business entities to complain about a State's failure to enforce its environmental law, including those deriving from international obligations.

Recent bilateral agreements also provide for public participation. The 1991 Canada–United States Agreement on Air Quality provides that the International Joint Commission previously established shall invite comments, including through public hearings as appropriate, on each progress report prepared by the Air Quality Committee established to assist in implementing the agreement.[15] A synthesis of public views and, if requested, a record of such views shall be submitted to the Parties. After submission to the Parties, the synthesis shall be released to the public. The Parties agree to consult on the contents of the progress report based in part on the views presented to the Commission. Further, in Article 14, the Parties shall consult with State or Provincial governments, interested organizations, and the public, in implementing the agreement.

The Agreement on Environmental Cooperation between Canada and Chile lists among its objectives to promote transparency and public participation in the development of environmental law, regulations, and policies.[16] The obligations of the Parties include periodically preparing and making publicly available reports on the state of the environment. In more detail, Article 4 provides that each Party shall ensure that its laws, regulations, procedures, and administrative rulings of general application respecting any matter governed by the agreement are promptly published or otherwise made available to enable interested persons and the other Party to become acquainted with them. To the extent possible, each Party is to publish in advance any such measure that it proposes to adopt and provide interested persons and the other Party a reasonable opportunity to comment on the proposed measures.

The Right to a Remedy for Environmental Harm

Principle 10 of the Rio Declaration provides that "effective access to judicial and administrative proceedings, including redress and remedy, shall be provided." Agenda 21 calls on governments and legislators to establish judicial and administrative procedures for legal redress and remedy of actions that affect the environment and that may be unlawful or infringe on rights under the law, and to provide access to individuals, groups, and organizations with a recognized legal interest. UNCLOS also provides that states shall ensure that recourse is available for prompt and adequate compensation or other relief concerning damage caused by pollution of the marine environment by natural or juridical persons under their jurisdiction (Article 235(2)).

Some instruments make it explicit that the right to a remedy is not limited to nationals of a State, for example, the OECD Recommendation on Equal Right of Access in Relation to Transfrontier Pollution.[17] Some international agreements contain obligations to grant a potential or *de facto* injured person a right of access to any administrative or judicial procedures equal to that of nationals or residents. Equal access to national remedies has been considered one way of implementing the "polluter-pays" principle. Implementation of the right of equal access to national remedies requires that States remove jurisdictional barriers to civil proceedings for damages and other remedies in respect of environmental injury. Both the Espoo Convention and the Helsinki Convention on the Transboundary Effects of Industrial Accidents call for equality of access. The United Nations Convention on the Non-Navigational Uses of International Watercourses, Article 32, formulates the same principle under the title "nondiscrimination."

The 1997 Agreement between Canada and Chile Concerning Environmental Cooperation contains broad remedial guarantees in addition to obligations of State enforcement of environmental laws and regulations. Article 6 requires each State Party to ensure that interested persons may call on authorities to investigate alleged violations of the State's environmental laws and regulations. In addition, each Party must ensure that affected persons have access to administrative quasi-judicial or judicial proceedings for the enforcement of the applicable environmental laws and regulations. Private access shall include, in accordance with local law, rights to sue for damages; to seek sanctions or remedies such as penalties, emergency closures, or orders to mitigate the consequences of violation; and to request authorities to take appropriate enforcement actions to protect the environment or avoid environmental harm.

The Aarhus Convention

The various international efforts to promote environmental rights in environmental instruments produced a landmark agreement on 25 June 1998, when thirty-five States and the European Community signed a *Convention on Access to Information, Public Participation and Access to Justice in Environmental Matters.*[18] The Convention builds on prior texts, especially Principle 1 of the Stockholm Declaration, incorporating and strengthening its language. The Preamble expressly states that "every person has the right to live in an environment adequate to his or her health and well-being, and the duty, both individually and in association with others, to protect and improve the environment for the benefit of present and future generations."

The following paragraph adds that to be able to assert the right and observe the duty, citizens must have access to information, be entitled to participate in decision making, and have access to justice in environmental matters. These provisions are repeated in Article 1, where States Parties agree to guarantee the rights of access to information, public participation, and access to justice. The Convention acknowledges its broader implications, expressing a conviction that its implementation will "contribute to strengthening democracy in the region of the UNECE."

The Convention obliges States Parties to collect and publicly disseminate information, and respond to specific requests (Articles 4 and 5). Each Party is to prepare and disseminate a national report on the state of the environment at three- to four-year intervals. In addition, it is to disseminate legislative and policy documents, treaties, and other international instruments relating to the environment. Each Party must ensure that public authorities, upon request, provide environmental information to a requesting person without the latter having to state an interest. Public authorities means, in addition to government bodies, any natural or legal person having public responsibilities or functions or providing public services. The information has to be made available within one month, or in exceptional cases, within up to three months. In addition to providing information on request, each State Party must be proactive, ensuring that public authorities collect and update environmental information relevant to their functions. This requires that each State Party establish mandatory systems to obtain information on proposed and existing activities that could significantly affect the environment. This provision is clearly aimed at the private sector and is supplemented by Article 5(6), which requires States Parties to encourage operators whose activities have a significant impact on the environment to inform the public regularly of the environmental impact of their activities and products, through ecolabeling, ecoauditing, or similar means. States Parties are also to ensure that consumer information on products is made available.

To enhance the effectiveness of the Convention, States Parties must provide information about the type and scope of information held by public authorities, the basic terms and conditions under which it is made available, and the procedure by which it could be obtained. The Convention also foresees the establishment of publicly accessible electronic sites that should contain reports on the state of the environment, texts of environmental legislation, environmental plans, programs and policies, and other information that could facilitate the application of national law.

The treaty provides numerous exceptions in Article 4(4) to the duty to inform in the light of other political, economic, and legal interests. Thus, the State may refuse to provide the information if the information is not in its possession; the request is manifestly unreasonable or too general; material is incomplete or internal communication of a public authority; or the disclosure would adversely affect

- the confidentiality of public proceedings;
- international relations, national defense, or public security;
- criminal investigations or trials;
- commercial and industrial secrets (however, information on emissions relevant to the protection of the environment shall be disclosed);
- intellectual property rights;
- privacy (that is, personal data);
- the interests of a third party;
- the environment, such as the breeding sites of rare species.

The Convention does state that all exceptions are to be read restrictively and the State may provide broader information rights than those contained in the Convention. In addition, where nonexempt information can be separated from that not subject to disclosure, the nonrestricted information must be provided. In spite of these interpretive provisions, many environmental groups have expressed concern that the exceptions will result in the withholding of extensive and crucial information.

Any refusal to provide information must be in writing and with reasons given for the refusal. Reasonable fees may be charged for supplying information. The government has special disclosure obligations in case of any imminent threat to human health or the environment.

Public participation is guaranteed in Articles 6 through 8 and is required in all decisions that regard whether to permit or renew permission for industrial, agricultural, and construction activities listed in an Annex to the Convention as well as other activities that may have a significant impact on the environment. The public must be informed in detail about the proposed activity early in the decision-making process, and be given time to prepare and participate in the decision making. During the process, the public must have access to all relevant information on the proposal, including the site, description of environmental impacts, measures to prevent or reduce the effects, nontechnical summary, outline of the main alternatives, and any reports or advice given. Public participation can be through writing, hearings, or inquiry. All public comments, information, analyses, or opinions shall be taken into account by the Party in making its decision. All decisions shall be made public, along with the reasons and considerations on which the decision is based.

In addition to providing for public participation regarding decisions on specific projects, the Convention calls for public participation in the preparation of environmental plans, programs, policies, laws, and regulations. Further, States Parties are to promote environmental education and to recognize and support environmental associations and groups.

The provisions of Article 9 on access to justice mirror many human rights texts in requiring proceedings before an independent and impartial body established by law. Each State Party must provide judicial review for any denial of requested information, and a remedy for any act or omission concerning the permitting of activities and "acts and omissions by private persons and public authorities which contravene provisions of its national law relating to the environment." Standing to challenge permitting procedures or results is limited to members of the public having a sufficient interest or maintaining impairment of a right; however, the Convention provides that environmental nongovernmental organizations "shall be deemed" to have sufficient interest for this purpose. Standing to challenge violations of environmental law is open to the public, including NGOs "where they meet the criteria, if any, laid down in national law" (Article 9(3)).

The Convention's topic has induced the drafters to take small steps toward the creation of compliance procedures and enhancement of public participation on the international level. Primary review of implementation is conferred on the meeting of the Parties, at which nongovernmental organizations "qualified in the fields to which this Convention relates" may participate as observers if they have made a request and if not more than one-third of the Parties present at the meeting raise objections (Article 10). This provision is common in international environmental agreements. The Convention adds, however, a provision on compliance review (Article 15), which mandates the establishment by the Meeting of the Parties of a "non-confrontational, non-judicial and consultative" optional arrangement for compliance review, which "shall allow for appropriate public involvement and may include the option of considering communications from members of the public on matters related to this Convention." This tentative language marks the first time a petition procedure has been contemplated in an international environmental agreement.

If the compliance procedure is established when the Aarhus Convention comes into force, it will mark an important step in enhancing the effectiveness of international environmental agreements. At present, nearly all environmental agreements vest authority over issues of implementation and compliance in the Conference or Meeting of the Parties, a plenary and political body. In some cases small Secretariats are created, but they lack broad competence. Environmental compliance mechanisms should be further developed and the creation of an international body, a commission that could play the role of the United Nations Human Rights Commission or a High Commissioner for the Global Environment who could act as an ombudsman, should be seriously considered.

NOTES

1. United Nations, Forty-fifth Session, General Assembly, Resolution 45/94, Document A/RES/45/94, *Need to Ensure a Healthy Environment for the Well-Being of Individuals,* 1990.

2. Article 24.

3. Article 11.

4. UNEP, UNEP/FAO/PIC/INC.5/3, Report of the Intergovernmental Negotiating Committee for an International Legally Binding Instrument for the Application of the Prior Informed Consent Procedure for Certain Hazardous Chemicals and Pesticides in International Trade on the Work of its Fifth Session, Annex, 1998.

5. Vienna, 5 September 1997, reprinted in 36 ILM 1431 (1997).

6. See, for example, Directive 76/160, O.J. number L 31/1 of 5 February 1976, on bathing water quality, which states that "public interest in the environment and in the improvement of its quality is increasing; the public should therefore receive objective information on the quality of bathing water." Article 13 requires member states to submit regularly to the commission a "comprehensive report on the bathing water and most significant characteristics thereof." The commission publishes the information "after prior consent from the Member State concerned." However, the consent may limit the information provided, undermining its "objective" nature.

7. Council Directive 85/337/EEC, 27 June 1985, O.J. number L 175/40 of 5 July 1985, chap 6.

8. Council Directive 90/313/EEC, 7 June 1990, on the freedom of access to information on the environment, O.J. number L 158, 23 June 1990.

9. European Charter on Environment and Health, adopted 8 December 1989 by the First Conference of Ministers of the Environment and of Health of the Member States of the European Region of the World Health Organization.

10. Conference on Security and Cooperation in Europe, Sofia Meeting on Protection of the Environment (October–November 1989) (CSCE/SEM.36, 2 November 1989).

11. Ministerial Declaration on Environmentally Sound and Sustainable De-

velopment in Asia and the Pacific (Bangkok, 16 October 1990), A/CONF.151/PC/38. Paragraph 27 affirms "the right of individuals and non-governmental organizations to be informed of environmental problems relevant to them, to have the necessary access to information, and to participate in the formulation and implementation of decisions likely to affect their environment."

12. The Arab Declaration on Environment and Development and Future Perspectives, adopted by the Arab Ministerial Conference on Environment and Development (Cairo, September 1991), A/46/632, cited in United Nations, Document E/CN.4/Sub.2/1992/7, 20.

13. See also Articles 10(2)(e), 13(1)(b), 14(2), 19, and 25. Other agreements referring to public participation are the:

- Protocol to the 1979 Convention on Long-Range Transboundary Air Pollution Concerning the Control of Emissions of Volatile Organic Compounds or Their Transboundary Fluxes, Geneva, 18 November 1991, Article 2(3)(a)(4);
- Convention on the Protection and Utilization of Transboundary Rivers and Lakes, Helsinki, 17 March 1992, Article 16;
- Convention on the Transboundary Effects of Industrial Accidents, Helsinki, 17 March 1992, Article 9;
- Convention for the Protection of the Marine Environment of the Baltic Sea, Helsinki, 9 April 1992, Article 17;
- Convention for the Prevention of Marine Pollution of the North-East Atlantic, Paris, 22 September 1992, Article 9;
- Convention on Civil Responsibility for Damage resulting from Activities Dangerous to the Environment, Lugano, 21 June 1993, Articles 13 through 16;
- North American Convention on Cooperation in the Field of the Environment, Washington, D.C., 14 September 1993, Article 2(1)(a), 14;
- Convention on Cooperation and Sustainable Development of the Waters of the Danube, Sofia, 29 June 1994, Article 14;
- Protocol to the 1975 Barcelona Convention on Specially Protected Zones and Biological Diversity in the Mediterranean, Barcelona, 10 June 1995, Article 19;
- Joint Communique and Declaration on the Establishment of the Arctic Council Ottawa, 19 September 1996, Preamble and Articles 1(a), 2, 3(c);
- Kyoto Protocol to the United Nations Framework Convention on Climate Change, 10 December 1997, Article 6(3).

14. See, for example, Kenya-Tanzania-Uganda, final act of the Conference of Plenipotentiaries on the Establishment of the Lake Victoria Fisheries Organization, Kisumu, Kenya, 30 June 1994; Bangladesh-India Treaty on Sharing of the Ganges Waters at Farakka, New Delhi, 12 December 1996; India-Nepal Treaty Concerning the Integrated Development of the Mahakai River, New Delhi, 12 February 1996.

15. Ottawa, 13 March 1991.

16. Ottawa, 6 February 1997, reprinted in 36 ILM 1193 (1997).

17. C(76)55, 11 May 1976, Final.

18. The convention was sponsored by the United Nations Economic Commission for Europe (UNECE) and is open for signature by the fifty-five members of the UNECE, which includes all of Europe as well as the United States, Canada, and states of the former Soviet Union. States having consultative status with the UNECE may also participate.

3 Agenda 21 and Human Rights

The Right to Participate

Romina Picolotti

ONE OF THE PRIMARY OBJECTIVES of this compilation of works is to show how human rights and environment relate. When thinking about this relationship, the first question that came to my mind was this: *Is there any value added if we relate them?* To further analyze this question we thought to approach the issue from both sides; that is, from the environmental side and from the human rights side. One of the most seductive areas where environmentalists may look to strengthen the relationship with the human rights world is in the existence of international legal fora. That is, the existence of a quasi-judicial or judicial international process to force States to comply with international human rights law. Presently, international environmental law lacks this kind of mechanism. Hence, an important value added through linking these two areas of international law may be the use of international human rights mechanisms and systems for environmental claims. Several authors in this publication refer to such possibilities in their respective chapters.

Let's look at the human rights side. What is the value added to the environmental world if it is related to the human rights world? The human rights world already has an international forum to which to take claims for violations of human rights recognized by international instruments, and has been using this forum for the past several decades. The current struggle of human rights actors therefore is not to create these mechanisms but to strengthen and develop them. It is here, then, where the environmental world receives an added value. The clever introduction of environmental claims in international human rights fora could lead to the further development of environmental concepts and consequently help broaden the sphere of environmental protection.

The human right to participate in Agenda 21 is an example of using human rights fora in such a way. The human right to participate is recognized in international human rights treaties and is included in international environmental documents, resulting in the broadening of its concept and the development of what the right implies.

This discussion starts with a brief introduction of the existing links between human rights and the environment. Immediately afterward, it analyzes the way in which human rights are dealt with in Agenda 21. Finally, it refers to the right to participate, conditions for the effective exercise of this right, and the advantages and disadvantages that participation implies.

Human Rights and the Environment

Few are the issues of major concern in the international agenda as those of human rights and the environment. These two fields are intrinsically connected and constitute a common theme dealt with in the course of international conferences taking place during the last decade of the twentieth century. This connection gave rise to the United Nations Conference on Environment and Development (Rio de Janeiro 1992), the Second Universal Conference on Human Rights (Vienna 1993), the International Conference on Population and Development (Cairo 1994), and the United Nations Conference on Human Settlements (Habitat II; Istanbul 1996).[1]

We arrived at the end of the twentieth century with the firm conviction that human life is not conceivable without perfect functioning and integral natural ecosystems, which conviction constitutes an urgent and unpostponable need for the achievement of sustainable development. In this regard, practices that don't sustain the ecosystem represent a crucial threat to the right to life. Nonetheless, the intrinsic connection between human rights and the environment cannot be reduced to the right to life only, since the existence of a healthy environment becomes a condition *sine qua non* for the enjoyment of other basic human rights. The following examples of the links between human rights and the environment illustrate this fact:

- The right to health is clearly connected to the environment, as without a clean environment we would hardly enjoy this human right.
- The right to own property is not only individually but collectively violated by environmental abuses. For instance, atmospheric pollution

reduces property value, while the intrusion into indigenous territories for the sake of irrational exploitation of natural resources violates collective rights to property.

- The right to development is essential to consider within the framework of sustainability.
- The right to equality is violated due to the existence of marked disparities in the ways certain social sectors face disproportionate environmental abuses and degradation.
- The right to participate is essential in every democratic society in order to ensure the implementation of efficient and sustainable environmental policies.

For the sake of brevity, this discussion does not extend to other links that emphasize the inherent interdependence, complementarity, and indivisibility of human rights and the environment as these examples sufficiently illustrate the matter.

Human Rights in Agenda 21

The main concern of Agenda 21 is to meet the basic needs of human beings, such as nutrition, health preservation, decent housing, and education, each of which has a corresponding human right. In this respect, the Rio Declaration as well as Agenda 21 are significantly involved with elements that rightly belong to the conceptual universe of human rights; human beings are the main concern for sustainable development that highlights the right to a healthy and productive life in harmony with nature. We should also emphasize that the right to development must be achieved in a way that equitably meets developmental and environmental needs of present and future generations. Moreover, poverty is recognized as a threat to sustainable development and the right to life.[2]

Along this line of thought, it is suitable to point out the specific reference included in Agenda 21 to two instruments that address human rights: The Universal Declaration on Human Rights and the International Covenant on Economic, Social, and Cultural Rights, specifically when dealing with the right to decent housing.

Of special importance concerning the right to participate is the right to appropriate access to information as well as to effective jurisdictional resources.[3] At this point, we will analyze the right to participate, the central topic of this presentation.

Right to Participate as Presented in Agenda 21

The Rio Declaration and Agenda 21 have drawn special attention to the right to participate in environmental management and development, and to the promotion of sustainable development. The declaration explicitly refers to the right to participate (Principle 10), highlighting the role of women (Principle 20), youth (Principle 21), indigenous people and local communities (Principle 22). The exercise of the right to participate presented in Agenda 21 is worthy of a more detailed study, which includes the integration of women in all development activities (chapter 24), children and youth (chapter 25), indigenous people and their communities (chapter 26), nongovernmental organizations (chapter 27), workers and trade unions (chapter 29), business and industry (chapter 30), farmers (chapter 31), and the scientific and technological community (chapter 32). Finally, in chapter 23, Agenda 21 emphasizes the fact that the commitment and genuine involvement of "all social groups" for the achievement of a "real social partnership" in support of a common effort for sustainable development will have decisive importance in all program areas of Agenda 21. It also recognizes that the fundamental prerequisite for the achievement of sustainable development is broad public participation in decision making.

We may conclude that any attempt to develop a local agenda in any given locality should not disregard a broad and active participation of all social sectors. Such disregard would imply not only an inexcusable contradiction with respect to the global agenda, but also a futile effort that detours financial and human resources from their principle target of sustainable development.

When analyzing a determined issue, we must first define the concepts that will be used. In this specific case, we refer to what we understand as the right to participate. Within the context of this article we define participation as the genuine involvement of all social actors in social and political decision-making processes that potentially affect the communities in which they live and work. We do not consider participation merely as an end, but as an effective tool to establish priorities; offer solutions; and prepare, execute, and apply the most accurate decisions possible. As has been wisely stated by the world community and expressed within the framework of the Rio Declaration, it is essential to invest in the integration of civil society actors, the private sector, educational centers, and other key sectors of societies when developing a local agenda.

Local government is the closest public sector institution with respect to the community. The local arena, furthermore, has a particular advantage and capacity to identify and understand local problems, and consequently is the most appropriate level at which to foster democratic mechanisms. Recent promotion of community participation at the local administrative level stems from the fact that the traditional role of the State as supplier of services and the community as passive recipient of the services no longer reflects global circumstances. Participation guarantees a more efficient and more rational functioning of local public activities and use of resources. This attitude is grounded in the fact that no other actor is better poised to identify problems with public services and develop solutions to address them than the user of the services. Participation proposes a change in the dynamics between government and the governed, from a system of representative democracy toward one of participatory democracy. The community is hence transformed into a promoter of ideas and an active actor in the public realm, while government fosters a rapprochement of the community to local government mechanisms. The government is hence transformed into advisor and technical implementer of publicly agreed-upon works.

We can conclude that when developing a local agenda for any given locality, it is fundamental to consider the incorporation of the right to participate, which aims at achieving effective and sustainable local development, by means of the implementation of democratic procedures and mechanisms for the involvement of the community at all levels of policy- and decision-making processes. Having established the purpose of incorporating the right to participate, we now look at the various participatory modalities that may be used in the participative process.

Participation is not a static homogenous process, but has many different shapes and grades subject to local administration, and to society- and government-specific circumstances. It is important that the promoter of participation (in this case, local government) understand the advantages and disadvantages that theses modalities may imply, since each of them will generate different expectations by the actors.

Participation implies not only negotiation, convergence, and cooperation of interests and actors, but also disagreement and confrontation; it does not entail a mere approval of proposals made by a regional Administrator, but genuine involvement of all relevant stakeholders in the process. Participation can manifest itself as approval of *or* opposition to a particular issue.

We identify four basic modalities of participation:

1 *Informative participation*:[4] Informative participation implies an exchange of information and knowledge on certain issues of concern to the community. The community provides information to the State and vice versa, enabling each to make proper decisions about how they administer resources, which leads to more optimal resource management.
2 *Consultative participation*: Consultative participation implies expression of opinions and inquiry into the position of the actors involved in a given situation, but it is not directly binding to the authorities. One of the available legal mechanisms for consultative participation is the public hearing in which the State calls the affected actors to a given site, to hear their ideas on a specific issue; the conclusions reached during this type of proceeding, however, are usually not binding for the State.
3 *Participation in decision making*: Participation in decision making implies commitment and exercise of power in the decision-making process. An example is participation in budget allocation in which the State calls all social actors affected not only to express their ideas and opinions, but also to decide on what, when, and how investment resources will be allocated. In this modality the decisions that result from the participatory process are binding to the State.
4 *Participation in management* (comanagement or joint management): Participation in management implies the exercise of power and commitment for the effective implementation of policies, projects, public works, and services. This is the highest stage of participation, in which the State empowers social actors to become the executors or monitors of the public activities. A typical example might be a community-led construction of a housing project.

In each of these instances, participation will have diverse dynamics creating different expectations of the actors who participate. Moreover, the role of the provincial or municipal authorities will vary according to the modality selected.

A Framework to Exercise the Right to Participate

As for most human rights, some basic conditions are needed to ensure the enjoyment of the right to participate. Some of these conditions follow:

1 *Access to information*: For participation to be effective and fruitful, it should be informed. The design and implementation of a local agenda involve the development of effective mechanisms of access to information. Likewise, information shall be clearly systematized and intelligible as far as possible.
2 *Autonomy*: Participation requires autonomy of the actors, that is, the independence or nonsubordination of actors with respect to one another.
3 *Political willingness*: Participation is not possible if the State authority that promotes it does not have the true intention to open itself to community opinion. The executive must foster this space. Without true political will to create a participatory space, participation will not have fruitful results.
4 *Stakeholder identification*: The exhaustive incorporation of the stakeholders involved is essential for successful and meaningful participation, since without the incorporation of the opinions of all of the interested parties, true representation will not be achieved. This includes stakeholders who may be positively or negatively affected, or indirectly affected by omission. Considering the importance that stakeholder identification has in the participative process, it is essential to analyze this aspect in detail.

We might first ask, who assumes the task of identifying the stakeholders? In the development of a local agenda for the achievement of sustainable development, it is the State, province, or municipality that grants the opportunity to participate. Consequently, the State is in charge of identifying *prima facie* the affected actors, or more commonly, stakeholders.

There are many ways of identifying stakeholders, which we will not cover in this chapter. Whatever the methodology selected for the identification of the social actors involved, however, the following caveats are in order.

- The institutionalization of the State (that is, its formal and informal structures) will likely result in a parallel institutionalization of the possible affected social actors. From the very moment when the identification process takes place, the State will naturally rely on its own categorization and identification system with preconceived social sectors (such as the grass roots sector, industrial sector, trade unions). Because the formal State institution may not have formal or even informal contact with *all* of the real stakeholders, this categorization could lead to the exclusion of certain of those social actors who, although affected, are not viewed or recognized by the State, the so-called "invisible sectors."

- The identification of leaders representing a specific sector does not necessarily imply that the leaders will always respond to the needs or demands of that particular sector. Therefore, the incorporation or consultation of the formal leaders in the participatory process does not necessarily mean that the sector is represented in the process. It is often difficult to determine the degree to which representation is or is not achieved in a given issue. The following example illustrates the point. In a particular municipality the mayor decided to consult with the community on the needs of their neighborhood. Thinking he was giving the community a participatory opportunity to help direct public investment, he approached the elected representatives of the neighborhood association to hear requests. The representatives indicated that the community requested the creation of a green open space for the recreation of the children. The mayor's subsequent move to construct a park in the neighborhood gave rise to mass protest from the community. Follow-up consultation with multiple residents of the community showed that, in fact, the desire of the majority was for improvements to the sewage system; few actually wanted a park.

By citing this example, we do not mean to diminish the value of democratic representation through elected officials, but we wish simply to show that different mechanisms of participation may yield divergent results. The promoter of participatory mechanisms needs to be especially attentive to the dynamics of the community and ensure that he or she is properly identifying stakeholders.

Benefits of Participation

- It improves the level of transparency favoring communication between the affected social sectors and public authorities.
- It facilitates the access to information, establishing mechanisms and procedures that permit easy access to information.
- It encourages the design and execution of public policies, better identifying the basic needs of the community and the use of public resources. Such information is essential to the implementation and review of environmentally sound and socially responsible sustainable development.
- It promotes a revitalization of the State by fostering planning and

decentralization of the governance process. The participatory process requires that the State establish procedures for consultation and conciliation in the decision-making processes so as to avoid a mere act of receiving or providing solutions and remedies to the complaints presented by the community.

- It promotes the commitment and genuine involvement of all social groups in the decision-making process. In this way, the community becomes the agent of its own development.
- Participation promotes a positive change in the relationship between representative and represented as a result of improved representation.
- It transforms the nature and perceived value of the public good, contracting the indifference of society toward public matters and developing a sense of belonging and ownership in the community.
- It tends to increase public revenues proportional to the level of increase in perceived value and ownership of the public good, and the subsequent increase in willingness to pay taxes associated to public investments.
- It increases the legitimacy of the State.
- It permits the identification of priorities and corresponding solutions.

We can also cite a few of the costs of participation:

- Participation creates expectations that, if not fulfilled, can work against the political capital of the governing body.
- It can generate conflicts that, if not solved, may obstruct or cripple the administration.
- It requires ample time dedicated by the governing authority.
- It requires the attention and dedication of public human resources.
- As the participative process has a compelling force, it is difficult to control once it has been launched.

Conclusion

It is fitting to stress the extraordinary worldwide changes that took place during the last decade of the twentieth century. These changes constitute a landmark of political and social transformation. They are characterized by a deep reflection on the foundations of our societies, on the relationship between the governors and the governed, and on the relationship between the State and its citizens. The twenty-first century will see a worldwide revaluation of matters that affect humankind. One of our biggest challenges will be to ensure sustainable development. One of the ways to achieve it will be through initiatives such as local Agenda 21. As the international community wisely recognized in Agenda 21, the human right to participate and the implementation of a local agenda will be essential to achieve sustainable development. The international community has agreed in the Rio Declaration on the content of the human right to participate and is developing more sophisticated notions of political participation. The relationship between human rights and environment becomes fundamental in the exercise of our right to participate.

NOTES

1. A. A. Cancado Trindade, "Relations between Sustainable Development and Economic, Social, and Cultural Rights: Recent Developments," *Human Rights, Sustainable Development, and the Environment,* IIDH-BID, 2nd ed. (1995): 357–78.

2. The Rio Declaration also refers to humanitarian international law, applying it to the protection of the environment (Principle 24), to the protection of human health (Principle 14), and to the interdependence and indivisibility of environmental protection, development, and peace (Principle 25).

3. See supra note 2.

4. There is a distinction between informative participation and access to information. In the former, the State becomes an active participant that fosters and provides information, while in the latter, the individual (either particular or collective) becomes the active participant while the State is passive with respect to the obligations assumed. That is to say that in the first modality the individual becomes a passive receptor of the information, and in the second, the individual receives the information because he or she has requested it.

4

Public Participation in the Era of Globalization

Claudia Saladin

PUBLIC PARTICIPATION HAS long been recognized in domestic legal systems as critical to implementing the rights of individuals and communities to be informed about and be meaningful participants in decisions that affect the quality of their lives and environment. These decisions include those that affect the quality of the air they breathe, the quality of the water they drink, and the quality of other natural resources on which they depend. The need for public participation is often justified on the grounds that it results in better decisions. Increasingly, however, public participation is recognized as a right of individuals and communities to participate in decisions that affect their lives, including the right to know and the right to review.

While public participation has evolved in many domestic legal systems, in the international arena civil society voices have not been as effectively heard, despite the increasing importance of international organizations in the day-to-day lives of people around the world. Particularly in developing countries, international economic institutions, such as the World Bank Group, International Monetary Fund, World Trade Organization (WTO), and regional development banks, can profoundly affect national macroeconomic policies and governance structures, as well as development priorities and projects. These institutions write the rules that govern the global and national economies. They are simultaneously blamed for causing and heralded as solving international financial crises, such as those in Mexico, Asia, and Russia.

Despite the profound reach of these international institutions into the lives of ordinary citizens and the relatively questionable record of these institutions to date, civil society is still largely excluded from most of these institutions' operations. Public participation in these institutions often takes place on an informal and ad hoc basis, which often favors participation of powerful economic interests, such as multinational corporations, over the broader interested public. The corporations have the resources and time to develop informal contacts and keep abreast of what decisions are being made. While such decisions have a direct impact on the general public, it is often not aware of the decisions of these institutions until after they have been made or it is too late to affect the outcome. If international financial and trade institutions are given the power to dictate and constrain domestic policy making and to override domestic policy decisions, then they must institutionalize and guarantee a genuine and substantive role for civil society in their decision-making processes.

Increasing Recognition of the Right of Participation at the International Level

The importance of public participation in environmental decision making has achieved international recognition. The 1992 United Nations Conference on Environment and Development (UNCED) recognized the many benefits of public participation to government, regulated communities, individuals, groups, and society as a whole, and stressed public participation as one of the fundamental means for moving governments toward sustainable development. The Rio Declaration and Agenda 21 endorsed the principle of public participation at the national and international levels. Principle 10 of the Rio Declaration states that

> Environmental issues are best handled with the participation of all concerned citizens, at the relevant level. At the national level, each individual shall have appropriate access to information concerning the environment that is held by public authorities . . . and the opportunity to participate in decision-making processes. States shall facilitate and encourage public awareness and participation by making information widely available. Effective access to judicial and administrative proceedings, including redress and remedy shall be provided.[1]

Agenda 21, Article 27(9), elaborated on this principle for international finance and development agencies, stating,

> The United Nations system, including *international finance and development agencies,* and all intergovernmental organizations and forums should, in consultation with non-governmental organizations, take measures to: . . . enhance existing or, where they do not exist, establish mechanisms and procedures within each agency to draw on the expertise and views of non-governmental organizations in policy and program design, implementation

> and evaluation; [and] ... [p]rovide access for non-governmental organizations to accurate and timely data and information to promote the effectiveness of their programs and activities and their roles in support of sustainable development *[emphasis added]*.[2]

Although the broad goal of public participation was widely endorsed, the precise content of the concept of "public participation" had not been developed. The United Nations Economic Commission for Europe (UNECE), through the Environment for Europe process, sought to define the idea of public participation within the UNECE region. As a result, in 1995 the Environment Ministers of the UNECE countries endorsed the Sofia Guidelines on Public Participation and Access to Information in Environmental Decision-Making. The Guidelines gave more concrete expression to the Rio Declaration and Agenda 21 within the European context. They also set in motion a process to negotiate an instrument that would elaborate on the principles of the Guidelines to create binding legal obligations on the Parties to incorporate the principles of transparent, accountable, and democratic governance into their environmental decision-making processes.

In June 1998, the member countries of UNECE adopted the Convention on Access to Information, Public Participation in Decision-Making and Access to Justice in Environmental Matters (UNECE Convention).[3] The Convention establishes *minimum* standards for civil society participation that will be legally binding on the Parties to the Convention once it enters into force. The majority of the provisions are not addressed to international organizations. Rather, they are addressed to the institutions of national governments. Once in force, however, the Convention would require each Party to "promote the application of the principles of this Convention in international environmental decision-making processes and within the framework of international organizations in matters relating to the environment."[4] The UNECE Convention is a regional instrument. It is nonetheless useful as one model of minimum standards for public participation, as it was one of the first international efforts to give concrete content to the concept.

Participation Rights as Human Rights

Participation rights also find some support in international human rights instruments.[5] Participation rights are procedural in nature and are implicit in such rights as the rights of individuals to take part in government, to equal access to public service,[6] freedom of association,[7] the right to seek and receive information,[8] the right of equal access to courts,[9] and equality before the law.[10] The Special Rapporteur on Human Rights and the Environment of the Sub-Commission on Prevention of Discrimination and Protection of Minorities (the Special Rapporteur) of the Commission on Human Rights also addressed the issue of public participation in her report and in the draft Declaration on Human Rights and the Environment.[11] The Special Rapporteur found both the right to information and the right to meaningful participation, including equal access to judicial and administrative actions, to be highly relevant to the issue of human rights and environment.[12] She found broad support for these rights within the United Nations system, including the Universal Declaration of Human Rights,[13] the Covenant on Civil and Political Rights,[14] and the World Charter for Nature.[15] The Draft Declaration on Human Rights and the Environment includes a section on participation rights, including the rights to information, meaningful participation, and effective remedy and redress.[16] Public participation at a domestic level is relatively well established. The following section briefly discusses the current status of public participation rights in international economic institutions.

Public Participation in International Economic Institutions

A difficult task at the domestic level, structuring meaningful and effective public participation is even more complex at the international level. Implementing the right of public participation at the international level can take the form of a public relations exercise directed at mollifying civil society without providing meaningful opportunities for participation. Often such processes are actually barriers between civil society and decision makers, as opposed to the more direct access to decision makers and government delegations afforded to corporations. For example, in the Free Trade Area of the Americas (FTAA) negotiations, a Committee of Government Representatives on Participation of Civil Society was created, ostensibly to channel civil society participation into the FTAA negotiations. The Committee has been more of a blockade to civil society participation, however, than a conduit for civil society input into the process. The Committee was established without a clear understanding of how it would feed civil society input into the negotiating process. To date the Committee has not been able to reach an agreement on the publication of documents it received from civil society, let alone how they will be incorporated into the negotiating process. Institutionalizing and harmonizing the right of public participation in international institutions and providing some uniform minimum standards would go a long way toward providing for meaningful participation.

Broadly stated, participation can be divided into three distinct groups of rights. The public should have access to information, with limited, explicit exceptions (access to information). The public should have a right to participate in the decision-making process and have that participation taken into account in the final decision (access to decision making). The public should ultimately have access to an independent and impartial review process, capable of binding institutions, to allege their rights have been infringed (access to justice).

Access to Information: The Right to Know

Access to information includes the right of citizens to obtain information, subject to certain limited and explicit restrictions, without having to show an interest in the information. Responses to such requests should be timely; refusals to provide information should be in writing and should state the reasons for the refusal. The right of access to information should create a presumption in favor of information disclosure. Institutions should be able to deny a request for information only on the basis of a list of specific, narrow, and clearly defined grounds for refusal, such as if disclosure of information would impair the ability of a person to receive a fair trial, or disclosure of sensitive economic data would distort the market. Categories of information that will not be disclosed should be precisely and narrowly defined and interpreted. Where a request for information has been denied, the requestor should have access to an independent body to review the denial.

An important element of the right of access to information is the duty of institutions to inform the public of their participation rights. It is not enough for these participation rights to exist; the institution must make an affirmative effort to inform the public of those rights. For example, when denying requests for information, institutions should inform the requestor of the availability of a review mechanism under the access to justice provisions. Institutions should inform the public of a decision to be made and their ability to participate in it. Access to information also entails informing the public of the opportunities and procedures for review of the institution's decision.

A final, essential element of the right of access to information is that international institutions should regularly and systematically collect and disseminate information on the state of the environment, labor rights, human rights, poverty, and other areas of importance to civil society. They should also know the environmental and social impacts of their activities and disseminate this information to the public. Such information should be in a language and format appropriate for communicating with the relevant public.

Several international institutions, particularly multilateral development institutions, have taken some steps to implement this principle, albeit imperfectly. Institutions dealing with the private sector and those not dealing directly with development assistance have done less to implement the right to know.

The World Bank[17] significantly reworked its information disclosure policy beginning in 1994. The current World Bank Policy on Disclosure of Information creates a presumption of disclosure,[18] except in certain cases, including proceedings of the Board of Directors,[19] information provided to the Bank on the understanding that it will not be disclosed,[20] documents related to the Bank's country strategies and analysis of country creditworthiness,[21] internal documents and memoranda,[22] and information disclosure of which would be detrimental to the interests of the Bank, a member country, or Bank staff.[23] Importantly, the loan covenants are disclosed, but only after the loan agreement is finalized.

The International Finance Corporation (IFC)—a part of the World Bank Group that lends to the private sector—adopted an Information Policy in 1994 (updated in 1996 and 1998) that creates "a presumption in favor of disclosure where disclosure would not materially harm the business and competitive interests of clients." Clients are defined by IFC as its private sector borrowers. The constraints on disclosure are quite broad, including business confidential information, which is not narrowly defined to protect competitive business interests, but is widely defined to include anything that business does not wish to be disclosed. In contrast to the World Bank, no portion of IFC loan documents, including environmental and social conditionalities, are disclosed. For both IFC and the World Bank, significantly more information is made available for projects with the greatest environmental impacts (category A projects) than for other types of projects.

The United Nations Development Program (UNDP) has developed an interesting and potentially innovative mechanism for information disclosure through its Public Information Disclosure Policy. The UNDP Information Policy was designed to ensure that information on UNDP operational activities was publicly available "in the absence of a compelling reason for confidentiality."[24] The UNDP Information Policy creates a presumption in favor of disclosure, subject to specific exemptions.[25] Requests must receive a response within thirty business days and a denial of the request must state the reason.[26] The Information Policy also creates mechanisms for reviewing denials of requests for information.

In 1996, the WTO adopted a Decision on Procedures for the Circulation and the Restriction of WTO Documents (Document Procedures),[27] which provides for the eventual public availability of some WTO documents, including final panel decisions, but excluding other documents related to dispute settlement proceedings. Under these procedures, official WTO documents are now circulated as unrestricted, unless they fall into a category specifically identified as restricted in the Appendix to the Document Procedures.[28] Unfortunately, the list of restricted documents includes most of the documents pertaining to pending policy decisions.

That many institutions now have information disclosure policies is an important development. All of these examples of information policies can be traced back to pressure from civil society for greater disclosure and transparency. Most contain a presumption in favor of disclosure, but all contain extremely broad exceptions or qualifications of that presumption. Except for the UNDP Information Policy, there is no means to appeal a denial of a request.

Moreover, the information policies of these institutions are not consistent with one another. It has proven difficult to harmonize policies, even within the World Bank Group, which is composed of closely related institutions with a single president. Those institutions dealing directly with development have moved more quickly to develop disclosure policies. The important aspect of the policies within an institution is that they level the playing field, giving all members of the public equal access within that institution. The failure to harmonize policies across institutions, however, means that the public right to know is contingent upon what institution they are dealing with. That the public has different levels of access to information at different institutions is not consistent with the right to know as a right.

Access to Decision Making: The Right to Speak and Be Heard

Meaningful and effective participation requires that the public know that a decision is being made and that they have a right to participate in the making of that decision, and the opportunities and procedures for such participation. The procedural elements of the principle of access to decision making must be designed to ensure that the public is able to participate in decision making in a meaningful and effective way. Notice of the pending decision-making process should come early enough for the public to review relevant documents and prepare input. Notice should also be made in a way reasonably calculated to reach the public in general, but more importantly that portion of the public most directly interested in and affected by the decision to be made, for example, by making information available in local languages and in culturally appropriate ways.

The process must also allow adequate time for the decision makers to process the public input and incorporate it into their decision-making process. For the public to be willing or interested in participating they must be certain that their views will be taken into account. Providing that final decisions be in writing and that they state the reasons for the decision ensures both that the decision makers adequately consider public input and that the public feels their input has been treated seriously. Failure to take public input into consideration or to comply with other procedural requirements of this right should be a basis for challenging the outcome of the decision-making process.

Several international financial institutions have taken steps to implement this right. The World Bank provides for consultation with affected peoples and local NGOs in its Policy on Environmental Assessment (EA Policy).[29] The EA Policy provides that consultations should occur after the project has been screened into the appropriate category—category A having the most environmental impacts—and again when a draft EA has been prepared. The Board must release the EA to the public 120 days prior to consideration of the project. Unfortunately, the policy does not involve the public at all in the process of screening the projects, often with the result that projects are screened incorrectly. If a project is not categorized as A, then no EA is required and consultation with the public is minimal. Failure by the Bank to comply with the consultation procedures laid out in the EA policy does give project-affected people some right of review through the World Bank Inspection Panel.

The IFC's Policy[30] also requires consultation with project-affected groups for all category A projects after the screening process and once an EA is prepared. IFC has also prepared a good practices manual to guide project sponsors in conducting public consultations. The Board must release the EA to the public sixty days prior to consideration of the project. The World Bank Inspection Panel does not apply to the IFC, but a Compliance Advisor Ombudsman was recently created to provide some review for project-affected people to ensure greater IFC compliance with its policies.

In contrast to the World Bank Group, the WTO provides virtually no formal role for public participation. The Marrakech Agreement, which established the WTO, provides that "the General Council may make appropriate arrangements for consultation and cooperation with non-governmental organizations concerned with matters related to those of the WTO."[31] In July 1996, the General Council adopted the Guidelines for Arrangements on Relations with Non-Governmental Organizations[32] (Guidelines). These do little, however, to improve the situation of NGOs in the WTO. The Guidelines themselves are less than a full page long and bestow no right of participation on NGOs. NGO participation is largely at the discretion of the Secretariat.

As with information disclosure policies, there is little consistency across institutions. Implementation of the right is largely at the discretion of the particular institution. Policies tend to be designed from the narrow point of view of what is most convenient for the institution, as opposed to what level of participation the public ought or needs to have. For example, multilateral development banks often draw a distinction in their operations between public-sector and private-sector projects and apply different levels of participation to each. Within the World Bank Group, for example, the private-sector–focused IFC provides less time for disclosure of information to the Board and the public, and discloses less information to the public, than the public-sector–focused World Bank, despite recent efforts to harmonize environmental and social policies within the World Bank Group. In revising its environmental and social policies in 1998, the IFC did not demonstrate (or even seem to ask) whether effective consultation can be conducted with only sixty days notice of a project, as opposed to the 120 days required by the World Bank. Nothing in the nature of private-sector operations, however, changes the minimum time periods and information necessary for meaningful and effective public consultation and disclosure of information, or the rights of the public to such participation. Such discrepancies are not consistent with the right of participation. For example, a community impacted by a resource extraction project funded by the World Bank will know more and will know it earlier than if the same project is funded by the IFC. The reality for the community in both cases would be the same, however. Moreover, many of the policies have not been consistently implemented and applied, highlighting the importance of review and accountability.

Access to Justice: The Right to Review and Hold Accountable

No right is effective unless it is enforceable by the holder of the right. In order to ensure that the law is respected, including the right of access to information and access to decision making, civil society must have access to an independent and impartial body. The procedures of such a body must be fair and equitable and not prohibitively expensive to use. In order for any review process to be meaningful, it must offer effective remedies, including injunctive relief. The review body should have the ability to create a binding obligation on an institution and must issue a decision in writing that is publicly accessible. The public must also be informed of the access to such review procedures and have adequate information to be able to avail themselves of the right of access.

Provisions on access to information should include a right to review by an independent body when a request for information is denied. Review by an independent body ensures that institutions implement their procedures effectively and in ways that do not undermine the right of access to information. Such review ensures that, in weighing the interest to be protected by nondisclosure against the interest of the public in disclosure, appropriate weight is given to both interests. It also ensures that limitations on the right of access truly are interpreted as restrictively as possible.

Provisions on access to decision making impose procedural obligations on institutions to ensure meaningful and effective public participation. Access to an independent review body when institutions fail to properly implement these procedural requirements is crucial. If institutions disregard such procedural requirements, then the substantive outcomes of those decision-making processes are illegitimate and must be vacated. Without such a remedy these procedural safeguards on the public's right to participate are meaningless.

Several of the international institutions discussed above have incorporated some aspects of the right of access to justice. In 1993 the Board of the World Bank established the World Bank Inspection Panel (the Panel) to bring greater public accountability to World Bank lending.[33] The Panel was created after several Bank projects proved to be environmental and social disasters. The Panel is a quasi-independent body designed to evaluate the World Bank's compliance with its own policies and procedures in project planning and implementation. Local people can turn to the Panel when they believe that violations of World Bank policies have harmed them, but their efforts to raise their concerns with Bank staff have been unsatisfactory. Although the Panel process has become seriously politicized, most of the claimants have managed to receive some benefit from filing claims. Both the Inter-American Development Bank and the Asian Development Bank have created accountability mechanisms, although they are significantly less independent and effective than the Panel.

In 1998 World Bank Group President Wolfensohn created the position of the Compliance Advisor Ombudsman (CAO) for the IFC and Multilateral Investment Guarantee Agency (MIGA). The CAO, like the Inspection Panel in the World Bank, is designed to provide a mechanism for local communities adversely affected by IFC- and MIGA-supported projects to raise their concerns. The CAO is independent of line management and reports directly to the President. It is designed to be a practical, problem-solving office. The first CAO took office in July 1999 and as of this writing had not yet received any complaints.

The UNDP Information Policy also creates a semi-independent panel to review denials of information requests, the Public Information and Documentation Oversight Panel (Oversight Panel). The Oversight Panel's functions are both to ensure full implementation of the policy and to reconsider denials of requests for information.[34] The Oversight Panel is composed of five members, appointed by the UNDP Administrator. Three of the members are UNDP professional staff and two are individuals from the nonprofit sector, one from a donor country and one from a program country. Implementation of the UNDP Information Policy is still weak, and the Oversight panel has not yet established rules of procedure or reviewed any denied requests.

Accountability and review mechanisms are newer and less common in international financial institutions in contrast to human rights regimes, for example. Nonetheless accountability mechanisms are a critical component of public participation. Without them policies on information disclosure and participation can potentially go unimplemented. Accountability mechanisms are needed to give meaning and full effect to policies on information disclosure and participation. Accountability mechanisms can be used, for example, to ensure that there are effective means for taking public participation into account in making decisions and avoiding the temptation to turn consultation processes into mere public relations exercises.

Implementing Public Participation in International Organizations

Although many of the attempts of some of the international development institutions do not go as far as they should in incorporating civil society into the international policy-making process, they represent movement in the direction of transparency and accessibility in international institutions and decision-making processes. Such mechanisms will become increasingly necessary as economic regulation moves to the international level.

A challenge for public participation in the era of globalization will be to create an agreed minimum standard for information disclosure, participation, and accountability. As can be seen from the examples given above, there is a lack of harmony across institutions in terms of the amount and quality of public participation they allow. This results at least in part because such policies have been adopted on an ad hoc basis, typically as the result of international civil society campaigns directed at particular institutions. In the case of the World Bank, for example, it took fifteen years to get basic environmental and social policies and an accountability mechanism. Once the World Bank had them, civil society attention shifted to the IFC and recently to the International Monetary Fund (IMF). The idea of a right to public participation suggests that minimum standards exist for implementing that right.

As the importance of administrative agencies in national governments grew in the twentieth century, the rules for how such agencies conducted their business—including their transparency, accountability to the public, and the role of the public within them—developed in tandem. We are now in an era where international institutions are becoming increasingly important regulators of what were once domestic issues, including important issues related to development and economic policy, which can profoundly impact the environment. The rules for how such institutions will conduct their business and establishing the minimum standards for how these institutions will incorporate the participation rights discussed in this paper have yet to be written.

An International Administrative Procedures Act (IAPA), by establishing minimum standards for public participation, would give content and definition to public participation at the international level. An IAPA would standardize such issues as public access to information, the procedures by which decisions are made, the opportunities for public access that would apply equally to civil society and industry, and standards of accountability for international institutions. The Rio Declaration, Agenda

21, the UNECE Convention, and the work of the Special Rapporteur on Human Rights and Environment, among others, all represent important efforts to define and give substance to the right of participation. States need to develop and implement an IAPA in order to set such *minimum* standards for public participation common to all international institutions, and they need to do so with the involvement of civil society as active participants.

NOTES

1. United Nations, Document A/Conf.151/26, vol. 1.

2. Ibid., vol. 3 *[emphasis added]*. The World Bank Group is part of the United Nations system.

3. United Nations Economic Commission for Europe, Document ECE/CEP/43, *Convention on Access to Information, Public Participation in Decision-Making, and Access to Justice in Environmental Matters,* 21 April 1998 (hereinafter UNECE Convention).

4. Ibid., Article 3.7. A more detailed discussion of this provision of the UN-ECE Convention and its implications for international institutions can be found in Claudia Saladin and Brennan Van Dyke, *Implementing the Principles of the Public Participation Convention in International Organizations* (European ECO Forum, June 1998).

5. Whether and how international human rights norms apply to international institutions are questions beyond the scope of this essay. The logic of policy coherence between international law and the activities of international institutions, however, argues for international institutions to act in a manner consistent with international law, regardless of whether, as a legal matter, they are bound to do so.

6. The right to equal access to public service is evident in United Nations, General Assembly, Resolution 217, Volume 2, Article 21, *Universal Declaration of Human Rights,* 1948 (hereinafter UDHR); *International Covenant on Civil and Political Rights,* 999 UNTS 171, 1966 (hereinafter ICCPR).

7. UDHR, supra note 6, Article 20; ICCPR, supra note 6, Article 22.

8. UDHR, supra note 6, Article 19; ICCPR, supra note 6, Article 19.

9. UDHR, supra note 6, Article 8; ICCPR, supra note 6, Article 12.

10. UDHR, supra note 6, Article 7; ICCPR, supra note 6, Article 26.

11. United Nations, Human Rights and the Environment, Final Report, Document E/CN.4/SUB.2/1994/9, *Review of Further Developments in Fields with which the Sub-Commission Has Been Concerned,* prepared by Fatma Zohra Ksentini, Special Rapporteur, 6 July 1994 (hereinafter Special Rapporteur's report).

12. Ibid., paras 203–23.

13. UDHR, supra note 6, Articles 19 and 21.

14. ICCPR, supra note 6, Articles 19 and 21.

15. United Nations, General Assembly, Resolution 37/7, "World Charter for Nature," 28 October 1982, para 23.

16. Annex I to Special Rapporteur's report, supra note 11, part 3, paras 15–20.

17. The World Bank Group is composed of four major institutions: the International Bank for Reconstruction and Development (IBRD), which lends money to governments; the International Development Association (IDA), which lends money on more favorable terms to the poorest governments; the International Finance Corporation (IFC), which lends money to private sector enterprises for investment in developing countries; and the Multilateral Investment Guarantee Agency (MIGA), which sells political risk insurance to private sector enterprises who invest in developing countries. The World Bank refers to the two public-sector lending arms of the World Bank Group—IBRD and IDA.

18. The presumption of disclosure is in World Bank, *Policy on Disclosure of Information,* para 4, 1994.

19. Ibid., para 50.

20. Ibid., para 51.

21. Ibid., para 52.

22. Ibid., para 53.

23. Ibid., para 54.

24. UNDP, *Public Information Disclosure Policy,* para 1.

25. Ibid., para 6.

26. Ibid., para 19.

27. WTO, *Procedures for the Circulation and Derestriction of WTO Documents,* WT/L/160/Rev.1 (hereinafter Document Procedures). For a more detailed discussion of the Document Procedures, see L. Brennan Van Dyke and John Barlow Weiner, *An Introduction to the WTO Decision on Document Restriction* (undated).

28. Document Procedures, supra note 27, para 1.

29. World Bank, Operational Directive 4.01.

30. IFC, Operational Procedure 4.01.

31. Marrakech Agreement, Article 5:2.

32. WTO, General Council, *Guidelines for Arrangements on Relations with Non-Governmental Organizations,* WT/L/162.

33. IBRD, Resolution 93-10/IDA 93-06, *Resolution Establishing the Inspection Panel,* 22 September 1993. For more information on the operations of the panel, see *Inspection Panel Operating Procedures,* as adopted by the panel on 19 August 1994; and Dana Clark and Michael Hsu, *A Citizen's Guide to the World Bank Inspection Panel* (CIEL 1997).

34. UNDP Information Policy, supra note 24, paras 20–23.

5
The Right to Water as a Human Right

Ignacio J. Alvarez

WATER, WHETHER CONSUMED DIRECTLY or used for such basic needs as sanitation, cleansing, and growing food, is essential to human life. Since three-quarters of the water consumed by humans is used in agriculture, water shortages or contamination can lead to famine, disease, and even death.[1]

The United Nations Department of Technical Cooperation for Development has said,

> No resource is more basic than water. Water is essential for life, crucial for relieving poverty, hunger and disease and critical for economic development. Despite enormous improvements over the past 15 years, hundreds of millions of men, women and children still do not have proper water for drinking and sanitation. Many remain unemployed because water resources cannot support agricultural or industrial growth. Water problems ultimately end up as "people" problems.
>
> As world population increases and development efforts expand, water needs can only increase. By the end of the century, global water use is expected to reach twice the level of 1980.[2]

While the consumption of water has increased constantly through the years and the number of human beings using and relying upon it continues to multiply at an alarming rate, the amount of water on Earth remains finite and constant, being that the total supply of water neither grows nor diminishes. It is believed to be almost precisely the same now as it was 3 billion years ago.[3] In this sense, there exists a steady and continuing reduction of the amount of fresh water on Earth per individual that will inevitably lead to intensified competition for increasingly scarce water.[4]

The demand for water stimulates invention, and the facility of obtaining it is forever increasing the demand. In light of this observation, it is perhaps not surprising that the most technologically advanced societies consume the most water on a per capita basis. The average person living in the United States, for example, consumes more than seventy times as much water annually as the average resident of Ghana.[5]

Therefore, the point concerning whether water is a human right is very important. Equally important is the consequence of deciding whether States have an obligation to provide their citizens with water of adequate quality and quantity for their health and sanitation needs.

Legal Framework

The right to water is not specifically mentioned in the 1948 Universal Declaration on Human Rights; in the 1966 Covenant on Economic, Social and Cultural Rights; or in the 1966 Covenant on Civil and Political Rights. Nevertheless, the right to water is understood as part of the right to life, as a component of the right to health, and as part of the right to food. However, little attention has been given to the question of whether there is a specific *right to water*; and, if so, what the contours of such a right may be.[6]

The right to life comprises the right of every human being not to be deprived of his life, and the right of every human being to have the appropriate means of subsistence and a decent standard of living.[7] In this sense, construed as including the right to appropriate means of subsistence, the right to life would clearly encompass the right to sanitary drinking water.[8]

The right to water can also be viewed as part of the right to health. The Constitution of the World Health Organization (WHO) in 1946 declared the "enjoyment of the highest attainable standard of health" to be a "fundamental right" recognized by the international community.[9] In this respect, one common definition of health is a "state of complete physical, mental and social well-being and not merely the absence of disease or infirmity."[10] It has been argued that applying these standards, the right not to suffer from cancer, liver damage, disorders of the nervous system, or birth defects as a result of drinking contaminated water, is fundamental.[11] Water is also a component of the right to food. The right to food should be interpreted as the right to receive life-sustaining nourishment, or sustenance, so that it would include the right to potable drinking water sufficient to sustain life.[12] The principal importance of distinguishing under which right water falls, as noted infra, is to determine what States' obligations are related to this right, and therefore, which methods will be used to enforce it.

Universal Declaration on Human Rights

Article 25 of the Universal Declaration on Human Rights proclaims that "[e]very one has the right to a standard of living adequate for the health and well-being of himself and of his family, including food. . . ." McCaffrey sustains that the right to water is implicit in the right to an adequate standard of living, because "it seems obvious that such a standard of living could not exist without an adequate supply of water suitable for drinking. Further, unless food were imported from other states, the 'right' to an adequate standard of living presumes an adequate supply of water to sustain agriculture to the extent necessary to feed a state's population."[13]

The word "including" in Article 25 of the Declaration implies that there can be other components of the right to an adequate standard of living. In this sense the right to water, whether conceived as part of the right to health or the right to food, or as an autonomous right, is a fundamental component of the right to an adequate standard of living.

COVENANT ON ECONOMIC, SOCIAL AND CULTURAL RIGHTS The Covenant on Economic, Social and Cultural Rights establishes more detailed provisions from which the right to water can be inferred. Article 11(1) establishes that the States recognize the right of everyone to an adequate standard of living for himself and for his family, including adequate food. This part of the article is similar in nature to Article 25 of the Declaration, from which, as noted above, the right to water has been inferred.

Article 11(2) refers to State obligations related to the right of everyone to be free from hunger, saying that States shall take measures to improve methods of production of food by developing or reforming agrarian systems in such a way as to achieve the most efficient development and utilization of natural resources. The right to water could also be inferred from this part of the article. Evidently, the most efficient development and utilization of natural resources in order to improve methods of food production shall take into special account aspects related to quality, distribution, and utilization of water.

Article 12 of the Covenant, which is related to the right to health, includes as part of the necessary steps States must take to achieve the full realization of this right those necessary for the reduction of infant mortality and those necessary for the improvement of all aspects of environmental and industrial hygiene. Given the close relationship between safe drinking water and infant mortality, as well as the link between environmental and industrial hygiene, it could be very well argued that the right to water is also implied in Article 12 of the Covenant.

COVENANT ON CIVIL AND POLITICAL RIGHTS Article 6 of the Covenant establishes that every human has the inherent right to life, which has to be protected by law. There are disagreements on whether the right to life could imply the right to water. It has been said that "[t]he human right to life per se . . . is a civil right and does not guarantee any person against death from famine or cold or lack of medical attention."[14] In this line of thought, Article 6 would not require the State to take affirmative actions to ensure that its citizens have access to adequate sustenance, but only would oblige it to refrain from practicing or tolerating arbitrary deprivations of life. Therefore, it would be difficult to infer a right to water under this interpretation of Article 6.[15]

On the other hand, more recent and progressive doctrine adopts a more expansive interpretation of Article 6. Cancado Trindade, Judge of the Inter-American Human Rights Court, says in this sense that "under the right to life, in its modern and proper sense, not only is protection against any arbitrary deprivation of life upheld, but furthermore States are under the duty to pursue policies which are designed to ensure access to the means of survival for all individuals and all peoples."[16] The Human Rights Committee has also stated that "[The Committee] has noted that the right to life has been too often narrowly interpreted. The expression 'inherent right to life' cannot properly be understood in a restrictive manner, and the protection of this right requires that States adopt positive measures. In this connection, the Committee considers that it would be desirable for States Parties to take all possible measures to reduce infant mortality and to increase life expectancy, especially adopting measures to eliminate malnutrition and epidemics."[17] Within this modern view, the right to life comprises the right of every human being not to be deprived of his life, and the right of every human being to have the appropriate means of subsistence and a decent standard of living. In this context, the right to life would clearly encompass the right to sanitary drinking water.[18]

UNITED NATIONS CONVENTION ON THE RIGHTS OF THE CHILD This modern Convention, which is a comprehensive human rights treaty comprising economic, social and cultural, civil and political, and humanitarian rights has been ratified by nearly all countries of the world. It establishes in Article 24 that States Parties recognize the right of the child to the enjoyment of the highest attainable standard of health and the right to facilities for the treatment of illness and rehabilitation of health. To the end of pursuing the full implementation of this right, States shall take appropriate measures to "combat disease and malnutrition, including within the framework of primary health care, through, *inter alia,* the application of readily available technology and through the provision of adequate nutritious foods and clean drinking-water. . . ."

This treaty is therefore the main universal instrument that explicitly refers to water as a human right. Within this context, water is seen as part of the measures needed to ensure the right to health. Nevertheless, it is important to highlight that the above article makes some distinction between food and water, assuming that the right to water is not the same subject as the right to food.

HUMANITARIAN LAW Under humanitarian law (the laws governing war), the right to water is recognized and protected. McCaffrey points out that "It is a well established rule of the law of armed conflict that the enemy's water supply may not be poisoned or contaminated."[19] In this respect, Article 54, paragraph 2, of the 1977 Protocol I Addition to the Geneva Conventions, related to the protection of civilians in conflicts of an international nature, states, "It is prohibited to attack, destroy, remove or render useless objects indispensable to the survival of the civilian population, such as foodstuffs, agricultural areas for the production of foodstuffs, crops, livestock, drinking water installations and supplies and irrigation works, for the specific purpose of denying them for their sustenance value to the civilian population or to the adverse party, whatever the motive, whether in order to starve out civilians, to cause them to move away or for any other motive."[20]

UNITED NATIONS STANDARD MINIMUM RULES FOR THE TREATMENT OF PRISONERS The United Nations has also explicitly established the right to water in its Minimum Rules for the Treatment of Prisoners. In its Article 20, titled "Food," the mentioned instrument says,

1 Every prisoner shall be provided by the administration at the usual hours with food of nutritional value adequate for health and strength, of wholesome quality and well prepared and served.

2 Drinking water shall be available to every prisoner whenever he needs it.[21]

It is interesting to note that although the right to drinking water is located under the title of food, it is construed in a paragraph different from that dealing with the right to food. This could be another manifestation of the fact that it is not quite clear whether the right to water is comprised in the right to food, in the right to health, or as a right by itself.

Inter-American Human Rights Instruments

Although neither the American Declaration of the Rights and Duties of Man nor the Inter-American Convention on Human Rights establishes an explicit right to water, the Declaration understands the right to food as part of the right of every person to the preservation of his health. Within this context, the Inter-American Commission has dealt with the right to water. For example, in its 1997 Report on the Development of Human Rights in Cuba, the Commission analyzed the impact of the United States embargo on Cuba and cited a report of the American Association for World Health: "The deteriorating water supply in Cuba has increased the incidence of water-borne illnesses such as typhoid fever, dysentery and viral hepatitis. For example, the mortality caused by acute diarrhea rose from 2.7 per 100,000 inhabitants in 1989 to 6.7 per 100,000 in 1994. The rate of illness from amoebic and bacillary dysenteries showed a sharp increase during the same time."[22]

National Laws

The right to water is diversely treated in national laws. While many countries do not have this right in their laws, there are examples in which the right is given such importance that it is placed in the Constitution, while others have enacted specific laws on the matter.

The 1996 South African Constitution, for example, states in its section 27(b) that "Everyone has the right to have access to . . . sufficient food and to sufficient water." The United States for its part has the Safe Drinking Water Act of 1974, which directs the Human Health Sub-Committee of the United States Environmental Protection Agency (EPA) to ensure that both public and noncommunity water systems meet minimum standards for protecting public health.[23]

Components of the Rights and State Obligations

To accept that water is a human right would presume at least a right to a sufficient supply of safe drinking water to sustain life. This right would entail a correlative obligation of the State to provide such a supply of water.[24] The right to water comprises two main aspects: the water consumed directly by human beings and the water used for such basic needs as sanitation, cleansing, and agriculture.

Regarding water consumed directly by human beings, or safe drinking water, the Human Health Sub-Committee of the United States Environmental Agency (EPA) Science Advisory Board, states that contamination of drinking water is one of four categories classified as a "relatively high risk" to human health. The Sub-Committee adds that it can become contaminated at the original water source, during treatment, or during distribution to the home. If the drinking water originates from surface water, such as river or lake, "it can be exposed to acid rain, storm water run-off, pesticide run-off, and industrial waste." If drinking water originates from ground water such as private wells and some public water supplies, it generally takes longer to become contaminated, but the natural cleansing process also may take much longer.[25]

The quality of the water used for such basic needs as sanitation, cleansing, and growing food is equally important. An example of such water quality is a situation in Chile, in which much of the agricultural land is irrigated with water from the same rivers into which most domestic and industrial waste is dumped. This practice resulted in an outbreak of cholera in 1991, largely because Santiago, Chile's capital, has no water treatment plants.[26]

From the point of view of the individuals, the human right to drinking water comprises both the right to an adequate supply of water and the right to quality water. The State obligations correlative to this right would differ depending on whether the right to water is understood as part of the right to life or as part of the right to health, of the right to food or as a proper right in itself.

If the right to water is an element of the right to life, thus protected under Article 4 of the Covenant on Civil and Political Rights and under other regional instruments, States have "an immediate obligation to 'respect and to ensure' this right and to take whatever other necessary measures to bring about that result."[27] On the other hand, if the right to water is viewed as forming part of the right to health, or of the right to food, or even as an independent right included in an adequate standard of living, it should be understood as recognized by Article 11 or Article 12 of the Covenant on Economic, Social and Cultural Rights. In this sense, from a traditional point of view, the States' obligations related to the water would be determined by Article 2 of the Covenant, according to which States agree to take steps to their maximum available resources to achieve progressively the full realization of the rights recognized in the Covenant.

The result of these various approaches to State obligations under the two Covenants seems odd, to say the least. As McCaffrey says, it causes one to wonder whether there are indeed sound reasons in the nature of the obligations undertaken by States Parties under the two covenants, and it reveals several defects in the differential approach to the obligations under the two covenants. In particular, it seems questionable whether all of the rights under the Covenant on Economic, Social and Cultural Rights are appropriate for progressive implementation, according to available resources, since

> It may well be that certain rights under that instrument either are not of a fundamental nature or would require the establishment of governmental infrastructures and the like to ensure their fulfillment. . . . But other rights under the E.S.C. Covenant can hardly be described as being anything but fundamental. Indeed, Article 11 itself refers to the "fundamental right of everyone to be free from hunger." This basic right can only be interpreted as a right to life-supporting sustenance, which would include potable water.[28]

In this sense, and taking into account the importance of the rights under the Covenant on Economic, Social and Cultural Rights concerning basic needs such as food and water, a strong argument can be made that the standard to be applied in determining whether governments have adequately safeguarded those rights approaches the level of obligations under the Covenant on Civil and Political Rights.[29] For these reasons, it could be affirmed that water is a basic human right that States have the immediate obligation to respect, to promote, to protect, and to fulfill.

Therefore, the State has the obligation to fulfill the right to water for every individual. This obligation is the State's most important regarding the right to water, because the State usually has control over water resources and water distribution machinery. The State also has the obligation to respect the right to water of those who are able to provide themselves with it. This implies respect for water resources owned by the individual and respect for his freedom to take necessary actions to satisfy his own water needs. The State has the obligation to protect, which means active protection of the existing water resources against public or private subjects, such as contaminating industries. The final State obligation is related to promotion; the State has the obligation to facilitate the opportunities by which the rights can be enjoyed. In regard to the right to water, for example, the State, under Article 11(2) of the Covenant on Economic, Social and Cultural Rights, should take steps to improve methods of production of food by making full use of technical and scientific knowledge, which would include aspects related to the best use of irrigating water.

Measurement of States' Compliance and Implementation of the Right

Measurement of States' compliance with their obligation to provide safe water can be achieved in various ways. One is by measuring the general population's access to water. Both UNICEF[30] and the United Nations Development Programme, which shows measures in its annual Human Development Report, measure access to water. In that Report, the Programme offers data in the profile of human development and in the profile of human deprivation related to the percentage of population with access to safe water and to the percentage of population without access. In this sense, the 1996 Human Right Development Report shows that in countries with high human development indicators, an average of 84 percent of the population has access to safe water (showing 100 percent for Singapore and 71 percent for Argentina), while in countries with low human development indicators the average falls to 55 percent (97 percent for Bangladesh and 12 percent for Afghanistan).[31] As usually happens with these indicators, these figures reveal that for different reasons, there are countries with high average human development indicators in which the percentage of population with access to safe water is substantially inferior to some other countries with lower average human development indicators.

Another manner of measuring a State's compliance with its obligation of providing safe water is through the personal consequences of the lack of access to it. For example, if a child dies because of illness resulting from not having access to safe water (for example, diarrhea), it could be very well argued, as indicated supra, that the State has violated his right to life.

In implementation of the right to water, there are other ways of measuring compliance. One is through the reporting systems of the Covenant on Economic, Social and Cultural Rights and of the Convention on the Rights of the Child. For example, States could be required to include in their reports measures adopted and progress made in achieving the full realization of the right to water. The reporting Guidelines of the Committee on Economic, Social and Cultural Rights require, for example, States Parties to provide (where available) indicators defined by the World Health Organization (WHO) relating to population access to safe water, disaggregated by urban and rural areas.[32]

Another form of measurement is through the individual petition system of complaints of the Covenant on Civil and Political Rights and of the Inter-American Convention on Human Rights. For example, individuals can file petitions in cases of violations of right to life related to lack of access to the right to safe water. At the national level, it is very important to ensure the enjoyment of the right by establishing a specific right to water in national laws, as is done in South Africa in its 1996 Constitution, and in the United States in its Safe Drinking Water Act of 1974.

It is interesting to note that there is a nongovernmental organization called the International Water Tribunal (IWT), seated in Amsterdam, that receives "complaints" concerning water use and establishes multidisciplinary "juries" of independent experts to pass judgment on them and to make recommendations for their solutions. This tribunal heard a case in which the complainants charged that at least half of some seventy Arab communities in the center and north of Israel are not recognized by the State and are not connected to national drinking networks. This situation was said to have led to serious health problems caused by Israel to pressure those Arab communities to evacuate their place of residence and relocate against their will.[33]

In conclusion, there are several ways of measuring and ensuring States' compliance with their obligations related to the right to water. Certainly, one of the first and main tasks is to raise awareness about the existence of the right to water, and about the importance of this right.

Conclusion

Water, whether consumed directly or used for such basic needs as sanitation, cleansing, and growing food, is essential to human life. Although the right to water is not specifically mentioned in the 1948 Universal Declaration on Human Rights in the 1966 Covenant on Economic, Social and Cultural Rights, or in the 1966 Covenant on Civil and Political Rights, it can be clearly inferred from those instruments and from other international human rights instruments. Given the importance of the right to water, and on the basis of the analysis made, the right to water is a human right that States have the immediate obligation to fulfill, to respect, to promote, and to protect.

Although there are several ways of measuring and ensuring States' compliance with their obligations related to the right to water, one of the first steps should be to raise awareness about the existence of the right to water and about the importance of this right. One very important aspect of this is to take into account that water is a resource that remains constant and finite.

NOTES

1. Stephen C. McCaffrey, *A Human Right to Water: Domestic and International Implications,* 5 Geo. Int'l Envtl. L. Rev. 1, at 5 (1992).

2. United Nations, Department of Technical Cooperation for Development of Water Resources, undated brochure, cited in McCaffrey, supra note 1, at 8.

3. Luna B. Leopold and Kenneth S. Davis, *Water* 33 (1966), cited in McCaffrey, supra note 1, at 3.

4. McCaffrey, supra note 1, at 2.

5. Ibid., at 4.

6. Ibid., at 1.

7. United Nations, Human Rights Committee, General Comments adopted under Article 40, paragraph 4, of the Covenant on Civil and Political Rights, Document CCPR/C/21/Rev. 1, 19 May 1989, at 5.

8. McCaffrey, supra note 1, at 10.

9. See Preamble to the Constitution of the World Health Organization as adopted by the International Health Conference, New York, 10–22 June 1946; signed on 22 July 1946 by representatives of sixty-one States (Official Records of the World Health Organization, 2, 100), and entered into force on 7 April 1948.

10. Ibid.

11. Satvinder Juss, *Global Environmental Change: Health and the Challenge for Human Rights,* 5 Ind. J. Global Leg. Stud. 121, Fall 1997, at 150.

12. McCaffrey, supra note 1, at 23.

13. McCaffrey, supra note 1, at 8.

14. Yoram Dinstein, The Right to Life, Physical Integrity, and Liberty, in The International Bill of Rights, at 114 (L. Henkin ed., 1981); cited in McCaffrey, supra note 1, at 9.

15. McCaffrey, supra note 1, at 9.

16. Antonio A. Cancado Trindade, *The Parallel Evolutions of International Human Rights Protections and of Environmental Protection and the Absence of Restrictions on the Exercise of Recognized Human Rights,* 13 Revista Instituto Interamericano de Derechos Humanos 35, 51 (1991).

17. United Nations, Human Rights Committee, General Comments adopted under Article 40, para 4 of the C.P. Covenant, Doc. CCPR/C/21/Rev. 1, 19 May 1989, at 5.

18. McCaffrey, supra note 1, at 10.

19. McCaffrey, supra note 1, at 20.

20. Protocol I, Article 54, *Additional to the Geneva Convention of 12 August*

1949, and Relating to the Protection of Victims of International Armed Conflicts, 7 December 1978, at Article 54, para 2, reprinted in 16 ILM 1391.

21. *Standard Minimum Rules for the Treatment of Prisoners,* 30 August 1955; Doc. E/3048 (1957), adopted 30 August 1955 by the First United National Congress on the Prevention of Crime and Treatment of Offenders, Document A/CONF/611, Annex I, ESC Resolution 663C, 24 US ESCOR Supplement 1, at 11, amended ESC Resolution 2076, at 62; UN ESCOR Supp. (No. 1) at 35, U.N. Doc. E/5988 (1977).

22. Inter-American Commission on Human Rights, OAS/SER.L/V/II.98, *Annual Report,* 1997, at 950.

23. Juss, supra note 11, at 13.

24. McCaffrey, supra note 1, at 12.

25. Cited by Juss, supra note 11, at 130.

26. Nathaniel C. Nash, *Scrubbing the Skies Over Chile,* New York Times, July 6, 1992, at 7, cited by McCaffrey, supra note 1, at 7.

27. McCaffrey, supra note 1, at 9, citing Thomas Burghental, *International Human Rights in a Nutshell* (St. Paul, Minn.: West, 1988), 29–33.

28. McCaffrey, supra note 1, at 13.

29. McCaffrey, supra note 1, at 15.

30. See, for example, UNICEF, *The State of the World's Children 1996,* New York, 1996, at 29.

31. United Nations Development Programme, *Human Development Report,* 1996, at 145.

32. Alston Philip, 63 *The International Covenant on Economic, Social and Cultural Rights, in United Nations Centre for Human Rights: Manual on Human Rights Reporting,* 1991, cited by Audrey R. Chapman, *Monitoring Women's Right to Health under the International Covenant on Economic, Social and Cultural Rights,* 44 Am. U.L. Rev. 1157 (1995), at 1167.

33. McCaffrey, supra note 1, at 6.

6 Women's Rights and the Global Population Crisis

Michael G. Shaw

[C]ontraception and abortion were the true revolutions of the twentieth century, constituting not a power-sharing between women and men, but a transfer of power from men to women. Women alone could decide on maternity, they could determine whether they chose to live with the child's father, to be married and to recognize the father's rights. They [women] alone currently had the power in the family under the law.

—HENRY STEINER and PHILIP ALSTON

THERE ARE DIFFERING OPINIONS on the gravity of the global population problem.[1] Some population analysts believe that there could be an environmental doomsday.[2] Other analysts believe that the problem exists only in individual countries and not globally.[3] Almost all analysts, however, share the common belief that lowering birth rates will improve either the global or local situations.[4]

The epigraph of this chapter quotes the French representative to the United Nations Convention on the Elimination of All Forms of Discrimination Against Women[5] (CEDAW), who stated that women in France had the sole power in the family to decide on maternity.[6] Whether this was an accurate statement at the time is not as important as the point it made—there is great tension in the family over the decision to have a child.[7] The decision itself is hugely important to the global population problem.[8] A decision that fails to take into account consequences will almost surely be detrimental to the global population problem.[9]

Countries have taken various approaches to lowering their birth rates. Some countries have implemented extremely coercive programs including strict limits on the number of children per family, forced sterilization, and forced abortion.[10] More recent attempts to control population have been increasingly cognizant of human rights and hence less coercive; these attempts emphasize making contraception more readily available.[11]

International law states that the family has the ultimate authority to make decisions regarding the number of children they will have.[12] International law also states that women and men should have equal rights.[13] These two statements, unfortunately, are not in harmony with each other. In most countries, the culture, government, religion, and patriarchal system combine to give men most of the power to make decisions regarding the number of children in the family.[14] Women do not have equal rights.[15]

This chapter examines whether a transfer of power within the family is required to cause a desired drop in the world population growth. The first part explores the current state of the population problem and the main impediments to controlling population growth. The second part discusses existing international law on population and women's equal rights. The third part analyzes the differences between the theory and practice of the treaties that on the one hand give the family the right to decide on the number of children, and on the other hand give women equal rights. The fourth part discusses the definitions of coercive programs and whether it is possible for coercive programs to work in harmony with human rights. The fifth part recommends that international law be interpreted differently and a coercive element added so that women have the ultimate power to decide on the number of children they have. Giving women this power will result in better decisions on the number of children in a family and will lower the global population growth rate.[16]

The Population Problem

Ever since Malthus[17] first warned of the harm caused by increasing population, analysts have disagreed as to its severity.[18] The worst situation, according to some analysts, is that if the population continues to grow as it has, the result could be an environmental doomsday where population is reduced by mass famines and diseases.[19] More moderate warnings are that vital global systems will be damaged beyond repair.[20] The result of this damage will be, according to different analysts, either that large numbers of people will die[21] or that large numbers will be caught in cycles of misery and poverty.[22]

The main methods for rectifying problems caused by overpopulation are to slow the increase of population,[23] decrease the consumption of resources,[24] and increase the amount of resources.[25] Until recently, population planners focused on decreases in reproduction, with public and private initiatives concentrated, *inter alia*, on sterilizing women, providing easier access to contraceptives, and imposing quotas on family size.[26] Some of these initiatives have been successful but the problem remains: predictions are that the 1995 global population of 5.7 billion will double in forty-three years.[27]

Both developing and developed countries must participate in solving the population problem.[28] While the developing countries are expected to account for 90 percent of the future population growth, the developed countries currently consume 75 percent of the global resources.[29] Thus, all countries must undertake population planning; countries that currently have low fertility rates have as much responsibility to reduce fertility and consumption as do countries with high fertility rates.[30] Additionally, countries with low fertility rates often have specific problems that should be addressed.[31]

The population problem is global; hence, a global solution is warranted. The United Nations is the appropriate forum for such a solution. Many international treaties and conferences have provisions related to population,[32] including population programs, development strategies, human rights, and specifically women's rights.

Existing Law: Women's Rights, Population Growth, and the International Covenant on Civil and Political Rights

International human rights groups traditionally regard the International Covenant on Civil and Political Rights[33] (ICCPR) as a core instrument of the human rights movement.[34] The ICCPR contains guarantees to the right to life, the right not to be subjected to medical or scientific experimentation, the right not to be subjected to inhumane or degrading treatment, the right to liberty and security of person, the right not to be subjected to arbitrary or unlawful interference with privacy or the family, and the right to marry and found a family.[35] The ICCPR endorses the general principle that there should be no sexual discrimination when implementing its guarantees.[36] Many of the activities associated with population policies, however, violate these civil and political rights and discriminate on the basis of sex.[37]

International Conference on Population and Development

PRINCIPLES CEDAW still provides the basic law regarding women's rights and includes statements on population.[38] A major enhancement to CEDAW's statements on population occurred in 1994 when the International Conference on Population and Development[39] (ICPD or Cairo Conference) was held in Cairo. The Cairo Conference was the first conference to combine population and development[40] strategies. It shifted the emphasis from trying solely to slow the population growth to combining decreased population growth with increases in human rights.[41] Quotas and targets were deemphasized, and the focus became the need for greater access to education and information so women could make better decisions about the number of children they conceive.[42]

The Cairo Conference also agreed that human rights must be the foundation of governmental population programs.[43] The delegates believed that these human rights were already recognized in existing national laws and international human rights documents;[44] therefore the next step was to apply the existing human rights to population programs.[45] The Cairo Conference gave individuals the right to make informed choices about reproductive activity.[46] This newly articulated right was of particular significance to women, who were not empowered to make their own reproductive decisions.[47]

The Cairo Conference focused on the fact that empowering women would result in better choices in family planning,[48] give women control over their bodies,[49] and serve an important human rights objective.[50] The implication was that empowering women would result in women choosing to have fewer children.[51] The delegates understood that women are not empowered in the current world to make family planning choices.[52] Restrictions and pressures are placed on women by the State, religion, culture, and male partners.[53] Examples of the restrictions and pressures include violence,[54] laws against owning land,[55] marriage at a young age,[56] and lack of education.[57]

THE CAIRO PROGRAMME OF ACTION An output of the Cairo Conference was the Programme of Action[58] (Cairo Programme or Programme), a set of goals and recommendations for population and development. The Programme is today considered the fundamental paradigm for population programs.[59] The implementation of the recommendations contained in the Programme, however, as in most documents of this kind, was at the discretion of each country.[60] The language of the Programme allowed each country to avoid implementation of a recommendation if the recommendation was inconsistent with national laws and development priorities.[61] This, along with the lack of enforcement so often existing in international treaties and declarations,[62] resulted in actualization well short of the stated goals.[63]

Even though the recommendations were not uniformly implemented, the Programme contained considerable language supporting the empowerment of women.[64] For instance, it stated that gender equality,[65] empowerment of women, and elimination of violence against women are the cornerstones of population and developmental programs.[66] It provided for countries to take full measures to eliminate all forms of exploitation, abuse, harassment, and violence against women,[67] take actions to prohibit female genital mutilation,[68] and take a more forceful position on child marriage.[69]

On the other hand, the Programme took a very moderate approach to abortion.[70] It stated that in no case should abortion be promoted as a method of family planning, but if countries allow abortion, measures should be taken to make abortion safe and to provide follow-up services.[71]

The Programme defined reproductive health as the state of complete physical, mental, and social well-being, including the ability to have a satisfying and safe sex life.[72] Statements on laws that affect population were not limited to those directly regulating reproductive matters, but also included laws regarding the minimum age of marriage, education, status of women, health care, employment, child care, welfare, and old age security.[73] The Programme required States to avoid coercion in all family planning programs.[74]

The Programme failed to acknowledge the collective rights of society.[75] Collective rights were recognized, however, by the 1974 Bucharest World Population Plan of Action,[76] which stated that family planning must take into account the needs of not just the living, but the needs of future children as well.[77]

Effect on Population Programs

The goal of population programs is to adjust fertility, mortality, migration, and consumption to achieve a better balance in economic and resource demographics.[78] One of the main assumptions of many population programs is that women will choose to have fewer children if given the choice.[79]

The Cairo Programme emphasizes voluntary, informed choices by individuals and couples rather than the coercive measures employed by some States.[80] This approach intends to provide women with sufficient education and economic opportunities so that there are options other than having large families.[81] This human rights–based approach is criticized by some, however, for being too slow when a quicker resolution is necessary.[82] Alternatives to the human rights approach propose direct State action by setting quotas or by providing contraceptive or sterilization programs; these kinds of programs are often considered coercive.[83]

The Cairo Conference provided the framework for major enhancements to population programs. One of the impediments to progress, however, is the role the family plays in reproductive choices.

Family Planning

The Rights of the Family in Theory

The 1948 Universal Declaration of Human Rights (UDHR) describes the family[84] as the natural and fundamental unit of society.[85] Later, as a result of the Tehran Conference in 1969, the United Nations General Assembly published the Declaration on Social Progress and Development.[86] This was the first United Nations resolution to urge governments to protect families' rights to determine freely and responsibly the number and spacing of children.[87]

The Cairo Programme has many pronouncements on the family. First, it states that the family is the basic unit of society but acknowledges that various forms of the family exist in different social, cultural, legal, and political systems.[88] Second, the Programme states that all couples and individuals have the basic right to decide freely and responsibly the number, spacing, and timing of their children.[89] Third, the Programme states that men and women must equally participate in all areas of family and household responsibilities including family planning, and actions should be taken so that men and women have more choices regarding the balance between domestic and public responsibilities.[90] The Programme also proposes to raise the status of female children by eliminating the root causes of son preference, which results in female infanticide and prenatal sex selection.[91]

None of the aforementioned treaties discusses the definition of a family, apparently silently acknowledging the differences in the various countries and cultures.[92] What is usually thought of as the "normal" family in Western cultures—one wife, one husband, and children—is not the norm throughout the world and is even changing in Western cultures.[93] The definition of a family is nourished even more today by single parents, same-sex partnerships, and new reproductive technologies that make it easier than before for traditional couples, individuals, and partners to become parents.[94]

The Rights of the Family in Practice

PATRIARCHAL SYSTEMS In contrast to the stated goals of the treaties that promise equality within the family for deciding the number of children,[95] the power within the family is not with the woman.[96] The power is with the male partner or with other male members of the family.[97] Women do not have an equal role in deciding the number and spacing of children.[98] Patriarchal[99] systems control the family and reproductive decisions with respect to the number and spacing of children,[100] and are often reinforced by religion and tradition.[101]

Patriarchal systems, particularly in developing countries, leave women without political, social, economic, and judicial power.[102] Patriarchal systems essentially assign women the roles of service to family, husband, and children and eliminate the image of women as individuals entitled to self-determination.[103]

Men generally control the decision to reproduce, as well as other aspects of women's lives,[104] but are generally reluctant to use contraceptive methods themselves, thereby leaving women largely responsible for contraception.[105] In developing countries, for instance, only 26 percent of contraceptive users utilize male contraceptive methods such as vasectomies, condoms, withdrawal, or the rhythm method.[106] In some cultures, men are the major objectors to family planning because having children is considered a demonstration of their virility;[107] in others, men believe that pregnancy is a way of keeping women faithful.[108] Some population programs exacerbate these problems by directly requiring the woman to obtain the husband's consent for obtaining contraceptive services.[109]

REPRODUCTIVE DECISIONS AND POPULATION PROGRAMS One of the first statements that proposed giving a woman the sole right to decide on the number of children was from the Yugoslav delegation at the United Nations Conference on Human Rights at Tehran, where the delegation stated that the right to family planning should be the fundamental right of women to conscious motherhood.[110] That kind of statement, however, has not often been voiced and has not become part of international law.[111] Discrimination against women remains pervasive throughout the world, particularly in developing countries with the most serious concerns about population growth.[112] This discrimination denies women their rights of self-determination and reproductive autonomy.[113]

Most population programs focus on women's reproductive behavior.[114] On the surface, this may seem logical since it is women who bear children. In most societies seeking to reduce birth rates, however, men dominate most, if not all, of the decisions in the family, including reproductive decisions.[115]

An additional problem with population programs, whether based on utilitarian perspectives[116] or on human rights perspectives, is that they fail to take into account the underlying sexual behavior between partners.[117] Thus, even when family planning programs focus more on the interests and needs of the family unit as opposed to coercive programs that focus solely on decreasing fertility, they often ignore the realities of the family decision-making process where men believe they have the right to control the sexuality and fertility of the woman.[118]

The level of equality within a marriage affects the success of family planning and population programs.[119] When reproductive decisions are made through unequal power dynamics caused by patriarchal control, higher fertility rates tend to result than when the decisions are achieved through a truly joint decision-making process.[120]

PUBLIC AND PRIVATE SPHERES "Public spheres" and "private spheres" are terms that are often used as categories for assigning men and women to different roles.[121] In the areas of international law and population programs, these terms complicate the discussion of human rights.[122] State court systems[123] and delegates to international conferences may think that anything within the private sphere is outside of their scope.[124] For instance, many think that reproductive rights are different from other human rights since reproduction is more involved with private settings, social custom, and policy,[125] and is therefore part of the private sphere. Thus, these people might think that reproductive rights are outside of the scope of treaties because States have not traditionally taken action regarding the private sphere.[126]

Thinking in terms of private sphere versus public sphere complicates even the basic qualities of human rights. Many believe that private sphere rights exist only theoretically and can be exercised only after a government intervenes to actualize them.[127] Public sphere rights are inherent to the individual and can be taken away only by governments.[128] Possibly because of this differentiation, the international human rights community has traditionally been more interested in civil and political rights than it has been in social, economic, cultural, and women's rights.[129]

If countries change their thinking on the role the family plays in reproductive decisions, the question then becomes how to incorporate those changes into population programs. An obstacle to incorporating the changes is the confusion over the definition of "coercive" population programs.

The Coercive Element

Coercive Population Programs

There is no consensus on the definition of a coercive population program.[130] One reason for the confusion may be that the dictionary provides definitions of "coercion" involving force or threat, but also provides alternative definitions involving "compel" or "nullify" without any mention of force or threat.[131] The definitions of coercive population programs can therefore be relatively narrow, such as defining coercive programs as those involving physical force or the threat of severe deprivation, to compel individuals to do what they otherwise would not do.[132] Or the definitions can be much broader, such as defining coercive programs as any program compelling people to submit to family planning demands of any type against their will.[133]

Some writers believe that population programs necessarily include a coercive element.[134] They also believe that terminology is important. The term "family planning programs" in and of itself does not necessarily involve State regulation of fertility since a family planning program that merely educates individuals and couples on contraception and assists with birth planning does not regulate fertility.[135] A "population control program," in contrast, includes State actions or regulation intended to influence the size of families.[136]

Generally, there is agreement that the more draconian measures concerning limits on the number of children per family are coercive.[137] There is far less agreement, however, on whether other measures, such as government propaganda, are coercive.[138] It could be argued that any government advertising that changes the will of the people is coercive, but more probably the answer depends on the underlying target of the advertising; if the measure that the advertising attempts to promote is coercive, then the advertising itself is coercive.[139] A similar question deals with incentives.[140]

Supporters of incentives argue that incentives are only inducements to change behavior and hence are not coercive.[141] Critics of incentives, however, argue that people who are poor are in no position to make free choices and hence are coerced.[142]

Treaties

The treaties themselves, including CEDAW and the Cairo Conference, do not define coercive programs, and in some cases imply that each country should decide itself whether its programs are coercive.[143] Additionally, there are seeming contradictions. For instance, the Cairo Conference repeatedly states that coercion must not be used.[144] It then contradicts itself, however, by stating that government population programs should take affirmative actions to ensure the rights of individuals and families to make decisions concerning reproduction free of discrimination, coercion, and violence.[145] By failing to define coercion, the Cairo Conference leaves each country to decide, for instance, whether population program elements such as incentives to families and local program directors, or advertisements for condoms, are coercive.[146]

In light of prevailing international human rights law, the vagueness of a definition of a coercive program is troubling for a number of reasons. Some argue that coercion means any action that influences behavior and that any use of coercive practices is antithetical to human rights.[147] The same people argue that even when the goal of coercive practices is to strengthen human rights by making certain conduct compulsory for the benefit of all,[148] the coercive programs should not be used because the ends never justify the means.[149] People with those beliefs never want governments to take any action related to family rights.[150]

Human rights, however, are of a legal character, and they imply, or sometimes even explicitly invoke, the use of coercion or compulsion to achieve certain ends.[151] For example, the UDHR states both that everyone has the right to education and that education shall be compulsory, thus implying that a coercive element is necessary to ensure that the right is achieved.[152] The same could be said for coercive elements in population programs; governments can take actions to ensure that human rights are achieved.[153]

Although the average global birth rate has been decreasing,[154] it is not sufficient to eliminate the population problem. All countries must undertake further steps.[155] Recently, programs based on human rights have been successful, especially those that concentrate on the education of women and improvement in the status of women.[156] Coercive population programs that attempt to meet target fertility rates through measures such as forced sterilization, contraception, and abortion have sometimes been successful but only at the expense of human rights.[157] Nevertheless, coercive programs are generally considered to provide faster results because they force quicker change.[158]

Recommendations

The ideal programs for the future would use a human rights–based approach but at a greater speed than in the past.[159] The international treaties, particularly CEDAW and the Cairo Programme, provide human rights–based approaches; they call for the empowerment of women in reproductive decisions by allowing women to make more informed choices.[160] As with all such treaties, however, there is no enforcement power.[161] There are many exceptions within the treaties, and States can comply or not comply based on their current political, religious, and cultural situations.[162]

There is currently a dichotomy between the international treaties. Many treaties specify that there must be equality between women and men,[163] but at the same time define the family as the basic unit of society and as the entity having the right to make decisions as to the number and spacing of children.[164] In theory, this makes sense; however, in reality, a large majority of women have no power within the family.[165] This dichotomy must be reconciled in the international treaties. The wording of the treaties need not change since, in an ideal system where all States and individuals comply with the treaties, the wording would be appropriate. The interpretation of the treaties, however, should change in order to take into account the realities of the current patriarchal systems.

As an impetus to change, and as further acknowledgment of the empowerment of women, this chapter suggests that the specific treaty language of "individuals and families shall have the right to freely and responsibly determine the number, spacing, and timing of their children"[166] and "the family is the basic unit of society"[167] be interpreted differently. The decision for the number of children should not be given to the family, since the reality is that the family is part of the patriarchal system and hence males usually make the decision.[168] A better interpretation is to concentrate on the wording that specifies "individuals" and to give sole power for having a child to the woman and not to the family.[169] In the typical partnership of woman and man, since the woman today has far fewer rights than the man, the result of this change of interpretation would be to increase the rights of the woman. Because of the well-regarded proposition that women, when given the choice, will opt for fewer children,[170] giving women this right would result in a decrease in the number of children.[171]

This suggestion is a human rights–based approach. It moves toward equality in the rights of men and women, as all of the treaties specify must be done.[172] Critics may say that this approach is coercive because it infringes on the rights of men and that it causes changes in the current patriarchal systems.[173] The better way to look at it, however, is that it moves toward equality. Patriarchal systems that infringe on the rights of women must be replaced.[174] Coercion that creates more equality should be encouraged.[175] CEDAW, without defining its terms, testifies to the legitimacy of coercive elements by stating that "temporary special measures aimed at accelerating *de facto* equality between men and women shall not be considered discrimination."[176] Given the changes in many societies today regarding partners, marriage, and divorce, and given the changes in technology that provide new methods for individuals—including same-sex partners—to have children, this movement away from the traditional concept of "families" makes even more sense.

This suggested change in interpretation will further true equality of women and men and will reduce the population problem by reducing the birthrate.[177] It will not, of course, lead to any immediate change, given the lack of enforcement in international treaties[178] and the embedded patriarchal systems, cultures, and religions.[179] It will, however, better direct the thinking of the international community and provide a commonality as international organizations and States endeavor to solve the global population problem.

Conclusion

A global population problem truly exists. All countries and international organizations have an obligation to take steps to avoid a potential environmental doomsday. In order to decrease the birth rate, it is not sufficient to state theory in the international treaties. Until practice matches theory, coercive steps need to be taken to give women the ultimate power within the family to decide the number of children they will have. These steps will have the added benefit of moving toward the goal of complete equality between women and men.

NOTES

1. See generally Gary E. McCuen, ed., *Population and Human Survival: Ideas in Conflict* (1993); David Bender and Bruno Lecne, eds., *Population: Opposing Viewpoints* (1995).

2. See Paul R. Ehrlich and Anne H. Ehrlich, "The Population 'Explosion' Is a Serious Threat in Population and Human Survival: Ideas in Conflict," in McCuen, 21.

3. See, for example, Michael Fumento, "There is No Population 'Explosion,'" in McCuen, 26–31. But see also Ehrlich and Ehrlich, "The Population 'Explosion'" (1990).

4. See John R. Weeks, *Population: An Introduction to Concepts and Issues* 456 (1994).

5. United Nations, General Assembly, Thirty-fourth session, Resolution 34/180, Document A/RES/34/180, 1980 (hereinafter CEDAW). CEDAW was held in 1980, became effective in 1981, and is generally considered the basic treaty in the field of international women's rights. See generally, United Nations, Document A/48/38, *Consideration by CEDAW of Country Reports: Political Participation* (excerpted from the annual country report of the French representative to the CEDAW Committee in regard to Article 7 of the Convention) 1993, at 887–924 (hereinafter CEDAW Country Report), in Henry J. Steiner and Philip Alston, *International Human Rights in Context: Law, Politics, Morals* 964 (1996). CEDAW condemned discrimination against women in all forms and required States to take all appropriate measures without delay in order to end the discrimination. See CEDAW, Article 2. Most of the world governments have ratified CEDAW but the United States has not. See generally Malvina Halberstam, *United States Ratification of the Convention on the Elimination of All Forms of Discrimination Against Women,* 31 Geo. Wash. J. Int'l L. & Econ. 49 (1997).

6. See CEDAW Country Report, at para 329.

7. See infra notes 95–109 and accompanying text.

8. See infra note 79 and accompanying text.

9. See infra note 79 and accompanying text.

10. See, for example, John S. Aird, *Slaughter of the Innocents: Coercive Birth Control in China* (1990).

11. See generally Paul R. Ehrlich et al, *The Stork and the Plow* (1995), 72–98.

12. See, for example, United Nations, General Assembly, Twenty-fourth Session, Resolution 2542, Article 4, Supplement 30, Document A/7630, *Declaration on Social Progress and Development* (1969).

13. See United Nations, General Assembly, Third Session, Resolution 217, Article 2, Document A/810, *Universal Declaration of Human Rights* (hereinafter UDHR), 1948, at 71; United Nations, General Assembly, Twenty-first Session, Supplement 16, Article 3, Document A/6316, *International Covenant on Civil and Political Rights* (hereinafter ICCPR), 1966, at 52; United Nations, General Assembly, Twenty-first Session, Supplement 16, Article 3, Document A/6316, *International Covenant on Economic, Social and Cultural Rights* (hereinafter

ICESCR), 1966, at 49; United Nations, General Assembly, Twenty-second Session, Resolution 2263, Supplement 16, Document A/6716, *Declaration on the Elimination of Discrimination Against Women,* 1967, at 35.

14. See infra notes 95–109 and accompanying text.

15. See ibid.

16. See infra note 79 and accompanying text.

17. See Joel E. Cohen, *How Many People Can the Earth Support?* (1995) 61–67; see generally Weeks, supra note 4, at 380–81.

18. See Stanley P. Johnson, *World Population—Turning the Tide: Three Decades of Progress* 221 (1994).

19. See Cohen, supra note 17, at 88–90; Ehrlich et al, supra note 11, at 3–6.

20. See Ehrlich et al, supra note 11, at 2.

21. See ibid., at 21 and 30.

22. See Paula Abrams, *Symposium on Population Law: Population Control and Sustainability: It's the Same Old Song but with a Different Meaning,* 27 Envtl. L. 1111, 1111 (1997).

23. See Carl Haub and Martha Farnsworth Riche, "Population by the Numbers: Trends in Population Growth and Structure," in *Beyond the Numbers: A Reader on Population, Consumption, and the Environment,* ed. Laurie Ann Mazur (hereinafter *Beyond the Numbers*) (1994), at 95–99. Haub and Riche conclude that declining mortality, and not birth rates, is the main problem today. See also Erla Zwingle, *Women and Population,* Nat'l Geographic, October 1998, at 39. Birth rates have fallen in most parts of the world over the last forty years but because people are living much longer, the absolute number of births (and the total population) continues to increase.

24. See Paula Abrams, *Reservations about Women: Population Policy and Reproductive Rights,* 29 Cornell Int'l L.J. 1, 1 (1996).

25. See generally Ehrlich et al, supra note 6, at 145–54.

26. See Meredith Marshall, *United Nations Conference on Population and Development: The Road to a New Reality for Reproductive Health,* 10 Emory Int'l L. Rev. 441, 444–50 (1996). An example of a government-sponsored program was India's law that allowed its States to mandate sterilization. See Betsy Hartmann, *Reproductive Rights and Wrongs: The Global Politics of Population Control,* rev. ed. (1995) 157, 223, 298–300. See Jodi L. Jacobson, "China's 'One-Child' Program: An Overview," in McCuen, 117, 120, 121. See Amartya Sen, *Fertility and Coercion,* 63 U. Chi. L. Rev. 1035, 1056–57 (1996). This article provides statistics on Kerala, India. Kerala is generally considered one of the great success stories of population planning. See Zwingle, supra note 23, at 40. The other program credited for a large part of the decrease in population is the program that makes small loans available to women. See Zwingle at 41.

27. See Cohen, supra note 17, at 13, 25–28. See Ehrlich et al, supra note 11, at 19. See Zwingle, supra note 23, at 38. See Ehrlich et al, supra note 11, at 99. See Paul R. Erlich and Anne H. Erlich, *The Population Explosion: Why We Should Care And What We Should Do About It,* 27 Envtl. L. 1187, 1188–91 (1997).

28. See Ehrlich et al, supra note 11, at 28.

29. See Marshall, supra note 26, at 442.

30. See Ehrlich et al, supra note 11, at 102.

31. See, for example, Zwingle, supra note 23, at 50.

32. See infra notes 38–83.

33. See ICCPR, supra note 13.

34. See Steiner and Alston, supra note 5, at 117.

35. See ICCPR, supra note 13, Articles 6, 7, and 23.

36. See ICCPR, supra note 13, Article 3.

37. See Reed Boland et al, "Honoring Human Rights in Population Policies: From Declarations to Action," in Gita Sen et al, eds., *Population Policies Reconsidered: Health, Empowerment, and Rights* 89 (1994).

38. See CEDAW, supra note 5, Article 16.

39. See United Nations, Annex, Document A/CONF. 171/13, *Report of the International Conference on Population and Development, Programme of Action of the International Conference on Population and Development* (hereinafter Report of ICPD), 1994, at 5. Previous conferences that contributed to the changes of the Cairo Conference included the 1974 World Population Conference in Bucharest. See Johnson, supra note 18, at 109–24; Weeks, supra note 4, at 380–81. The 1984 International Conference on Population in Mexico City was marred by the reversal of the United States from its previous view that population growth must be slowed in order to promote economic development. See United Nations, Document E/CONF/76/19, *Report of the International Conference on Population* (1984); Weeks, supra note 4, at 380. The 1993 World Conference on Human Rights in Vienna occurred the year before the Cairo Conference. See Steiner and Alston, supra note 5, at 928–30.

40. See Abrams, supra note 22, at 1117–18.

41. See Johnson, supra note 18, at 326. But see also Ehrlich et al, supra note 11, at 102.

42. See Marshall, supra note 26, at 443.

43. See Report of ICPD, supra note 39, Preamble para 1.15.

44. See ibid.

45. See ibid., Annex, para 7.3.

46. See ibid., chap 4, which proclaims the goals for gender equality, equity, and empowerment of women.

47. See Abrams, supra note 24, at 1, which states that the Cairo Conference gave women, who often lack control over their reproductive decision making, hope for change.

48. See Marshall, supra note 26, at 451–52.

49. See ibid., at 451.

50. See ibid.

51. See infra note 79 and accompanying text, which states that in every country in which women have had the choice, they have chosen to have fewer children.

52. See Report of ICPD, supra note 39, chap 4.

53. See infra notes 95–109 and accompanying text.

54. See Marshall, supra note 26, at 452, which provides examples of infanticide, rape, sexual abuse, battering, and bride burning.

55. See Seager, supra note 5, at 120, and Marshall, supra note 26, at 452.

56. See Nafis Sadik, "Investing in Women: The Focus of the '90s," in *Beyond the Numbers,* supra note 23, at 209, 214, which provides examples that three out of four teenage girls in Africa are mothers, that the average age of marriage in Bangladesh is 11.6 years, and that 58.5 percent of teenage girls in Jordan are married. The Cairo Programme calls on governments to strictly enforce laws concerning the minimum age at marriage. See Report of ICPD, supra note 39, para 4.21.

57. See Seager, supra note 5, at 120. Nafis Sadik (*Investing in Women,* at 209, 212) states that parents with little income are far more likely to spend on education for their sons than for their daughters. Report of ICPD, supra note 39, para 4.2 details that two-thirds of the illiterate adults worldwide are women, that 70 percent of children not enrolled in primary school are girls, and that girls in certain developing countries attend secondary school at a rate less than one-third that of boys.

58. See Report of ICPD, supra note 39.

59. See Abrams, supra note 24, at 1.

60. See Report of ICPD, supra note 39, chap 2, which affirms that each country may take into account its local factors when deciding whether to implement the recommendations.

61. See ibid., which states that the "implementation of the recommendations is the sovereign right of each country, consistent with national laws and development priorities, with full respect for the various religious and ethical values and cultural backgrounds of its people, and in conformity with universally recognized international human rights."

62. See Louis Henkin, *International Law: Politics, Values and Functions,* 216 Collected Courses of the Hague Academy of International Law, 4 Receuil des Cours 13 (1989), excerpted in Steiner and Alston, supra note 5, at 350–51.

63. See Abrams, supra note 24, at 2, 3.

64. See Report of ICPD, supra note 39, chap 4.

65. See UDHR, supra note 13, Article 2; ICCPR, supra note 13, Article 3; ICESCR, supra note 13, Article 3; Declaration on the Elimination of Discrimination against Women, supra note 13, Articles 1, 4, 6, 9, 10.

66. See Report of ICPD, supra note 39, chap 2.

67. See ibid., chap 4, para 4.9, which states further actions should be taken to prohibit trafficking in women, adolescents, and children, and exploiting women through prostitution. It also states that special attention should be paid to those who are potentially exploitable, such as migrant women, women in domestic service, and schoolgirls.

68. See ibid., chap 4, para 4.22.

69. See ibid., chap 6, para 6.11.

70. See ibid., chap 8, para 8.25.

71. See Report of ICPD, supra note 39, chap 8, para 8.25, which adds that prevention of unwanted pregnancies must be given the highest priority and every attempt should be made to eliminate the need for abortion.

72. See ibid., chap 7, para 7.2.

73. See ibid., chap 7, paras 3.17, 4.21, 6.17.

74. See ibid., chap 7, para 7.3, which states that all women and men must have the right to make their own decisions about reproduction without discrimination, coercion, or violence.

75. See Report of ICPD, supra note 39.

76. United Nations, Document E/CONF 60/19, *Report of the United Nations World Population Conference,* 1974.

77. See ibid., chap 1, para 14(f). "Collective rights" is another term for future rights. Luke T. Lee, *Population: The Human Rights Approach,* 6 Colo. J. Int'l. Envtl. L. & Pol'y. 327, 338–39 (1995).

78. See Abrams, supra note 22, at 4, citing Ruth Dixon-Mueller, *Population Policy and Women's Rights: Transforming Reproductive Choice* 5 (1993).

79. See Zwingle, supra note 23, at 39, who observes that in every place in which women have had the choice, they have chosen to have fewer children. See also Ehrlich et al, supra note 11, at 80.

80. See Report of ICPD, supra note 39, chap 4.

81. See James A. Joyce, ed., *World Population 1589–1789* 3 (1976). Numerous studies have shown that the most consistent factor in reducing birth rates is change in the legal and social status of women.

82. See Abrams, supra note 22, at 1115.

83. See ibid., which states that most governments agree that coercive measures violate human rights but that there is a great deal of disagreement about what constitutes coercive practices and regulation. The earlier population programs focused on distributing contraceptive and sterilization services. See Abrams, at 1122.

84. See *Black's Law Dictionary* (abr. 6th ed.), s.v. "family," which gives the definition as "[a] group of persons consisting of parents and children . . . [and] immediate kindred," but providing various alternate definitions including "a collective body of persons who live in one house and under one head or management."

85. See UDHR, supra note 13, Article 16. There is some indication that the intent of the wording about families in this and other treaties was to differentiate families from governments and therefore to protect "family" matters from government intrusion.

86. See *Declaration on Social Progress and Development,* supra note 12.

87. See UDHR, supra note 13, Article 4, which states that the family is a basic unit of society, that governments should assist and protect the family, and that parents have the exclusive right to determine freely and responsibly the number and spacing of their children. Subsequently, CEDAW restated the same proposition. See CEDAW, supra note 5, Article 16, which states that countries must provide women with the rights to decide freely and responsibly on the number and spacing of their children and to have access to the information, education, and means to enable them to exercise these rights.

88. See Report of ICPD, supra note 39, chap 5, para 5.1. Family planning has also been described as a basic human right. See Lee, supra note 77, at 328. The United Nations did not officially recognize the principle that family planning constitutes a basic human right until May 1968, when the United Nations Con-

ference on Human Rights in Tehran proclaimed that "parents have a basic human right to determine freely and responsibly the number and the spacing of their children." United Nations, Document A/CONF 32/41, Sales F 68 XIV, 2, *Final Act of the International Conference on Human Rights,* 1968.

89. See Report of ICPD, supra note 39, chap 7, para 7.3; see also *Final Act of the International Conference on Human Rights,* supra note 88, at 3.

90. See Report of ICPD, supra note 39, chap 4, para 4.26.

91. See ibid., chap 4 IV, paras 4.16–4.18.

92. See ibid.; CEDAW, supra note 5; UDHR, supra note 13; *Report of the United Nations World Population Conference,* supra note 76.

93. See ibid., para 5.2.

94. See ibid., para 7.17.

95. See supra notes 85–91 and accompanying text.

96. See Hartmann, supra note 26, at 46–47, which declares that "the harmonious household is largely a myth" and that where men make decisions, many women must battle to survive physically and emotionally. But see also 47, which suggests that poor women often have more power within the family because their labor is considered vital to family survival.

97. See ibid.

98. See Ehrlich et al, supra note 11, at 81. Even when women do have some independence, men use their power over the women to force sexual favors, and children often result.

99. See *Webster's Third New International Dictionary of the English Language,* 3d ed. (1986), s.v. "patriarchy," which gives the definition as a "social organization marked by the supremacy of the father in the clan or family in both domestic and religious functions, [and by] the legal dependence of wife or wives and children . . . ."

100. See Abrams, supra note 22, at 1123, which cites Dixon-Mueller, supra note 78, at 24–27. Abrams adds that patriarchal systems also have an impact on marriage age, divorce, and maternal health.

101. See Hartmann, supra note 26, at 53–54, which explains that the Catholic Church condemns all artificial forms of birth control while Islam's views on family planning are interpreted differently by various religious authorities.

102. See Dixon-Mueller, supra note 78, at 23–27, which discusses the patriarchal bases of social control and states that the patriarchal system is the most fundamental threat to a woman's right to self-determination.

103. See Julia O'Faolain and Lauro Martines, eds., *Not in God's Image* (1973): 144–53, 220–33.

104. See supra notes 102–103 and accompanying text.

105. See Zwingle, supra note 23, at 47.

106. See ibid.

107. See Zwingle, supra note 23, at 46.

108. See ibid.

109. See Dixon-Mueller, supra note 78, at 25.

110. See Lee, supra note 77, at 329, which provides the statement of the Yugoslav delegation.

111. See Report of ICPD, supra note 39; CEDAW, supra note 5; UDHR, supra note 13; *Report of the United Nations World Population Conference,* supra note 76.

112. See supra notes 95–109 and accompanying text.

113. See Abrams, supra note 24, at 1.

114. See ibid., at 11.

115. See supra notes 95–109 and accompanying text.

116. See Abrams, supra note 24 and accompanying text.

117. See Abrams, supra note 22, at 1123.

118. See Cynthia B. Lloyd, "Family and Gender Issues for Population Policy," in *Beyond the Numbers,* supra note 23, at 249.

119. See supra notes 99–103 and accompanying text.

120. See Abrams, supra note 24, at 12, which refers to studies that show family planning is affected by the level of equality within the family.

121. See CEDAW, supra note 5, introduction, which states that cultural patterns assign the public sphere to men and the private sphere to women.

122. See Elizabeth K. Spahn, *Waiting for Credentials: Feminist Theories of Enforcement of International Human Rights,* 44 Am. U. L. Rev. 1053, 1062 (1995). Spahn explains that categorizing women in the private sphere causes some critics to resist human rights for women because of possible conflicts with other types of human rights related to privacy, culture, and religion. Further confusion arises because of the categorizations of the marketplace and government as public sphere, and the family and civil society as private sphere. See also 1077–78.

123. See *Ankenbrandt v. Richards,* 504 U.S. 689, 703 (1992). This case declares that the "domestic relations" exception in the United States federal courts is still valid. But see Judith Resnik, *Revising the Canon: Feminist Help in Teaching Procedure,* 61 U. Cinn. L. Rev. 1181, 1188 (1993), which provides criticism of the "domestic relations exception"; Naomi Cahn, *Family Law, Federalism, and the Federal Courts,* 79 Iowa L. Rev. 1073, 1073 (1994), discusses the unimportance of "family law" in both the United States federal and state courts.

124. See Spahn, supra note 122, at 1077, for delegates' attitudes to the private sphere.

125. See Reed Boland, *Symposium on Population Law: The Environment, Population, and Women's Human Rights,* 17 Envtl. L. 1137, 1156 (1997). See generally Arthur H. Robertson and John G. Merrills, *Human Rights in the World* (1989).

126. See Boland, supra note 125, at 1156, which states that population programs are based on rights that do not fit the normal human rights models because they are more in the private sphere.

127. See ibid.

128. See ibid.

129. See ibid. The fact that reproduction in many ways deals directly with issues such as conception, pregnancy, and childbirth, which are unique to women, may also be a reason that the human rights community has been less interested in them.

130. See Aird, supra note 10, at 12, which states that seemingly innocent ex-

pressions such as "propaganda" or "persuasion" may actually disguise sinister intent.

131. See *Black's Law Dictionary* 177 (abr. 6th ed.), s.v. "coercion," which it defines as "[c]ompulsion; constraint; compelling by force or arms or threat. It may be . . . implied, . . . as where one party is constrained by subjugation to other to do what his free will would refuse"; see also *Webster's Third New International Dictionary of the English Language* 439 (1986). It provides one definition of "coercion" as "The application of sanctions or force by a government usu. accompanied by the suppression of constitutional liberties in order to compel dissenters to conform."

132. See Donald P. Warwick, "The Ethics of Population Control," in Godfrey Roberts, ed., *Population Policy: Contemporary Issues* 21, 28 (1990).

133. See Aird, supra note 10, at 17.

134. See Hartmann, supra note 26, at 153. Hartmann observes that even the Cairo Programme, while opposing direct coercion, supports what could be called "soft-sell" coercion through media channels.

135. See Abrams, supra note 24, at 4–5.

136. See ibid.

137. See Aird, supra note 10, at n.47, which implies that China's easing of the more overtly coercive practices of its population programs still contained the coercive practices of family planning targets, sterilization for couples with two or more children, forced abortion for unauthorized pregnancies, forced insertion of intrauterine devices, and absolute prohibition of more than two children per couple. Other examples of measures that are generally considered coercive are having cadres repeatedly visit the houses of women who have refused to comply with other coercive directives, and enforcing economic penalties on a woman or family that has not complied. See Aird, at 17. But see also Aird, at 16, which states that China did not consider most of its measures coercive because there was no overt physical coercion.

138. See ibid., at 12, which provides the example of propaganda that China "advocates" that each couple have only one child but that the "advocacy" is actually carried out by "ideological mobilization."

139. See ibid., at 4.

140. See Boland, supra note 125, at 1156, which provides the pronatal example of incentives given by Romania as special allowances for mothers with large families, indemnities for the birth of third and subsequent children, and increases of taxes on persons with no children.

141. See Hartmann, supra note 26, at 66, which explains the view of incentive supporters, that incentives are voluntary since people are free to choose either to accept or refuse them. The World Bank uses incentives extensively for its programs and does not consider them coercive.

142. See ibid., at 66–68; Abrams, supra note 24, at 7, states that incentives are inherently coercive.

143. See Aird, supra note 10, at 113, n.14.

144. See Report of ICPD, supra note 39, at n.27, para 5.5, and Principle 8.

145. See ibid., para 7.3.

146. See ibid.

147. See Abrams, supra note 24, at 25.

148. See Report of ICPD, supra note 39, para 7.3, which states that, while exercising their rights, individuals and families should take into account the needs of their living and future children and their responsibilities toward the community. It also states that government population programs should have as their basis the promotion of the responsible exercise of those rights.

149. See Lee, supra note 77, at 335.

150. See supra notes 121–129 and accompanying text.

151. See Lee, supra note 77, at 333–35, which observes that coercion may be an integral part of a legal order that makes specified behavior compulsory for the benefit of all.

152. See UDHR, supra note 13, Article 26(1).

153. See, for example, Lee, supra note 77, at 335, which provides examples of authorities who justify coercive measures in certain situations. The Universal Declaration of Human Rights states that "[e]lementary education shall be compulsory."

154. See supra note 23 and accompanying text.

155. See Ehrlich et al, supra note 11, at 28, which provides the example that the United States needs to take further steps, and that by continuing its current consumption levels, the United States seduces other countries into higher consumption, as well.

156. See Abrams, supra note 40, which states that a United Nations study concludes that there is extensive empirical evidence on direct and indirect correlation between fertility and education of women.

157. See Aird, supra note 10 and accompanying text.

158. See Hartmann, supra note 26, at 167.

159. See ibid.

160. See supra notes 64–69 and accompanying text.

161. See supra notes 60–62 and accompanying text.

162. See supra note 61 and accompanying text.

163. See supra note 13 and accompanying text.

164. See supra notes 88–90 and accompanying text.

165. See supra notes 96–103 and accompanying text.

166. See *Declaration on Social Progress and Development,* supra note 12, Article 4; CEDAW, supra note 5, Article 16; UDHR, supra note 13, Article 4.

167. See *Declaration on Social Progress and Development,* supra note 12, Article 4; UDHR, supra note 13, Article 4.

168. See supra notes 96–103 and accompanying text.

169. *Declaration on Social Progress and Development,* supra note 12, Article 4; CEDAW, supra note 5, Article 16; UDHR, supra note 13, Article 4.

170. See supra note 79 and accompanying text.

171. See ibid.

172. See supra note 13 and accompanying text.

173. See supra notes 96–103 and accompanying text.

174. See Abrams, supra note 24, at 12.

175. See Lee, supra note 77, at 334–35, which provides the example that the "right" to education usually includes a coercive element to ensure that children attend school.

176. See CEDAW, supra note 5, Article 4, which adds that these temporary measures should be discontinued when the objectives of equality have been achieved.

177. See supra note 79 and accompanying text.

178. See supra notes 60–62 and accompanying text.

179. See supra notes 97–103 and accompanying text.

7

How Human Rights Norms Can Contribute to Environmental Protection

Some Practical Possibilities within the United Nations System

Caroline Dommen

A RANGE OF PRINCIPLES and procedures has evolved in international law in response to specific kinds of issues. The precautionary principle,[1] for instance, has emerged as part of international environmental law. In international economic law, the global institution offers a unique, binding dispute-settlement system.[2] The human rights legal system offers quasi-judicial procedures that allow access to an international body when seeking redress for alleged human rights violations.

While international environmental law has continually adopted more stringent standards, norms, and techniques for its implementation over the last few years, it offers little recourse to individual victims of environmental harm. In most cases only States can implement environmental law or dispute-settlement procedures. Human rights mechanisms, conversely, are especially attractive in that they offer procedures that allow individuals or groups to appeal outside their national government to an international body. Such mechanisms are particularly interesting in the context of the quest for environmental protection. Human rights mechanisms allow individuals to seek redress despite national laws that might fail to defend against alleged violations. Furthermore, the most systematically affected victims of environmental harm tend to be individuals or communities with limited or nonexistent political recourse, such as members of racial and ethnic minorities, or individuals and communities who are geographically isolated from the locus of political power within their country.

This article presents some examples of how those seeking prevention or reparation of environmental harm can use the procedures provided for by international human rights law mechanisms. It will focus on opportunities for raising environmental issues within the United Nation's human rights bodies.[3]

The United Nations Human Rights Commission and Sub-Commission

The United Nations Human Rights Commission (the Commission) held its inaugural meeting in 1947 and is the global institution with comprehensive responsibility for promoting and protecting all human rights.[4] Although States are the only members of the Commission, its yearly six-week sessions are attended by more than two thousand people, including representatives of the Commission's fifty-three Member States, representatives of United Nations Specialized Agencies, nongovernmental organizations (NGOs), and a variety of other experts and interested individuals. The Commission is a highly politicized body; its decisions tend to be motivated more by political or economic considerations than by a real concern for human rights.

The Sub-Commission was set up in 1947 by the Commission to undertake studies and make recommendations to the Commission concerning prevention of discrimination. The Sub-Commission's members are twenty-six experts who are appointed by governments, but whose positions should be independent from those of any State. Despite its distinctive mandate and its members' supposed independence, in practice the differences between the Sub-Commission and the Human Rights Commission is minimal. The agendas of both bodies are vast and cover subjects ranging from human rights in occupied Palestine to the right to development, from conscientious objection to extrajudicial executions or contemporary forms of slavery. The procedures of the Commission and Sub-Commission do not allow for litigation-type action, but individual cases of human rights violations are frequently raised with the aim of alerting public opinion, promoting a resolution, decision, or a new mechanism (such as a Special Rapporteur or a Working Group[5]) set up to examine the issue.

Consideration of Environmental Issues by the Commission and the Sub-Commission

Environmental issues have been presented and considered as human rights issues both in the Commission and the Sub-Commission under a variety of different agenda items,[6] including those concerning indigenous peoples; economic, social, and cultural rights; and scientific and technological developments. They also have been the agenda under which human rights violations in specific countries are raised. The 1996 report on the situation of Human Rights in Cambodia, for instance, specifically mentioned the right to a healthy environment and to sustainable development, highlighting that logging and agribusiness in Cambodia might have potentially significant detrimental consequences for Cambodians who depend on the environment for their food, culture, and way of life.[7]

In 1989 the Sub-Commission launched the process that led to a Sub-Commission study of "the problem of the environment and its relation to human rights." The study, carried out by Sub-Commission member Fatma Zohra Ksentini, was completed in 1994,[8] but its recommendations have not been taken up by the Commission or Sub-Commission, nor has either body substantively discussed the Draft Declaration of Principles on Human Rights and the Environment[9] that was annexed to the final report. The Commission on Human Rights currently has an item, Science and Environment, that appears on its agenda each year, but nothing worthy of mention with respect to environment is ever addressed. In recent years, NGOs have been lobbying for a Commission Special Rapporteur on human rights and the environment, but it seems unlikely at the moment that the Commission on Human Rights will create such a mandate or set up any other thematic mechanism dealing with human rights and the environment.

The Commission on Human Rights has had a Special Rapporteur on toxic wastes and the environment since 1995. The position, however, despite its useful nature, has been the subject of criticism, most notably due to the fact that the Special Rapporteur has focused on generalities surrounding the issue of illicit movements and dumping of dangerous products and wastes, which are already within the mandate of other more competent and better financed bodies[10] than on specifically human rights–related aspects of such activities.[11]

The Commission and the Sub-Commission are the busiest among the international human rights bodies, attracting much diplomatic attention and media coverage; yet statements made during a Commission or Sub-Commission meeting or a resolution adopted by the Commission or Sub-Commission can go virtually unnoticed unless a great deal of time and energy is invested in publicizing the action and transmitting information to groups working on the same issue nationally or in other fora. Sub-Commission and Commission resolutions have relatively little legal weight, but States do go to great lengths to avoid criticism by these bodies. Further, an important number of NGOs devote extensive amounts of time and resources lobbying the Commission and Sub-Commission, indicating that they are indeed effective and accessible mechanisms of the system. Evidently, the Commission and Sub-Commission are useful mechanisms to uncover and shed light on cases of States' violation of rights and perpetration of environmental harm.

Environmentalists who wish to bring issues or cases before the Commission and Sub-Commission are best served by submitting information to relevant thematic or country rapporteurs. Engaging one of these rapporteurs or working groups is more effective and more likely to result in direct access to the Commissions than directly lobbying for adoption of a resolution or the creation of a new theme or country mandate. There is also the Commission's Special Rapporteur on toxic wastes,[12] which may be of particular interest to some environmentalist groups, or other Commission mechanisms such as those on racial discrimination and religious intolerance, or on the right to development. Finally, alternative inroads are offered by the Sub-Commission mechanisms, such as those that focus on indigenous populations or on income distribution.

The United Nations Human Rights Treaty Bodies

Several human rights treaties have been adopted[13] under the United Nations' auspices. Implementation of each of these treaties is monitored by a Committee of independent experts, usually set up by the treaty itself. These Committees are known collectively as the treaty bodies.[14] Monitoring is carried out mainly by examination of State reports. Three of the treaty bodies also have the competence to receive and consider individual complaints.[15] The treaty bodies' mandates are limited to the rights protected by the treaties they monitor. The right to a clean environment per se is not recognized by the United Nations' human rights treaties, but the treaty bodies can still provide a useful channel of recourse to environmental activists since other rights, such as the right to life or the right to health, relate closely to environmental issues.

States as well as treaty body members have for many years considered that environmental issues fall within the scope of their obligations under human rights treaties. In 1986, for instance, Tunisia reported at the International Covenant on Economic, Social and Cultural Rights (ICESCR) on measures taken to prevent degradation of natural resources, particularly erosion.[16] In 1995 the Ukrainian government provided details to the Human Rights Committee in the context of the right to life about the environmental situation following the Chernobyl disaster in that country. In 1992, Bolivia reported to the Committee on the Rights of the Child that it had taken steps to improve the health situation of women and children by promoting full attention to the economy, housing, environment, and education.[17]

In their periodic reports to the treaty bodies, States tend to present the situation in their country in a favorable light and avoid attracting attention to domestic problems of respecting human rights. For this reason, the members of the various treaty bodies usually welcome nongovernmental information, which can pad the State's descriptions and help members get a better sense of the actual situation in the country they are examining.

Environmental groups may find participating in the human rights treaties' reporting process useful for a number of reasons.[18] The process can provide an additional means of pressure on governments if used in conjunction with national campaigns on an issue within the scope of one of the human rights treaties. NGOs can respond to issues that have been dealt with in the State report or raise issues that the report has avoided. States are sensitive to information that can be perceived as criticism and may make very positive statements about their policies before a treaty body. NGOs can play a role in ensuring that these statements are picked up by the media or transmitted to national groups working on the issue and holding the State to its word. In addition, submission of NGO information to a treaty body can be a useful publicity peg, particularly when working with the media.

A limitation to using the treaty bodies' reporting mechanisms as an avenue for redress of environmental injustices is that Committees can generally consider only the situation within a country when that country's report is due to be examined, that is, once every two to five years. The Committee on Economic, Social and Cultural Rights and, to a lesser extent, the Human Rights Committee are, however, developing and improving procedures that allow them to consider information they have on urgent and serious situations in any State that is party to the respective treaty, regardless of whether this State has a report due for examination.[19]

The Treaty Bodies' Individual Complaint Procedures

Three treaty bodies—the Human Rights Committee, the Convention on the Elimination of all forms of Racial Discrimination (CERD), and the Convention against Torture (CAT)—implement individual complaints procedures.[20] Of these, the procedures of the Human Rights Committee and of CERD are perhaps the most relevant to environmentalists.[21]

Environmental harm often falls harder on vulnerable groups and is often linked to discrimination; thus a case regarding environmental discrimination brought to CERD would have a high chance of receiving attention.[22] So far, however, none of the cases that CERD has decided relate to environmental issues. The Human Rights Committee, on the other hand, has examined a number of cases that raise environmental concerns. From an analysis of these cases, it is possible to draw some conclusions as to how the Committee might approach future issues that would be likely to arise in the context of environment-related cases.

The environment-related cases considered by the Committee happen to fall into two categories: those that relate to nuclear weapons or radioactive materials, and those that relate to the rights of indigenous or minority groups. In *E.H.P. v. Canada*,[23] a communication was submitted to the Human Rights Committee on behalf of present and future generations. The communication complained that the storage of radioactive waste near the residences of the applicants was a threat to their right to life. The Committee considered the applicants' reference to future generations as "an expression of concern purporting to put into due perspective the importance of the matter raised in the communication." Although the communication was declared inadmissible for nonexhaustion of domestic remedies, the Committee recognized that it did raise legitimate environmental concerns and serious issues regarding the right to life.

In 1990, a communication submitted to the Committee[24] complained that in allowing cruise missiles to be stationed on its territory, the Dutch government was creating a threat to the plaintiffs' right to life. This case was submitted by 6,588 Dutch citizens and the Dutch government alleged that the number of authors made it an *actio popularis*, which would make it inadmissible. The Committee rejected this argument, saying that as long as each of the authors is a victim it is possible for a high number of authors to sign a communication submitted to the Committee without transforming the communication into an *actio popularis.* The Committee did find the complaint inadmissible, however, as the missiles had not actually been deployed, and thus, the authors of the communication were not actually victims of a violation or of a threatened violation of their right to life.

In 1995, a complaint concerning French nuclear testing in the Pacific was submitted to the Committee by Vaihere Bordes and John Temeharo.[25] The applicants claimed that the nuclear tests that France was planning to carry out in 1995 and 1996 in French Polynesia threatened their right to life and their right to a family life (Articles 6 and 17 of the ICCPR). The applicants submitted two requests for interim measures to the Committee, one with the initial communication in July 1995, before the testing started, and another in November 1995.[26] The Committee refused both requests and later considered the case inadmissible as Committee members were not satisfied that the applicants were "victims" in the legal sense as applied by the Human Rights Committee.

The Human Rights Committee has criticized nuclear testing as being a threat to the right to life in a 1984 General Comment.[27] General Comments, which have been said to be authoritative general interpretations of a provision of the ICCPR,[28] although not legally binding, are adopted from time to time by the Human Rights Committee in order to indicate to States how they can promote implementation of the ICCPR. In its 1996 decision on the admissibility of *Bordes and Temeharo v. France,* the Committee reconfirmed its 1984 General Comment on the threat posed by nuclear testing to the right to life.

Several cases that have been brought to the Committee concern practices that affect the environment on which indigenous groups depend for survival. In 1994, the Human Rights Committee adopted a General Comment on Article 27 of the ICCPR, which concerns minority rights.[29] In this General Comment the Committee observed that "culture manifests itself in many forms, including a particular way of life associated with the use of land resources, especially in the case of indigenous peoples. That right may include such traditional activities as fishing or hunting." This comment can be said to support the view that the resources on which indigenous groups traditionally depend should be used only in a way that is compatible with these groups' cultures. This view has been borne out by the Committee in the cases presented below.

In *Bernard Ominayak and the Lubicon Lake Band v. Canada,*[30] the author alleged that the Alberta government had deprived the Lake Lubicon Indians of their means of subsistence and their right to self-determination by selling oil and gas concessions on their lands. The Committee found that historical inequities and certain more recent developments, including oil and gas exploration, were threatening the way of life and culture of the Lake Lubicon band and were thus violating minority rights, contrary to Article 27 of the ICCPR.

O.S. et al v. Finland[31] was also brought under the ICCPR's article protecting minority rights by four Finnish citizens of Sami ethnic origin. The applicants, reindeer breeders, complained about a road construction and logging program that they thought would have a negative impact on the reindeer population in their area, thus violating their right to enjoy their own culture. The Committee found that the communication was admissible and that measures of interim protection were needed. In the decision on the merits, however, the Committee considered that there was no violation of the ICCPR. The Committee came to similar decisions in the cases of *Ilmari Länsman et al v. Finland*[32] and *Jouni E. Länsman et al v. Finland,*[33] although in the former case it considered that interim measures were not necessary. In these cases, as in other cases brought under Article 27,[34] the Committee said that the right to enjoy one's culture cannot be defined *in abstracto,* but has to be placed in context. In both the Länsman cases, the Committee considered that the scale of the activities in question (quarrying in the case of the Ilmari Länsman case and logging in that of Jouni E. Länsman) was not sufficient to threaten the authors' right to enjoy their own culture. However, the Committee specified that even if neither of these cases constituted a violation of the authors' rights, activities of the type complained of could constitute a violation of minority rights, and that the State Party is under a duty to bear this in mind when undertaking or authorizing certain kinds of activities.[35]

An analysis of the above cases allows one to draw a number of conclusions that will be positive for environmentalists who are considering turning to the human rights individual complaint procedures. Beyond the fact that the complaint procedures of the ICCPR offer a channel of recourse that allows a victim of environmental harm to appeal beyond his or her national government, the Human Rights Committee has shown itself sympathetic to the types of issues that arise in the environmental context, even when the actual decision of the case has not gone in favor of the author. This sympathy applies to interim measures (relevant to activities whose potential impacts are uncertain), sustainable use of resources, and complaints about human rights violations that can affect a large number of people. One can also recall as an example of the capacity and willingness of the Committee to respond to environmental problems the case of *E.H.P. v. Canada.* There is no doubt that the Committee found the case inadmissible since the authors had not addressed any domestic tribunal,[36] yet it went out of its way to point out that the communication "raised serious issues with regard to the obligation of States Parties to protect life" and acknowledged the submission of the case also on behalf of future generations as an indication of the importance of the issue at stake.

According to its rules of procedure, the Human Rights Committee can request a State to take interim measures of protection when an author of a communication would be unable to secure his or her rights if the Committee later found that there was a violation.[37] The Committee has said that what may constitute "irreparable damage" to the victim within the meaning of its rules of procedure cannot be determined generally,[38] and that the essential criterion is the irreversibility of the consequences in the sense of the inability of the author to secure his rights should there later be a finding of a violation of the Covenant on the merits. The Committee has most often—and successfully—asked a State to take interim measures of protection in cases concerning the death penalty. This possibility of asking the Committee to ask a State to take "preventive action" will naturally interest environmentalists, as environmental degradation is often irreversible and as the consequences of environmental harm that occurs now may not be immediate, thus requiring preventive action.

This consideration leads one to the main hurdle to bringing environmental cases under the Human Rights Committee's individual complaints procedure: the question of standing. The Human Rights Committee can consider only complaints from authors who are actual victims of a violation of their rights. The case of *Bordes and Temeharo v. France* shows that where there is uncertainty as to whether a planned activity will have a negative impact on the rights protected by the Covenant, the Committee may be reluctant to consider potential victims of this harm as victims. Some past cases have shown that the Committee is capable and willing to respond to a risk of a human rights violation, particularly in two cases concerning requests for extradition, Kindler[39] and Ng.[40] In Kindler, the Committee said that Canada could be guilty of a violation by exposing Mr. Kindler to a real risk of a violation of his rights under the ICCPR.[41]

One Human Rights Committee member told this author that had a similar approach to the Ng and Kindler been taken, the Committee might have found the *Bordes and Temeharo v. France* case on nuclear testing admissible. Other Committee members have indicated informally that their attitude to standing may become more flexible in the future. It is unlikely, however, that the Committee would be able to react to potential or future environmental harm if it cannot see a real risk of such harm occurring, or if the harm is not foreseeable.

Conclusion

The United Nations' human rights mechanisms offer a number of channels for environmentalists to appeal beyond their national governments and laws to seek prevention or reparation of environmental harm. If environmental activists infrequently use these possibilities, it is probably due to the fact that human rights procedures are not well-known in environmental circles. The United Nations in Geneva or New York may seem distant to activists working locally, but in fact procedures to submit information to the Commission on Human Rights or its Sub-Commission are relatively simple and can be a useful way of addressing environmental issues. The human rights treaties' reporting procedures can also provide a useful hook to raise domestic environmental issues, and information about environmental problems that fall within the mandate of one of the human rights treaties can be submitted—with relatively little expenditure of time or money—to treaty bodies in the context of examination of State reports or requests for urgent actions, or through the procedures allowing for examination of individual complaints. The individual complaint procedures hold particular promise when the risk of harm occurring is high or foreseeable.

It is probable that the most useful aspect of using any human rights mechanisms for environmental protection lies in the capacity of these mechanisms to serve as a hook for the "mobilization of shame." In addition, the quasi-judicial value of decisions of the Human Rights Committee and the Committee on the Elimination of Racial Discrimination does give these some added weight. In conclusion, it is the view of this author that the opportunities offered by international human rights mechanisms can usefully be used by environmentalists as an additional avenue for challenging activities of governments that go against international human rights or environmental norms.

NOTES

This chapter was completed in August 1999.

1. The precautionary principle, endorsed in Principle 15 of the Rio Declaration, states that where there are threats of serious or irreversible damage, lack of full scientific certainty should not be used as a reason for postponing measures to prevent such damage. United Nations, Document 1/CONF.151/26/Rev. 1, *Rio Declaration on Environment and Development,* 1992, reprinted in 31 ILM 874.

2. The binding dispute settlement system was offered through the 1994 *Un-*

derstanding on Rules and Procedures Governing the Settlement of Disputes of the World Trade Organisation; see http://www.wto.org/wto/legal/ursum__wp.htm

3. Other human rights or human rights–related bodies that environmentalists can usefully turn to are the European Commission on Human Rights, the African Commission on Human and People's Rights, the Inter-American Commission on Human Rights, UNESCO, and the ILO's Committee on Freedom of Association. See, for instance, Cees Flintermann and Evelyn Ankumah, "The African Charter on Human and Peoples' Rights," in Hurst Hannum, eds., *Guide to International Human Rights Practice* 153–74 (3d edition, 1999; hereinafter *Guide to International Human Rights Practice*); Maguelonne Déjeant-Pons, "The Right to Environment in Regional Human Rights Systems," in Kathleen Mahoney and Paul Mahoney, eds., *Human Rights in the Twenty-first Century: A Global Challenge* 595 (1993; hereinafter *Human Rights in the Twenty-first Century*); David Weissbrodt and Rose Farley, *The UNESCO Human Rights Procedure: An Evaluation,* 16 Human Rights Quarterly 391 (1994); Lee Swepston, "Human Rights Complaint Procedures of the International Labour Organization," in *Guide to International Human Rights Practice.*

4. For details about the mandates and functioning of the Commission and Sub-commission, see Nigel Rodley, "United Nations Non-Treaty Procedures for Dealing with Human Rights Violations," in *Guide to International Human Rights Practice,* 61–84; see also the United Nations human rights website at http://www.unhchr.ch/html/menu2/2/chr.htm and at http://www.unhchr.ch/html/menu2/2/sc.htm

5. The Commission and Sub-commission have a number of country-specific and thematic mechanisms that analyze and report on various issues. These include the Commission's Special Rapporteurs on extreme poverty or on country situations such as Burma or Congo (formerly Zaire), the Sub-commission's working group on indigenous populations and its Special Rapporteur on traditional practices that affect the health of women and children. For a complete list, see the High Commissioner for Human Rights' website on the Commission's thematic mechanisms at http://www.unhchr.ch/html/menu2/xtraconv.htm

6. For a more detailed discussion and evaluation of the work of the United Nations Commission on Human Rights and its Sub-commission, which can be of interest to environmentalists, see Caroline Dommen, *Claiming Environmental Rights: Some Possibilities Offered by the United Nations' Human Rights Mechanisms,* 11 Georgetown International Environmental Law Review 1–48 (1998).

7. See United Nations, Document E/CN.4/1996/93 (1996).

8. United Nations, Document E/CN.4/sub. 2/1994/9, *Human Rights and the Environment: Final Report,* prepared by Fatma Zohra Ksentini, Special Rapporteur, 1994.

9. See Neil Popovic, *In Pursuit of Environmental Human Rights: Commentary on the Draft Declaration of Principles on Human Rights and the Environment,* 27 Columbia Human Rights Law Review 487–603 (1996).

10. For the mandate of better-finance bodies, see, for example, the Secretariat of the 1989 Basel Convention on the Control of Transboundary Movements of Hazardous Wastes and Their Disposal.

11. For the Special Rapporteur, see United Nations, Document E/CN.4/1999/46, *Adverse Effects of the Illicit Movement and Dumping of Toxic and Dangerous Products and Wastes on the Enjoyment of Human Rights,* submitted by Fatma Zohra Ksentini, Special Rapporteur, 20 January 1999.

12. Information to be submitted to this or to any other of the Commission's or Sub-commission's thematic or country-specific procedures should be sent to [Name of procedure], Office of the High Commissioner for Human Rights, Palais des Nations, 1211 Geneva 10, Switzerland.

13. These treaties include the "International Covenant on Economic, Social and Cultural Rights" (1966); "International Covenant on Civil and Political Rights" (1966); "First Optional Protocol to the International Covenant on Civil and Political Rights" (1966); "International Convention on the Elimination of All Forms of Racial Discrimination" (1965); "Convention against Torture" (1984); "Convention on the Elimination of All Forms of Discrimination against Women" (1979); "Convention on the Rights of the Child" (1989).

14. For more information about the work of the treaty bodies, see the United Nations human rights website at http://www.unhchr.ch/html/menu2/convmech.htm. For their abilities to receive and consider individual complaints, see below.

15. See R. R. Churchill, "Environmental Rights in Existing Human Rights Treaties," in Alan Boyle and Michael Anderson, *Human Rights Approaches to Environmental Protection* (1996), at 89–108.

16. United Nations, Document: E/1986/3/Add. 9.

17. Cited by Susan E. Brice in *Convention on the Rights of the Child: Using a Human Rights Instrument to Protect Against Environmental Threats,* 7 Georgetown International Environmental Law Review 587 (1995).

18. See also Sandra Coliver, *International Reporting Procedures,* in Guide to International Human Rights Practice, at 175.

19. See Matthew Craven, "Towards an Unofficial Petition Procedure: A Review of the Role of the UN Committee on Economic, Social and Cultural Rights," in Krzystof Drzewicki et al, eds., *Social Rights as Human Rights—A European Challenge* (1994); see also Article 9 of CERD.

20. See Siân Lewis-Anthony, *Treaty-based Procedures for Making Human Rights Complaints Within the UN System,* in Guide to International Human Rights Practice.

21. For an overview of the procedure, see http://www.unhchr.ch/html/menu2/8/over.htm

22. For more details, see Caroline Dommen, *Claiming Environmental Rights: Some Possibilities Offered by the United Nations' Human Rights Mechanisms,* 11 Georgetown International Environmental Law Review 1 (1998).

23. Communication 67/1980 decision of 27 October 1982 in *E.H.P. v. Canada* (also known as the "Port Hope Environmental Group" case). In United Nations, *Selected Decisions of the Human Rights Committee* 2, 1990, 20.

24. Communication 429/1990 *(E.W. et al v. Netherlands),* decision of 8 April 1993.

25. Communication 645/1995 *(Bordes and Temeharo v. France),* decision of 22 July 1996, reproduced in 18 *Human Rights Law Journal* 36 (1997).

26. See Caroline Dommen, *Bordes et Temeharo v. France—Une tentative de faire protéger l'environnement par le Comité des droits de l'homme,* Revue juridique de l'environnement 157 (1997).

27. United Nations, General Comment 14 [23], *United Nations Covenant on Civil and Political Rights,* adopted on 2 November 1984, reprinted in Manfred Nowak, 5CPR Commentary 861 (N. P. Engel, ed., 1993).

28. Menno Kamminga, "The Precautionary Approach in International Human Rights Law: How It Can Benefit the Environment," in David Freestone and Ellen Hey, eds., *The Precautionary Principle and International Law* (1996), at 181.

29. United Nations, General Comment 23 [50], Document CCPR/C/21/Rev. 1/Add. 5, adopted on 6 April 1994.

30. Communication 167/1984 *(Bernard Ominayak and the Lubicon Lake Band v. Canada),* decision of 26 March 1990, *Annual Report of the Human Rights Committee* (A/45/40), vol. 2, Annex 9 A.

31. Communication 431/1990 *(O.S. et al v. Finland),* decision of 23 March 1994.

32. Communication 511/1992 *(Ilmari Länsman et al v. Finland),* decision of 26 October 1994 (available on the web at http://www.unhchr.ch/html/menu2/8/oppro/511hrc.htm)

33. Communication 671/1995 *(Jouni E. Länsman et al v. Finland),* decision of the 30 October 1996 (available on the web at http://www.unhchr.ch/html/menu2/8/oppro/decmen.htm).

34. See Communication 197/1985 *(Kitok v. Sweden),* decision of 27 July 1988 in United Nations, Document A/43/40, 1985, 22, and in United Nations, Document A/43/40, 1985, 221.

35. See Communication 511/1992, at paragraph 9.8, and Communication 671/1995, at paragraph 10.7, supra note 32.

36. As in other areas of international law, all domestic procedures must have been exhausted before an individual case can be brought to the United Nations Human Rights Committee.

37. See, for instance, Communication 538/1993 *(Charles E. Stewart v. Canada),* decision of 1 November 1996, available on the web at http://www.unhchr.ch/html/menu2/8/oppro/decmen.htm

38. Ibid.

39. Communication 470/1991 *(Joseph Kindler v. Canada*), decision of 30 July 1993.

40. Communication 469/1991 *(Charles Chitat Ng v. Canada),* decision of 5 November 1993.

41. Communication 470/1991, at paragraph 13. However, the Committee found that in this case there was no violation of the ICCPR.

8 Environmental Advocacy and the Inter-American Human Rights System

Jorge Daniel Taillant

WHAT FOLLOWS IS a guideline to encourage environmental and human rights advocates to use existing and experimental international human rights instruments for the defense of the environment. The guide is intended primarily for legal advocates, since the mechanisms described herein are legal human rights institutions of the American hemisphere, although channels for nonlegal advocacy may also be possible and are also described in this guideline.

This guideline should be useful to both environmental and human rights advocates, although it is primarily an introduction for the former to the Inter-American Human Rights System. Human Rights advocates, however, can gain important insight into environmental issues that can and should be considered in human rights litigation.

It is essential foremost to introduce and define the intricate relationship that exists between human rights and the environment. Although this relationship may seem obvious to many, it is not so obvious in the world of litigation and advocacy, and in fact it is often overlooked or ignored. The similarities, commonalities, and complementarities between human rights issues and the environment remain largely ignored by most human rights and environmental advocates. This paper is an attempt to encourage environmental advocates to familiarize themselves with human rights mechanisms and to consider expanding environmental protection into international human rights litigation mechanisms. As we discover the nature and dynamics of the relationship between these areas of international law, we recognize the aptness of human rights instruments for the defense of the environment. This guideline is also a first step for human rights advocates to expand their traditional approach to the defense of basic political and civil human rights to include economic, social, and cultural rights, or in this case, specifically environmental rights. Other materials and resources are available that focus more on the legal fundamentals that link human rights and the environment.

The idea of developing a guideline or tool for environmental advocates to use human rights instruments follows the growing tendency of organizations and individual advocates to experiment with the bridging of the human rights and environmental fields.[1] Since the end of 1999, several precedent-setting, nonpartisan case briefs (amicus curiae) presented before the Inter-American Court on Human Rights in Costa Rica and at the Inter-American Commission on Human Rights in Washington, D.C., have successfully influenced the Court and Commission to consider environmental degradation as a violation of human rights. Much research is also in progress on the links between human rights and the environment around the world. Inspired by such rulings, interpretations, and research, a new horizon appears for human rights and environmental advocates. While we are not advocating for an abrupt change of direction for human rights advocacy, or even offering an international legal panacea for environmental advocates, we do suggest that there is virgin international and even national grounds in which to expand our horizons and deepen our analysis from both angles, environmental protection and human rights protection.

Background on Human Rights, Environment, and International Law

Institutional Legal Structures

One principal hindrance environmentalists face with respect to international environmental advocacy is the lack of international legal structures in which to litigate in favor of victims of environmental degradation. Legislating the environment at an international level is a relatively new concept. The Rio Summit, for example, is a fairly recent move in this direction. The Stockholm Declaration of 1972 was a fundamental first step to attain this objective. Environmental legislation, however, remains largely a national issue, confined or limited to national laws and regulations, and often limited to select ministerial-level regulations. Even within nations, the environment and environmental legislation operate at the margins of the application of local law and custom. Attorneys, judges, law professors, and other legal actors simply ignore environmental legislation or don't have it on their radar screen. International environmental law has not succeeded in recognizing individuals as subjects of international law, leaving the victim of environmental abuses defenseless at the international level.

This is not the case for human rights law. Human rights *have* seen substantial legal attention from local and international bodies, especially in the last several decades. The international human rights arena developed last century in large part as a response to severe physical and psychological abuses by dictatorial regimes against individuals. Several international systems now address human rights, including the European and Inter-American Human Rights Systems. These systems have developed institutional instruments useful to defend human rights and have been largely successful in their effort to protect and promote the respect for human rights in the national and international arena. In many cases, national governments have adopted international law as national law and have even placed international law above national law. They have devoted important institutional resources to the protection and promotion of human rights. Through international jurisprudence, treaties, and declarations, human rights legislation has surfaced in many national arenas. One of the most important successes of international human rights law is that it has given victims direct access to international human rights fora. Thus in international human rights law, *individuals* are subjects of law and can legally claim against human rights abuses perpetrated by States.

Yet from an environmentalist standpoint, the approach in the defense of human rights with respect to the environment has been somewhat limited in scope. Although the treaties and declarations enumerating our human rights have a clear and expansive definition of human rights, the actual defense of those rights in the last century focused primarily on a select portion of these rights, namely, civil and political rights. This approach is largely due to the response and focus of the international community to the particular types of violations present in our societies. Human rights advocates in the past decades rightfully opposed dictatorial abuses of human rights, bringing cases of disappearances, torture, and murder before the courts, focusing legal argumentation on the rights related to these violations in particular. Few, if any, cases focus on social, cultural, or economic rights, and fewer, if any, on environmental matters.

What is interesting, nevertheless, from an environmental advocate's perspective, and also for human rights advocates willing to expand their focus, is that there is an experimental trajectory of international jurisprudence and cases of individuals litigating against Nation-States for rights violations. This trajectory can give us some indication of how international claims by individuals may fare in environmental issues. International Human Rights Systems offer a unique forum for individuals to litigate to defend against violations of their rights, including rights that relate to the environment.

This paper focuses specifically on the Inter-American Human Rights System (IAHRS or System), and the potential of this System to serve as a forum for environmental advocacy. The intention is to highlight areas where the System has been effective, where precedent-setting jurisprudence has paved the road for future advocacy, and where there may be inroads to defend the environment and promote environmental protection further. It is important to understand that the IAHRS is not merely a receptor of cases. In fact, although many cases were admitted at the Commission level, as we will see in the subsequent section, very few cases have actually been forwarded to the Court and even fewer have been decided. Yet this is not a story solely about litigation. This story is also about lobbying for better laws and better monitoring of existing circumstances. It is about civil society as an actor that provides international institutions with valuable information and research about human rights and the nature of human rights violations in the American Hemisphere. The IAHRS offers several pressure mechanisms to encourage States to defend and promote a healthier environment and more sustainable development. The IAHRS is a recognized and visible discussion forum, offering civil society an inroad to pressure and encourage States to respect human rights or face international repercussions.

Linking Human Rights and the Environment

One of the first issues we must address in the rapprochement of human rights and the environment is to better understand the fundamental commonalities that exist between our human rights and the environment. In his 1974 Hague Academy lecture, Nobel Prize winner René Cassin advocated that existing concepts of human rights protection should be extended in order to include the right to a healthful and decent environment.[2] Today more than ever, society is awakening to the links between our environment and human life. We are realizing that the anthropogenic destruction of our planet's sustainable biodiversity also negatively impacts humanity, placing human life at great risk. Human dependence on environmental quality is becoming so evident that it will surely be treated as a dimension of human rights.[3] In the words of Earthrights International, "without a habitable environment, all other human rights become either unattainable or meaningless."[4]

We easily make the connection between environmental degradation and the resulting severe threat to our basic *human right to life.* We are witnessing the frightful destruction, contamination, or elimination of many of the world's most significant natural resources. The exploitation of our forested lands is eliminating the oxygen supply, disturbing ecological biosystems, and intruding into the lives of peoples and cultures. The ozone layer is slowly depleted by the uncontrolled production of harmful emissions. Swamplands created by dam construction in numerous continents have created massive climatic changes and extinguished species. Meanwhile, the inhabitants of flooded valleys are faced with irreparable social, cultural, and economic damage, including not only a forced change of habitat, but also a drastic change of lifestyles and customs. The loss of nonforested habitat is also of great concern to humanity, disturbing wildlife's natural food chain and affecting local communities who live off of the natural resources offered by their lands. Areas once known for their pristine lakes and rivers that provided drinking and recreational water to millions of people face dangerous contamination by industry, which results in unsanitary living conditions for large portions of the population. Air and noise pollution from densely populated urban centers results in severe health problems for urban dwellers. This sort of irrational use and overexploitation of environmental resources directly affecting the quality of life of human beings continues at an alarming rate.

The links between environmental degradation and human rights violations are of even greater relevance when one considers that the victims of environmental degradation tend to belong to the more vulnerable sectors of society (racial and ethnic minorities or the poor), who regularly have their human rights disproportionately abused. Former President Clinton noted in October 1992 that it is no accident that in those countries where the environment has been most devastated, human suffering is the most severe.[5] Those who are able to defend themselves against such exposure would not tolerate such suffering. Yet in the development of international human rights and environmental jurisprudence, and in the way we choose to defend and promote environmental sustainability and human rights, we have yet to find ways to make this logical union. International jurisprudence, local and international organizations, governments, and other concerned actors continue to address the environment and human rights from separate institutional, thematic, and legal perspectives.

Most of our basic human rights are affected by environmental degradation. The right to health is affected by environmental abuse, such as water, air, and noise contamination. The right to property is often violated by commercial exploitation. A recurrent example is the intrusion of commercial ventures into indigenous lands for the extraction of natural resources. The value of our property is also affected by environmental pollution. The right to equality is greatly affected by the unequal burden shared by certain sectors of society who are the targets of environmental contamination. Toxic dumps systematically appear where certain sectors of the population are less able to defend themselves or to protest against such abuses, resulting in *environmental discrimination.*[6] The right to participate is a basic premise of democratic societies, understood as individuals' right to participate in decisions, such as investments, urban planning, and commercial policy, that directly or indirectly affect their habitat. Undoubtedly, few communities participate in the decisions that bring about severe environmental contamination in their areas.

In 1976, Gormley argued that the right to a pure, healthful, or decent environment is essentially a human right and that there is validity to the proposition that preservation of the ecology and environment is included within the scope of the inalienable rights of man. Gormley goes on to argue that at a philosophical level, the right to a pure and clean environment falls within the scope of the right to a mere physical existence, and that the exhaustion of the Earth's resources is a major threat to man's continued existence on this planet.[7]

Yet the laws that govern our human rights and those that govern the regulation and control of the environment rarely converge. International as well as national jurisprudence that address the environment and human rights have focused on these legal arenas through separate frameworks, separating inextricably linked issues, even though the links between environmental abuses and human rights abuses are unarguably evident. By maintaining this rift between the areas, we duplicate efforts, thin available resources, and miss the opportunity to leverage our actions. Society, particularly the actors who are behind the efforts to promote environmental awareness and legislation and those who are devoted to defending human rights, need to recognize the inextricable nature of these fields and understand that we cannot think of the environment as somehow removed from our human condition. Everything and anything that influences the environment directly influences our human condition, and a violation of the environment is a violation of our human rights.

Environmental and human rights advocates have developed resources and strategies designed to defend their specifically defined and prioritized issues. Human rights advocates and institutions have chosen a path specifically focused on political and civil rights, primarily on the protection against the types of human rights abuses perpetrated by dictatorial governments, abusive police and military forces, and limited political expression. Environmental advocates, meanwhile, have chosen to defend against the irrational and unsustainable exploitation of natural resources, often ignoring the human element contained therein.

In their respective strategies and instruments to address abuses, human rights advocates have focused on international institutions, aiming to "force" governments to comply with such laws through the treaties and declarations to which they say they adhere. Environmentalists have focused more on publicity campaigns. A perfect example is Greenpeace's worldwide and largely visible campaigns. Greenpeace uses public opinion to leverage protection and national regulations to enforce compliance with commonly accepted norms of environmental protection. Only recently has there been a significant international effort to develop international legislation to regulate the environmental arena. Yet neither group has addressed the links between the environment and people. Few have attempted to use the resources of one set of advocates to advocate for the other, despite the naturally complementary nature and frequent overlap of environmental issues and human rights issues.

Boyle and Anderson, in an important contribution to environment and human rights literature, suggest that the late twentieth century witnessed an unprecedented increase in legal human rights and environmental claims, and that historians will look back on the last quarter of the twentieth century as the period in which both environmental law and human rights law reached a kind of maturity and omnipresence.[8] Their rapprochement is imminent.

However, there is some resistance to linking human rights and the environment. This resistance is a result of the lack of communication between these actors and the parallel paths that they have paved for themselves. The human rights advocacy community simply does not communicate with their environmental counterpart, and the same is true in the other direction. More exchange is needed between the actors of each to make their available advocacy resources useful to each other.

In large part, this rapprochement will evolve and gain momentum when our society finally concludes that our human rights include a right to a healthy and sustainable environment. It has already been legislated.[9] We know it implicitly, or at least sense it; we now need to abide by it explicitly. This guideline is a single effort in a series attempting to begin to pave this road.

The Inter-American Human Rights System

History

CREATION OF THE SYSTEM The Inter-American Human Rights System (IAHRS) dates to 1948, the year the Organization of American States (OAS) was founded, and the year of the proclamation of the American Declaration of the Rights and Duties of Man.[10] The Inter-American Commission on Human Rights (the Commission) was created before the Court on Human Rights in 1959 to further respect for human rights in the American Hemisphere and is governed by the American Convention on Human Rights, which was signed in 1969 and came into force in 1978. The Statute and the Regulations of the Commission, detailing its faculties and procedures, were approved in 1979 and 1987, respectively.[11, 12]

In 1969, the Inter-American Specialized Conference on Human Rights, drawing upon the American Declaration, the European Convention on Human Rights, and the International Covenant of Civil and Political Rights, approved the American Convention on Human Rights (the Convention). Twenty-five of the thirty-five countries of the hemisphere have ratified the Convention and are legally bound to observe and protect the rights it contains.[13] The Convention significantly strengthened human rights protection in the hemisphere by standardizing more than two dozen rights within the Convention's eighty-two articles.[14] The Convention established a two-tiered, treaty-based structure (which includes the Inter-American Court on Human Rights, alongside the Commission) that has characterized the Inter-American System for the protection of human rights ever since.

The Inter-American Court on Human Rights, located in San José, Costa Rica, has been active since 1979. It was established by the Inter-American Convention, with twenty-two of the thirty-one Member States of the OAS recognizing its jurisdiction.[15] It is important to note that not all Member States accept jurisdiction of the Court to date.

A very useful OAS publication exists in each of the four official languages (Spanish, English, French, and Portuguese) that unites all of the basic documents pertaining to the Inter-American Human Rights System. This publication can be obtained by contacting the OAS or by visiting the OAS website.[16]

THE AMERICAN CONVENTION The American Convention was strongly influenced by the European Convention on Human Rights, the American Declaration on Human Rights approved in 1948, and the International Covenant of Civil and Political Rights. However, the American Convention, of all international instruments, covers human rights most extensively. The State Parties to the Convention agree to respect and ensure the free exercise of the rights enumerated in the Convention of all persons under their jurisdiction. In this context, governments of State Parties have both positive and negative duties. States have the obligation not to violate the rights of persons, and they must adopt reasonable and necessary measures to guarantee the free exercise of the rights of the individual.[17]

The American Declaration also contains a complete list of the rights that States should observe and protect. Apart from most of those contemplated in the Convention, the American Declaration includes various social and economic rights. The Convention is different in this respect because it provides only for States who are committed to adopt measures to achieve the recognition of cultural, social and economic rights. Nevertheless, the Convention establishes individual human rights in greater detail.[18]

While before the Convention the Commission acted as the primary human rights organ in the Inter-American System, conducting studies from its inception and receiving individual petitions, under the Convention the Inter-American Court can dictate binding decisions on Member States. Further, the Convention designates a dependent relationship between the Commission and Court, since a case cannot reach the Court without having first passed through and completed the duties of the Commission with respect to the case.

It is convenient at this point to determine how the System distinguishes between a convention and a declaration, and to clarify how the OAS's principal human rights institutions treat each. A convention is an international treaty, which, once ratified by a State, is a source of obligation, and in the specific case of American States, becomes part of internal law. The respect for the Convention is clearly an obligation of the State Party, and individuals may insist on compliance with its law before national and international tribunals.

The American Declaration is *not* an international treaty, but rather, as its name suggests, a declaration by the States Party. Declaration status does not mean adherence is not obligatory. What is interesting in terms of the System is that the Commission and Court on human rights have assigned obligations to the States based on the Declaration. In this respect, the System treats the Declaration with utmost importance, obliging Member States to comply with its laws. The American Declaration has been incorporated indirectly via Charter of the OAS, by means of Article 150, which calls for the Commission to protect the rights listed in the Declaration.[19]

THE COMMISSION The Commission, located in Washington, D.C., was created to promote the observance and defense of human rights and to serve as a consultative organ of the OAS. The Commission was intended as a working group chiefly concerned with conducting investigations into select human rights issues. The Commission's appeal as a forum for individual cases quickly gained popularity and soon expanded its role.

The Commission's Convention-based responsibilities are principally associated with its competence to receive, examine, report upon (in its annual report), and submit (to the Court) individual petitions. Article 1 of the Commission's Statute establishes it as an autonomous entity with the specific duty to promote the observance and protection of human rights in the hemisphere. Human rights in the System are understood as those rights set forth in the American Convention and the American Declaration of the Rights and Duties of Man.[20] In a subsequent meeting of the OAS General Assembly (GA, Rio 1965 and Buenos Aires 1967), the Commission's mandate was refined, establishing the Commission as a permanent organ of the OAS and generally strengthening the constitutional basis for an Inter-American Human Rights System.

The Commission is composed of seven Commissioners who are specifically recognized in the field of human rights and who work on a nonremunerated basis (except for the President of the Commission). The Member States submit up to three candidates who may be nationals of the State proposing them or of any other Member State of the organization. The commissioners serve four-year terms, and they may be reelected only once.

The Charter-based functions of the Commission specifically include the following[21]:

1 develop an awareness of human rights in the hemisphere;
2 make recommendations to governments on the adoption of progressive measures in favor of human rights in the framework of their legislation, constitutional provisions, and international commitments;
3 prepare country studies or reports focusing on human rights in Member States;
4 request that Member States report on matters of human rights;

5. respond to inquiries and provide advisory assistance to any Member State on matters concerning human rights;
6. submit an annual report on the state of human rights in the hemisphere;
7. perform on-site visits and investigations;
8. submit a program budget to the Secretary General;
9. act on petitions and other communications;
10. appear before the Inter-American Court of Human Rights in cases provided for in the Convention;
11. request the Inter-American Court of Human Rights to take such provisional measures as it considers appropriate in serious and urgent cases that have not yet been submitted to it for consideration, whenever this becomes necessary to prevent irreparable injury to persons;
12. consult with the Court on the interpretation of the American Convention on Human Rights or of other treaties concerning the protection of human rights in the American States;
13. submit additional draft protocols to the American Convention on Human Rights to the GA to include other rights and freedoms progressively under the System of protection of the Convention;
14. submit to the GA, through the Secretary General, proposed amendments to the American Convention on Human Rights.

The Commission meets for a period not exceeding eight weeks a year. Since the System's inception, there has been a steady increase in the workload of the Commission. It typically receives more than five hundred petitions for cases a year, and in special circumstances, many more.

The Commission can make recommendations to States, publish its conclusions regarding specific cases of human rights violations, and in certain cases, initiate legal action against a State on behalf of the victim before the Inter-American Court of Human Rights. The Commission's strength lies in its powers of persuasion and its freedom to publicize human rights abuses, since it cannot force Member States to take any course of action.[22]

THE COURT The Inter-American Court of Human Rights, seated in San José, Costa Rica, is an autonomous judicial institution whose purpose is the application and interpretation of the American Convention on Human Rights. The Court's Statute, adopted by the GA in 1979, provides for both advisory and contentious jurisdiction. The latter applies only to State Parties to the Convention. Advisory opinions, on the other hand, can involve Member States not party to the Convention, as well as specialized bodies within the Inter-American System. This ability is important since not all States accept Court jurisdiction. In this manner, even if the State in question in a given case is not party to the Convention, the Court may publish recommendations favoring remedies to abusive situations and may have a favorable influence on the case.

The Court is composed of seven judges nominated and chosen by the States who are party to the Convention. They must be nationals of an OAS Member State, but not necessarily party to the Convention. They serve six-year terms and can be reelected for one additional period.[23] Each State may nominate up to three candidates, nationals of the State that proposes them or of any other Member State of the OAS. Six months prior to the expiration of a term of a judge, the Secretary General of the OAS addresses a written request to each State who is party to the Convention that it nominate its candidates within the next ninety days. The Court meets in two regular sessions each year, one in each semester.

The Court received its first contentious case in 1986 and has received relatively few cases in its history. Some of the issues it has addressed have been notable for their complexity and novelty. Specifically, the Court has considered important questions concerning disappearances of persons *habeas corpus.*

ELECTION OF COMMISSIONERS AND JUDGES The electoral process of the commissioners and Court judges is an area where civil society, and specifically environmental advocates, can have an important lobbying function to ensure that the candidates for judge and commissioner are individuals favorable to a determined cause. The election of the commissioners and judges of the Court and Commission is largely a political affair in which Member States negotiate positions and vote for their preferred candidate. States or groups of States generally lobby in favor of a given candidate several months prior to the voting that takes place at the annual GA. Although the electoral process is formally an internal process, in practice, there is a strong lobby on behalf of civil society actors that can tilt the election in favor of one candidate or another. Additionally, and perhaps most importantly, this lobby has successfully impeded the election of individuals with highly questionable track records in the area of human rights. By the same token, if a candidate shows a questionable track record on environmental matters, the lobby can be an influential factor flagged by interested parties (civil society), and proper lobby may ensue to block election or reelection.

Commissioners are nominated on personal grounds and *do not* represent nominating States. The only risk that commissioners may be swayed by State positions is during reelection, when States may try to lobby for favorable treatment in exchange for reelection support. Commissioners may and often do lobby for themselves. Lobbying between States may go as far as exchanging favors in other international organizations such as the United Nations, that is, you vote for my candidate for commissioner, and I'll vote for your United Nations candidate.

NGOs have a fundamental role to play in the election process. In practice, NGOs provide States with information on candidates, suggest candidates, lobby for or against certain individuals, and secure voting by pressuring their contacts within State Parties. For environmental NGOs, the main concern is to be informed about upcoming vacancies, reelection possibilities, new candidates, and the "green" record of each. NGOs should encourage their State contacts in the System to secure the nomination of environmentally educated and sensitive candidates. Reelections are also an important moment to review the candidate's green track record during the term, and with such information, pressure to reconfirm or remove judges and commissioners who have been favorable or not to environmental issues within the System. We must remember, however, that the primary quality that candidates must have to be likely candidates is a strong background in human rights. Although we may lobby extensively for strong environmental candidates, if they do not have worthy human rights backgrounds, it is unlikely that the States will favor them. It is advisable that individuals and organizations who attempt to lobby in favor of a given candidate stress the background of the candidate on issues that have been assigned significant importance by the Human Rights System, such as a strong background with indigenous communities.

THE PERMANENT COUNCIL The Permanent Council (PC) is a political organ of the OAS. It is the main recurring forum for political discussion that concerns issues important to the hemisphere and debate on actions to be taken by the OAS. The PC meets one or two times monthly at OAS headquarters in Washington, D.C., and is the stepping stone to the GA, which takes place once per year. The GA agenda is negotiated at the various PCs. Also, issues and actions to be taken decided at the GA are generally planned and executed from the PC.

NGOs have observer status at the PC. They regularly attend the sessions and have fairly direct access to the Member State representatives present. The PC is an essential forum for civil society organizations to obtain information, debate issues with Member State representatives, make contacts with such representatives, and define strategies with like-minded States to promote or lobby for specific actions or votes on issues. It is also an essential forum to gain insight on initiatives or actions of States that may work against environmental interests. The agenda of the PC may or may not be circulated to NGOs prior to meetings; circulation will depend on the public nature of the content or on the will of a certain Member State to inform certain NGOs of upcoming agenda topics.

THE GENERAL ASSEMBLY The General Assembly takes place once a year in a different country each year. The GA is the culmination of the previous year's activity at which Member States take account of the OAS's ongoing work program and achievements with respect to previous GA commitments. Voting for such offices as judge and commissioner takes place at the GA. What is not defined or completed during PC sessions is finalized at the GA. Also, new commitments, initiatives, and program activities are usually presented, defined, and agreed upon, and working groups may be formed to address specific issues at the GA. It is especially important for NGOs who support specific issues that are up for vote to be present at the GA in order to lobby States to vote in favor of or against their issues of interest.

Legal Framework and Issues

The following section briefly reviews some legal issues relevant to the IAHRS, which are intended to help environmental advocates orient themselves with respect to the System. This guideline essentially describes how to use the IAHRS to litigate in favor of issues with environmental relevance.

VICTIM ACTION VS CLASS ACTION The IAHRS has been more flexible than the European System on accepting complaints on behalf of victims. However, the Commission, which acts as a filter or first step to the Court (see below) has been reluctant to accept class-action claims, stressing that there must be an identified victim. This requirement may be, although is not necessarily, a hindrance in cases involving entire communities. Environmental abuses are often characterized by their spatial and temporal dimension. The spatial dimension affects an important area, while the temporal effect is not only relevant to the present but may also affect future generations. Environmental advocates litigating in these types of cases before the System should be aware of the difficulties and reluctance of the System to process cases without a specific identification of at least one victim or in favor of future generations.

INDIVIDUAL RIGHTS VS COLLECTIVE RIGHTS Following its insistence on the identification of specific victims, the Commission interprets the Rights of the American Convention as individual, not collective, save for the right to free expression. One inroad explored by the Center for Human Rights and Environment (CEDHA), the International Human Rights Law Group, and the Center for International Environmental Law (CIEL) in an amicus brief presented to the Court would have all rights exercised *by the community,* especially in cases involving indigenous peoples. This approach to the System is innovative. The approach, however, may not be considered standard and may not always be successful. As jurisprudence may lean in this direction, such an approach may be further explored.[24]

STATES AND INDIVIDUALS AS SUBJECTS OF INTERNATIONAL HUMAN RIGHTS LAW The IAHRS is a forum for individuals to bring suits against States or for States to bring suits against other States. Unlike national fora, the System *cannot* be used to bring suits against corporations. This is an important issue that environmental advocates must consider since in many cases the perpetrator of environmental abuse is a corporation. One alternative way around this limitation, however, is to litigate against the State for not taking the necessary preventive measures to avoid corporate abuse. The System obligates States to take necessary measures to ensure the respect for the human rights embodied in the Convention.

CONFIDENTIALITY OF THE PROCESS When a given case is still at the Commission level (prior to the Court), the procedure is confidential and cannot be shared with the press. This restriction may limit alternative campaign strategies. Once the case is at the Court level, the case can be publicized.

The Commission may send to the State a report that summarizes the case facts and its recommendations (see below) that is also entirely secret. The report is an ultimatum for the State to comply before the facts and recommendations are revealed to the public. The costs of confidentiality for public advocacy of using the System must be considered before initiating legal action.

TIME FACTOR There are various time considerations that should be taken into account before committing to litigation in the IAHRS. A case can take from one to four years to run its course, depending on various factors. The first factor is the degree to which the advocates of the plaintiff party (the NGO, as the case may be) pressure the Commission and State to move the case. If the NGO is strongly behind the case, the NGO can speed up the process substantially. Also, the commissioner in charge of the particular country can greatly influence the time a case takes. Certain commissioners may move more quickly than others.

The State will always ask for extensions to the Commission, and these are normally granted. In practice, the petitioner only reacts against these extensions after several have been requested (at least two) by the State. Political pressure to react to such extensions sooner due to the delicate nature of a case may greatly influence its fluidity through the System. If the case is very high profile and generates pressures to the State, it can be resolved remarkably quickly, even in just a few months.

Further, some countries, due to their political presence or to their history of human rights abuses in the System, may receive more of the Commission's attention than others. Much also depends on the Commission's attorneys assigned to the cases, which can also greatly delay or speed up the case through its steps.

There is no clear indication or rule governing the time cases may spend in the System. There is a time risk that must be taken into account when choosing the IAHRS for litigation, and this may work as much against as in favor of the plaintiff. What is definite is that the plaintiff must be actively behind the case to ensure it moves as quickly as possible through the System.

EVIDENCE STANDARDS AND BURDEN OF PROOF Unlike most national courts, the Commission and Court have *low* standards of proof. In part this is due to the delicate circumstances that may exist to make collection of evidence difficult. The State, in many cases, has access to the evidence and has eliminated the available evidence for the case. The Court, as a result, has admitted circumstantial evidence as long as it assists the Court in clarifying the facts.

The burden of proof in a case is on the State. That is, according to Article 42 (Presumption) of the Commission Statute, the facts reported in the petition shall be presumed to be true if, during the maximum period set by the Commission, the government of the State in question has not provided pertinent information to the contrary. This article favors the petitioner.

Hence, if the State does not expressly deny the facts with supporting counterevidence, then the Commission recognizes the evidence submitted by the petitioner as true. If the State denies the evidence, it must specifically prove that the evidence is not valid. As a good rule, the petitioner should attempt to include *all* evidence possible, and not discard a fact because it cannot be proven, or because it may seem difficult to prove in a national court.

PRECAUTIONARY AND INTERIM MEASURES AND THE PRECAUTIONARY PRINCIPLE The Precautionary Principle is an emerging principle of international environmental law that requires anticipating and avoiding environmental damage before it occurs, especially where failure to do so would result not only in environmental degradation, but in human rights violations as well. Principle 15 of the 1992 Rio Declaration is the most widely accepted elaboration of the Precautionary Principle in international environmental law: "In order to protect the environment, the precautionary approach shall be widely applied by States according to their capabilities. Where there are threats of serious or irreversible damage, lack of scientific certainty shall not be used as a reason for postponing cost-effective measures to prevent environmental degradation."[25] Numerous international environmental law instruments both before and after Rio have endorsed the Precautionary Principle.

In essence, the Precautionary Principle shifts the burden of proof from those threatened by an environmentally destructive project, such as the petitioners, to those who want to proceed with the activity and who are more fairly required to make a showing that the project will not result in the threatened harm. This principle especially applies when the proponent of the project has not performed environmental impact assessment and has not even allowed participation by the affected peoples.

The Precautionary Principle may thus be seen as the environmental law analogue to the concept of precautionary measures that by statute and regulation can be employed by the Commission and Court on Human Rights.[26] When threats of irreparable harm to persons or the environment are posed, prudence dictates "erring on the side of caution" and preventing the threatened action until full consideration of the underlying issues can take place.

Article 29 of the Commission Regulations on Precautionary Measures states the following duties:

1 The Commission may, at its own initiative, or at the request of a party, take any action it considers necessary for the discharge of its functions.

2 In urgent cases, when it becomes necessary to avoid irreparable damage to persons, the Commission may request that provisional measures be taken to avoid irreparable damage in cases where the denounced facts are true.
3 If the Commission is not in session, the chairman, or in his absence, one of the vice-chairmen, shall consult with the other members, through the Secretariat, on implementation of the provisions of paragraphs 1 and 2 above. If it is not possible to consult within a reasonable time, the chairman shall make the decision on behalf of the Commission and shall so inform its members immediately.

Article 24 of the Rules of Procedure of the Inter-American Court on Human Rights states:

1 At any stage of the proceedings involving cases of extreme gravity and urgency and when necessary to avoid irreparable damage to persons, the Court may, at the request of a party or on its own motion, order whatever provisional measures it seems appropriate, pursuant to Article 63(2) of the Convention.

These articles of the Court and Commission regulations are important powers over Member States vested in the Commission and Court, and should not be underemphasized. In their history, the Commission and Court have acted on behalf of victims to force States to take immediate action in favor of the plaintiff party.

Procedures of a Case Entering the System

We highly recommend that interested parties refer to the Statute of the Inter-American Commission on Human Rights, which details the procedures of a case entering the System. There are also several publications available detailing and commenting on this procedure. The Commission also publishes a short manual intended to assist petitioners in the preparation of petitions.[27] We've included in appendix 2a the style to which the Commission requests petitions conform.

WHO MAY PRESENT A PETITION (CASE) TO THE SYSTEM Any person or group of persons or nongovernmental entities legally recognized in one or more of the Member States of the OAS may submit petitions to the Commission, on their own behalf or on behalf of third persons, with regard to alleged violations of a human right. This is an important point, since NGOs may actually identify and present a case before the System without having to convince a potentially unwilling party to confront the violator. This rule also permits *any* party to present a case on behalf of deceased victims or victims who have disappeared. This is an important difference between the Inter-American Human Rights System and the European System.

ADMISSIBILITY Before the Commission assesses the merits of a petition, the petition must meet certain basic requirements. Whether a petition is deemed admissible will determine the degree to which the entities charged with protecting the rights enshrined in the American Convention can hear, judge, and act upon a particular case or alleged violation.

When a petition enters the System, the Commission's Secretariat makes a preliminary judgment as to whether or not the petition conforms to the Convention's admissibility criteria. Articles 46 and 47 of the Convention (as well as provisions of the Commission's regulations) stipulate what admissibility criteria an individual petition must meet before the Commission can undertake a merit-based finding.

For a petition to be admitted by the Commission, three conditions must be met:

1 the accused State must have violated one of the rights established in the American Convention or the American Declaration;
2 the claimant must have exhausted the possibilities of legal redress in the State in which the violation occurred and his or her petition to the Commission must be presented within six months of the final judgment by the tribunal concerned; unless domestic legislation of the State involved does not afford due process, denies access, or prevents exhaustion of remedies, or causes an unwarranted delay in rendering a final judgment (Article 37, Statute);[28] and
3 the claim should not be the subject of some other international procedure.

REQUIREMENTS FOR THE PETITION All petitions should be in writing. There is no form or special format that must be followed, but a petition should contain all the available information on the case.

The petition should include the following:[29]

1 the name, nationality, and relevant contact information about the person or persons making the denunciations;
2 an account of the act or situation that is denounced, and if possible, the name of the victims of the violations;

3 an indication of the State that the petitioner considers responsible for the violation;[30] and
4 information on whether the remedies under domestic law have been exhausted or whether it has been impossible to do so.

RECEPTION AND OBSERVATIONS The Commission, through its Secretariat, receives the petition, and after entering it in its register, acknowledges receipt and, if the petition is accepted, determines its admissibility. Once the Commission begins inquiry, it contacts the government concerned, informs it that a claim has been received against it, and invites the government to reply to the accusations.

In serious or urgent cases or when it is believed that the life, personal integrity, or health of a person is in imminent danger, the Commission shall request a prompt reply from the government. This request is not considered a prejudgment with regard to the case.

COMMISSION'S ADMISSION OF THE CASE Once the Commission requests information from the State, the State has ninety days to provide the requested information. With justifiable cause the State may request a thirty-day extension, which generally and systematically occurs. In practice, the petitioner may, after several extensions, request that the Commission deny further extension requests. The Commission may, in order to gain a better understanding of the case, forward to the petitioner or the petitioner's attorney the documents supplied by the government and invite comments to the response.

PRELIMINARY QUESTIONS The Commission shall decide on the following matters:[31]

1 whether the remedies under domestic law have been exhausted and take measures to clarify remaining doubts;
2 other matters on admissibility or inadmissibility;
3 whether grounds for the petition exist or subsist, and if not, it shall order the case archived.

THE HEARING If the case file has not been closed, in order to verify the facts, the Commission may conduct a hearing following a summons to the parties and proceed to examine the matter set forth in the petition.[32] The hearing is a very powerful and useful instrument for the petitioner. Cases without hearings or with too few hearings are less likely to move quickly, press the State, or achieve desirable results. The hearing offers a meeting of the State, petitioner, and Commission in a situation in which the State confronts the accusation and petitioner via the Commission. Hearings are generally held to present documented evidence, discuss specific legal issues, show videos relevant to the case, present legal arguments, and so forth. In few other circumstances will the State offer to enter a dialogue with the petitioner about the case in the presence of a third party. Given that the Commission will tend to favor a friendly settlement, it will likely use the hearing to encourage the State to correct any wrongdoings and take appropriate steps toward reparations. The Commission has also used hearings to pressure the State with precautionary measures if it does not ensure the well-being of the petitioner. The petitioner may request the Commission to hold a hearing, usually to present new elements of the case. The request may not be granted. Considering the large caseload handled by the Commission, petitioners should justify why a special hearing is important to the case when they make the request. The petitioner should never excessively delay to file a case for lack of pertinent information, since this information can be presented at the hearing.

Since the Commission meets only twice a year, hearings may be formally scheduled only every six months. If petitioners need to move cases more quickly, they may request the Commission to hold special meetings (hearings). These sessions may take place at the Commission in Washington, D.C., or may sometimes be arranged in alternative sites. In some cases, the Commissioners may be able to meet with the parties in the country of the alleged abuse to review advances in negotiations toward a friendly settlement. It is unlikely that the Commission will agree to travel to a site merely for a meeting.

ON-SITE INVESTIGATION If necessary and advisable, the Commission shall carry out an on-site investigation, in which the States concerned shall furnish all necessary facilities.[33] In serious and urgent cases, only the presentation of a petition or communication that fulfills all the formal requirements of admissibility shall be necessary in order for the Commission to conduct an on-site investigation with the prior consent of the State in whose territory a violation has allegedly been committed.[34] Once the investigation stage has been completed, the case shall be brought for consideration before the Commission, which shall prepare its decision within 180 days.[35]

ACTIONS BY THE COMMISSION If the Commission decides that the government committed a violation of human rights, it will recommend that the government repair the breach, investigate what happened, compensate the victims, and desist from further violations of fundamental rights. The Commission cannot force this outcome, but it will try to achieve it in various ways.

FRIENDLY SETTLEMENT A friendly settlement may be reached at any stage of the examination of a petition. The friendly settlement in fact is one of the most useful and most used instruments of the System to address human rights violations. In a friendly settlement, the Commission acts as an organ of conciliation between the plaintiff and the defendant or State. By the Convention, the Commission first must take steps to reach a friendly settlement between the parties. Only in extreme cases, when the life of the petitioner or family may be in danger, may the Commission decide to skip this step.

As mentioned above, most cases do not proceed to the Court. States find it politically uncomfortable and risky to have the Court find against them. For this reason, the out-of-Court settlement is a preferred last resort for the State. For the plaintiff, friendly settlement can also be an effective means to obtain financial or political retribution and avoid a lengthy Court trial. The friendly settlement has allowed ample, timely, and effective remedies, that are often more favorable than the settlements that might otherwise be reached via Commission or Court intervention.

States are generally predisposed to and prefer a friendly settlement to the bad press generated by a case, not to mention the possible adverse outcomes and jurisprudence set in a Court decision, as well as possible international penalties faced due to noncompliance with international law. The Commission, meanwhile, will also try to resolve the case out of the Court through the friendly settlement mechanism.

THE COMMISSION REPORT If a friendly settlement is not reached, the Commission shall examine the evidence provided by the government and the petitioner, and evidence taken from witnesses or obtained from documents, records, official publications, or on-site investigations. It prepares a report that states the facts, conclusions, and recommendations regarding the case.

The Commission then presents its report to the State concerned. If within a period of three months the matter has not been settled, that is, if the State has not taken action to remedy the situation, the Commission may set forth an opinion and conclusions. The Commission may make pertinent recommendations and prescribe a period within which the government in question must take the measures necessary to remedy the situation. When the prescribed period has expired, the Commission shall decide whether to publish the report.

In the event the State in question is not party to the American Convention, the Commission's final decision shall include any recommendations the Commission deems advisable and a deadline for State implementation. If the State does not adopt the measure recommended by the Commission, the Commission may publish its decision.[36]

The publication of reports by the Commission is important leverage for States to act to avoid public hemispheric scrutiny. States generally do not wish to see an international institution such as the OAS publish information about human rights violations occurring in their territory. If at all possible, States will try to avoid, through intense lobby, the publication of such reports. Civil society actors may contribute to reports through various modalities, either by contributing information to the OAS on a given topic or case, or by following up State reports with Shadow Reports to clarify, extend, or contradict information therein contained.

GENERAL AND SPECIAL REPORTS As already briefly mentioned, the Commission prepares a series of reports during the year that are presented at the General Assembly, which can be useful to pressure States to remedy abusive situations. These are useful publications in which NGOs and other interested parties may find a space to lobby for the inclusion of a particular issue or matter. The details of these reports are listed in chapter 5 of the Statute. They are essentially draft reports; reports on the situation of human rights in a State; the Annual Report; and reports on Economic, Social, and Cultural Rights. It is important to remember that the Commission may make observations as well as recommendations for remedy in such reports.

The Commission Reports are considered jurisprudence by the IAHRS, particularly by the Commission itself. Therefore, any mention of pertinent legal issues, such as the importance of a healthy environment, can be considered as past jurisprudence of the Commission and should be cited in legal argumentation before the System. Commission reports can be consulted via the Commission website.[37]

PASSAGE OF THE PETITION TO THE COURT If a State who is party to the Convention has accepted the Court's jurisdiction, the Commission may refer the case to the Court. However, even if the State has not accepted the Court's jurisdiction, the Commission may call upon the State to make use of an existing option to accept Court jurisdiction in this specific case.

The importance of a case against a Member State is not to be understated. The State will have every incentive to divert the case from the Court, since it will most likely not want to face a possible unfavorable judgment. States prefer to settle at the Commission level (a sort of settlement out of Court) and not face a condemnation (see friendly settlement, above).

Unfortunately, the Commission does not have clear criteria on deciding what types of cases go to the Court. The American Convention does not have guidelines to clarify the process, nor do the IAHRS Statutes or regulations provide guidance in the matter. The Commission has generally tried to avoid exercising its right, under Article 51, to refer cases to the Court.

COSTS AND TIME INVOLVED AT THE COURT LEVEL As is the case for deciding to present a case to the Commission, the Court presents several delays and costs that should be taken into account before a case is pushed to this level. The Court is *not* a permanent body, and therefore meets only a few times per year. Parties must travel to Costa Rica, as must NGOs who wish to lobby and assist the Commission or to generate public hemispheric interest in the case. In terms of the actual case costs, the Commission cannot always pay for all witnesses to attend hearings. Often, the plaintiff must defray such costs. Hearings are often cancelled or postponed at the last minute. Lobbying parties should plan on arriving several days before the hearings to prepare strategies, prepare witnesses, hold press conferences, and meet with like-minded NGOs who support the cause in question. Interested parties should consider staying near or at the same lodging sites as the Commissioners, since location is a key to access the Commissioners during their stay.

STANDING Nongovernmental organizations *do not* have standing before the Court. Only the Commission and States have standing, and although NGOs often act as advisors to the Commission during Court sessions or as representatives of victims before the Commission, only the Commission can allow NGO intervention or opinion in the various stages of the case at the Court level. Conflict often arises with respect to how the victim's wishes are presented to the Court, since only the Commission assumes this representation at the Court level and may not revert to the NGO representative for input. NGOs are usually given standing during reparation hearings in order to provide pertinent information to the Court so that the victim is properly represented.

PUBLICITY OF THE CASE At the Court level, the case is no longer confidential. At this stage the press becomes a powerful tool to exert pressure on the State and parties to come to a favorable settlement. Proper lobbying of the press is essential to a successful advocacy campaign before, during, and after the hearings.

EVIDENCE The Court may, at the request of a party or on its own motion, obtain any evidence that it considers likely to clarify the facts of the case. The party requesting the production of evidence must assume the costs.

SENTENCE, RULING, SANCTIONING PROCESS The judgment of the Court shall contain, besides basic information about the parties and judges rendering the decision, the legal arguments of the case; the operative provisions of the judgment; the allocation of compensation; and the decision, if any, regarding costs.[38]

COMPLIANCE AND ENFORCEMENT There are no statistics concerning compliance of the decisions of the Commission and Court. Much depends on the will of the State to comply with the verdicts of the System's institutions. In its history, only a handful of cases have reached the Court, and in most of these, the State in question has been a relatively small State with little hemispheric political power to afford to ignore adverse decisions and rulings. In other more recent cases involving larger and more powerful States, States have conceded to calls for precautionary measures and cooperated in efforts to subdue or cease actions proving to result in human rights violations.

Noninstitutional Actors of the System

The Commission and Court and their role in the System, as well as the procedure to file a case in the System, are discussed above. While the litigation aspect of the System is the focus of this guideline, nonlitigant possibilities exist that can have an important impact on hemispheric affairs.

CIVIL SOCIETY ACTORS (NGOs) In most of the cases that have come before the System, an NGO has been the representative of the petitioner before the Commission and acted as an advisor to the Commission (as a sort of extension of the will of the victim) when before the Court. By charter, the System permits individuals or groups to bring complaints on behalf of themselves or on behalf of others. In fact, only a handful of NGOs has regularly represented victims of human rights abuses. These NGOs have extensive experience with the OAS and its human rights organs and are an important source of historical and procedural information. It is recommended that individuals seeking to address the System establish contact with experienced litigants to obtain guidance and assistance. Some NGOs that may be important sources of information are CEJIL, the International Human Rights Law Group, CELS, Comisión Andina de Juristas, CEDHA, and CIEL.

These nonofficial actors of the System are in fact fundamental facilitators of the System. They ensure that States, commissioners, and Court judges receive vital information about cases and help guarantee a transparent and effective process. Environmental NGOs interested in using the IAHRS are encouraged to familiarize themselves with these procedures and to participate in the various fora available to civil society to access the System.

For a case to have a useful impact in the hemisphere and in order to take advantage of the various lobby channels that become available throughout the process, the representative of the victim (the NGO, for example) before the Commission must mobilize all available resources in favor of the case, including press and other media tools to pressure the Commission to accept the case and to encourage the State to settle the dispute as quickly as possible.

NGOs have free access to the System and may participate in most fora of the System, including hearings, Permanent Council meetings, and General Assembly meetings. For the GA, a special request to attend should be sent to the Secretary General and permission must be granted.

AMICI CURIAE Another useful instrument of the System with growing importance, especially in the areas of environment and human rights, is the *amicus curiae* (or friend of the Court brief). The amicus curiae has been a useful tool to raise previously unconsidered legal issues and influence precedent-setting jurisprudence at the Commission and Court levels, especially those that concern the common grounds between human rights and environment. The amicus curiae is essentially a nonparty intervention in the form of a brief that outlines the legal issues of the case. Amici curiae that emphasize environmental circumstances in select cases have recently been successfully presented before the Court and Commission.[39]

The first amicus curiae to have an important environmental impact on the System was in the case of the Mayagna indigenous community of Awas Tingni and its effort to gain recognition of traditional lands. The brief argued that one of the major areas of intersection of international human rights law and environmental law is the area of indigenous peoples' rights. Since at least 1992, the indigenous community of Awas Tingni, Nicaragua, has been petitioning the government of that country to gain formal recognition of its traditional lands. For the first time, the OAS Inter-American Commission on Human Rights has sided with an indigenous community in its grievance over land rights and taken the extraordinary step of submitting that grievance to the OAS Inter-American Court on Human Rights. The outcome of the case will establish an international legal precedent regarding the extent of a country's obligation to recognize and protect indigenous traditional land and resource tenure.

Another amicus curiae that links human and environmental rights is currently before the System. It is the Wichi indigenous community case against Argentina, mentioned above. This brief analyzes the intricate relationship that exists between these indigenous peoples and their lands with respect to damages caused (and anticipated) by ongoing (and projected) public works in the indigenous territories. The document, a precedent-setting submission to the Commission, reviews international laws, treaties, and jurisprudence relevant to the defense of several indigenous communities of northern Argentina, promoting the special recognition and consideration of the interrelationship of human rights and environment, particularly as concerns the symbiotic relationship that exists between indigenous communities and their habitat.

State Reluctance to Reach the Inter-American Court

Although very few cases have actually been decided at the Court level, the Commission has been an effective tool to thwart human rights abuses and to settle numerous cases outside of the Court. Once a case reaches the Commission, the press it obtains and the resulting pressure on the Member State to resolve the case as quickly as possible (or face a Court trial) augments.

States will lobby the Commission to reject the case or will work with the petitioning party to withdraw the case from the System. The risk of facing trial may be pressure enough to warrant a correction of the abuse and a resolution for the victim.

If the Commission accepts the case, the State will usually make every effort possible to avoid its passage to the Court, usually including settlement with the victim in the form of remuneration. But pressure is also exerted on the State to remedy existing legislation and actions that are detrimental to human rights.

How Environmentalists Should Approach the IAHRS

The Inter-American Human Rights System (IAHRS), as its name suggests, is a regional institutional System that focuses on *human rights.* The institutions that comprise it, namely the Organization of American States and its various organs (the Commission, the Court, and others), are governed by human rights declarations and treaties. For this reason, the operative agenda of the System, the cases that it receives, and the initiatives that stem from the System *all* center on human rights. If we are to consider using the System for environmental advocacy, we must understand that the System will necessarily view our attempts through a human rights optic, and we must hence orient our advocacy so that it is in sync with this optic.

The System will always seek to defend human rights, and whatever environmental issues we may raise must take this into account. The human rights that are enumerated in the international treaties, declarations, and other legal documents to which the IAHRS regularly refers, cover a broad range of types of rights, including civil, political, social, economic, and cultural rights. Many of these rights have important environmental content or can be related to environmentally relevant issues. Some of these can be found in the United Nations Charter, the American Convention, the Universal Declaration of Human Rights, the Charter of the European Commission of Human Rights, the United Nations Covenant on Civil and Political Rights, and others. Some of the rights appearing in these documents are listed below:

- right to life;[40]
- right to equality before the law;[41]
- right to an effective judicial remedy;[42]
- right to residence and movement;[43]

- right to own property alone as well as in association;[44]
- right to religious freedom and worship;[45]
- right to the benefits of culture;[46]
- right to self-determination;[47]
- right to be free from discrimination;[48]
- right to health;[49]
- right to a clean and healthy environment;[50]
- right to be free from interference with one's home;[51]
- right of minorities;[52] and
- right to identity.[53]

There are many others. What we need to consider is that the IAHRS will heed a plea for a violation of environmental abuse if and only if the abuse can be shown to violate a human right in one of the legal instruments it defends. Human rights in the System are understood as those rights set forth in the American Convention and the American Declaration of the Rights and Duties of Man.[54] If an environmental abuse cannot be shown to have a direct link to one of these human rights, it is very difficult to present the plea in the System.

Consider an example. Assume that government A contaminates a river by releasing industrial waste into the river. Granted the waste may pollute the water, cause displeasing odor, death of plant life, death of fish, disruption of the biological chain, and more; if we cannot show, for example, that the contamination results in the health deterioration of persons, specific individuals, or a community, a case brought before the IAHRS to defend against this abuse will not likely be admissible. In order for us to approach the IAHRS with the case, we need to look at it through a human rights optic. We need to consider the consequences of this abuse to humans and present the case with environmental human rights arguments. We can transform the strictly environmental nature of this case by arguing the following:

1. the contamination of the river by government A violates the human right to health because the residents along the river are becoming sick from the contaminated water;
2. the human right to life is violated because individuals living along the river have died from the contamination of the water;
3. the human right to effective judicial remedy has been violated because despite the riverside communities' plea to the judicial system, nothing has been done to stop the contamination;

4 the human right to a healthy environment has been violated due to the multiple environmental impacts of the contamination.

Essentially, what we've done is to seek the impacts on human life caused by the environmental contamination, since if we argue the case simply for the environment's sake, the IAHRS and its organs will not have evidence or grounds on which to act.

We use another example to illustrate the point. Supposing government B allows company X to cut down one million hectares of rain forest per year for ten years. Part of the affected rain forest is in indigenous peoples' territory. Company X has promised to provide new housing for any displaced communities in an alternative forest region in another part of the country. The company will also replenish the cut forest with abundant new trees in twenty-five urban areas undergoing new park construction. The indigenous communities have fought for more than a year to halt the development project but have had their case rejected by the highest level of the national judicial system. We present a case to the IAHRS because of the massive negative environmental impact this cutting will have, and we request preliminary measures to halt the cutting until the case can be resolved. We argue that the cutting will eliminate one-third of the country's forestry resources in ten years, placing at risk the sustainable use of the forestry supply. Along with the trees, more than one thousand plant and animal species will die, and the country's climate will drastically change in that ten-year period. Further, we argue that Company X has not done a proper environmental impact assessment; therefore, it cannot anticipate what the extent of the environmental impact of the cutting will be, which according to World Bank environmental experts, will be much worse than calculated. Based solely on this information, our insistence on preliminary measures will likely have an unfavorable outcome in the System since, although we have shown obvious imminent environmental consequences of the timber cutting, we have failed to give the Commission enough evidence to link the potential impact of the cutting to human rights abuses.

We might consider a better defense of the case before the System. We could indicate, for example, that the peoples displaced by the cutting are indigenous peoples that have a symbiotic and cultural connection to their land. Removing them to another area is a violation of their human right to life. Further, the massive consumption of the trees will eliminate an invaluable part of the food chain for the communities living in the areas, not to mention the disruption to tribal hunting patterns caused by the cutting down of significant portions of the rain forest. We can focus our case on a number of rights, including the right to life, the right to an effective judicial remedy, the right to the benefits of culture, the right to be free from interference with one's home, the right of minorities, the right to identity, and others. All these rights can be defended using the IAHRS.

For the sake of typology and guidance, we've divided environmental advocacy before the IAHRS into three basic types or approaches. These are transformation, reinterpretation, and interpretation.

THE TRANSFORMATION APPROACH The transformation approach essentially strives to transform environmental claims into human rights claims. This approach follows the example of the river water contamination cited above. With this approach, we examine environmental degradation from a human perspective, answering the question, *what direct impact does the environmental abuse have on humans?* For this approach we need to break out of the strictly environmental arena and look at the contact humans may have with the environment, specifically with the case in question. Our approach needs to focus on the humans affected and their human rights.

THE REINTERPRETATION APPROACH The reinterpretation approach reinterprets basic human rights to include environmental rights. This approach requires more legal analysis and argumentation in an attempt to expand the IAHRS vision of basic human rights to include environmental issues. An example would be to expand the common understanding of the right to life to include the right to live in a healthy environment.[55]

THE INTERPRETATION APPROACH The interpretation approach allows for the inclusion of other national and international laws, treaties, declarations, and additional documents into the System. It is essentially a tool allowing the extension of such laws and treaties into the IAHRS, binding States in the hemisphere because they have subscribed to these laws and treaties. Article 29 of the Convention is the window to this approach.

ARTICLE 29 Article 29, Restrictions Regarding Interpretation, paragraphs (b), (c), and (d), of the American Convention, opens a window of opportunities to litigate before the IAHRS. It is worth reproducing them here:

> No provisions of this Convention shall be interpreted as:
> (b) restricting the enjoyment or exercise of any right or freedom recognized

> by virtue of the laws of any State Party or by virtue of another convention to which one of the said States is a party;
> (c) precluding other rights or guarantees that are inherent in the human personality or derived from representative democracy as a form of government; or
> (d) excluding or limiting the effect that the American Declaration of the Rights and Duties of Man and other international acts of the same nature may have.

Article 29 of the American Convention wisely articulates a mechanism that allows the American Convention to adapt itself to the evolution of international law, including the adoption of new concepts and trends. As a criterion to resolve potential conflicts between two or more human rights provisions, the criterion forces the application of the provision that establishes a human right in a manner that is most comprehensive and most favorable to the individual (principle *pro homine*). Article 29 similarly requires the adoption of the trends in effect in international law concerning the violation of rights. Thus, to more fully delineate States' responsibilities to afford petitioners special protection, petitioners must be able to resort to the body of international environmental law that has developed over the past several decades. They must also be able to resort to various human rights instruments, which collectively require governments to allow affected peoples to have information concerning development and to participate in matters that affect them.

Essentially, Article 29 gives us grounds on which to broaden the definition and content of rights that the individual and community have by understanding those rights based on the rights as defined by other treaties and international law to which the State is party, as well as according to national law of that State. Through this extension, States can be held responsible by the IAHRS to broader and more comprehensive understanding of basic human rights. Therefore, by *interpretation,* if the laws of a given State or the international treaties to which it subscribes protect the individual from certain environmental human rights that are cited in the IAHRS, and the State violates any one of those rights per one such treaty or law or does not provide for adequate protection against the abuse of one of those rights, the IAHRS can be used to litigate against the State.

THE SAN SALVADOR PROTOCOL The Additional Protocol to the American Convention on Human Rights in the area of Economic, Social and Cultural Rights, or more commonly, the San Salvador Protocol (SSP), was signed in San Salvador in 1988 by eighteen Member States but came into force only in 1998.[56] The SSP contains twenty-two articles that outline economic, social, and cultural rights. To date twelve countries have ratified the protocol.[57]

The SSP is an important international step in the recognition of the symbiotic links between the environment and human rights. Specifically, the SSP in its Preamble makes reference to "the close relationship that exists between economic, social, and cultural rights, and civil and political rights, in that the different categories of rights constitute an indivisible whole, . . . bearing in mind that . . . rights [in the Americas] be reaffirmed . . . on the basis of full respect for the . . . right of its peoples to development, self-determination, and the free disposal of their wealth and natural resources; . . . "[58] Article 11, the right to a healthy environment, is especially relevant to the environment and to environmental advocates seeking assistance of international law. It reads in part,

> Article 11: The Right to a Healthy Environment
>
> 1. Everyone shall have the right to live in a healthy environment and to have access to basic public services.
> 2. The States Parties shall promote the protection, preservation, and improvement of the environment.

Another important environmental right cited in the SSP with respect to workspace conditions is Article 7(e), which states that "State Parties undertake to guarantee in their internal legislation, particularly with respect to: safety and hygiene at work."[59]

The SSP defines useful parameters to encapsulate economic, social, and cultural rights, and, one hopes, will serve to bring economic, social, and cultural rights to the forefront of national and international law. The SSP delineates certain state and international organization responsibilities with respect to economic, social, and cultural rights, which may be especially useful to environmental advocates who seek redress before States for violations of human rights abuses related to environmental degradation. Some of these are listed below:

- **a** the obligation of States to Adopt Measures (Article 1), through national and international cooperation in order to fully observe the rights contained in the protocol;
- **b** the obligation of States to Enact Domestic Legislation (Article 2), to ensure the rights enumerated in the SSP;
- **c** the obligation of States of Non-Discrimination (Article 3);
- **d** that States, in order to protect these rights, must submit periodic

reports on the progressive measures taken to ensure due respect for the rights in the SSP; (Article 19 (1));

e with respects to Articles 8A and 13 (Trade Unions and Education), the Inter-American Commission on Human Rights may give rise to legal petitions against States for non-compliance with the Inter-American Human Rights System (Article 19 (6));

f the Commission may formulate such observations and recommendations as it deems pertinent concerning the status of economic, social and cultural rights established in the SSP (Article 19(7)).

The SSP is a fairly new international legal instrument that has yet to be used or applied. It is, however, cited in more recent analysis of international human rights law, and references to the SSP also appear in several precedent-setting briefs that aim to link environmental degradation to human rights abuses.[60] The SSP takes a bold step to reaffirm and regulate economic, social, and cultural rights. Due to the difficulty and reluctance of most States to ensure economic, social and cultural rights, these rights have been for the most part ignored by international tribunals. The rising awareness and debate over the importance of achieving sustainable development, however, as well as the growing importance of human rights to international tribunals and the ability to enforce them at an international level, have begun to change this deficiency in the international legal arena.

It is important to understand that the SSP is an addendum to the American Convention. The spirit of the SSP and the specific language it contains set out a series of useful and enforceable obligations and duties, while limiting the capacity of the System to achieve some of its objectives. Existing Inter-American human rights institutions *may not* use their full powers with respect to the rights outlined in the SSP. The SSP, for example, limits the Commission to very specific powers:

The Commission (and in certain cases the Court) can:

1. receive petitions against States based on violations of the Rights cited (only) in Articles 8A and 13 (Trade Unions and Education) of the SSP;[61]
2. receive Annual Reports of the States on the state of observance and protection of economic, social, and cultural rights (as submitted to the Secretary General by the States);[62]
3. formulate observations and recommendations on the status of Economic, Social and Cultural Rights in all States Parties in its annual reports or special reports and present these before the General Assembly.[63]

Of the actions it may take, the Commission may file reports, which have served as effective pressure on States to address circumstances in which human rights violations have or are occurring. Although the reporting system does not carry the weight of legal action, it has proved in the past to be a deterrent to States that systematically violate human rights.

In Article 1, the SSP makes States *progressively* responsible for the observation of the rights recognized by the protocol, depending on their level of development and available resources. Through this responsibility, States must uphold at least their level of compromise and protection of economic, social, and cultural rights, while striving to improve this level over time. This compromise can be important with respect to a State's past compliance with upholding such rights.

Another instrument of the Inter-American System is the injunction power. Through its Statute and regulations, the Commission may dictate precautionary measures and the Court may dictate interim measures to avoid imminent violations of human rights. This instrument has proven a very successful tool and power of the System, which has thwarted and prevented human rights violations in many of the hemisphere's countries. It has yet to be seen whether the Commission will go as far as to dictate precautionary measures in the case of rights enumerated in the SSP.

The SSP, despite its limitations, opens an important door to the defense of economic, social, and cultural rights. Its spirit, clearly cited in its Preamble, and the wide coverage of rights are well intentioned. Perhaps envisioning a warming to the defense of other economic, social, and cultural rights, Article 22 leaves an open door to the incorporation of other rights and an expansion of recognized rights, through an amendment procedure. Likewise, amendments may expand the powers of the Commission to act in the name of other existing rights covered by the protocol.

The SSP has at least overcome the initial resistance of most States to protect and ensure economic, social, and cultural rights to the individual. There are many aspects of the protocol and its use and application that remain to be explored and tested. The mechanisms through which the States Report to the System (frequency, content, person reporting, and so on), through the Secretary General are not established, for example. Its usefulness as an instrument to protect the environment remains unrealized. Once implemented, it will be a good first step toward the defense of economic, cultural, and social rights.

Civil environmental and human rights advocates who intend to use the Inter-American System as a forum for international environmental law should familiarize themselves with the SSP and follow developments and institutional interaction with respect to the protocol. Especially important will be the way in which the Commission and Court make reference to the

SSP and the ways in which Article 11 is referenced and applied in future human rights cases.

NGOs can take several concrete steps with respect to the rights, duties, and institutional powers contained in the SSP:

1 They can bring cases before the System that prove violations of Articles 8 or 13.
2 NGOs are encouraged to produce Shadow Reports to the State reports on the state of economic, social, and cultural rights submitted to the Secretary General.
3 NGOs may provide the Commission with valuable and relevant information on the state of economic, social, and cultural rights that the Commission prepares for the System.
4 NGOs may also introduce references to Article 11 of the SSP (the right to a healthy environment) in individual petitions before the Commission through the use of Article 29 of the American Convention.

Manner in Which Environmentalists Can Use the IAHRS

Prior sections discuss how the IAHRS is arranged, how human rights are addressed by the System, how a case makes its way through the System, and specifically, how an environmental case can be presented to the System. Environmental awareness is growing in many Member State societies and is slowly reaching the IAHRS. It is a new area of concern, and the OAS's and civil society's attention will likely grow. What is certain is that the System stands to grow considerably through increased environmental awareness. This guideline is about fostering that awareness and "greening" the Human Rights System as much as it is about offering an international legal forum to environmental advocates.

Litigation is one important ground for the development of environmental issues in the IAHRS. It is listed first since one would like to see more environmental cases reach the System. Yet there are several other ways in which the environment can be favored by the System, and these need not be legal in nature. Environmental advocacy can have multiple forms in the IAHRS. Some of these are discussed in the following paragraphs.

LITIGATION Cases that present human rights issues with high environmental content are relatively new to the System, yet they have a special and important place for the future of the System. More cases that focus on the environment as a human right, or on environmental human rights, are needed. By building a case history that addresses the environment, we can slowly build on international jurisprudence that favors the environment and increases the likelihood that the Commissioners and Judges will tend to environmental human rights concerns.

INFLUENCING THE ELECTION OF JUDGES AND COMMISSIONERS The nomination of candidates to the OAS organs is a highly politicized process that can be influenced by directed and informed lobbying. It is to the advantage of the System and to the environment that judges and commissioners be sensitive to green issues. This lobbying is open to the public, and interested parties should become informed about upcoming elections, judge and commissioner backgrounds, and other issues.

LOBBYING FOR NATIONAL AND INTERNATIONAL ENVIRONMENTAL PROGRAMS AND INITIATIVES By lobbying for recommendations or reparations to be sanctioned by the Commission and Court, and for OAS initiatives and programs, NGOs can help influence hemispheric environmental control, monitoring, education, programs, and legislation that protect the environment. These initiatives can range from education campaigns and programs in specific countries or regions to national or hemispheric laws, declarations, and conventions that foster environmental protection. The General Assembly is an excellent forum to promote new programs and initiatives, but important pre-GA groundwork is necessary.

PRECAUTIONARY MEASURES OR INTERIM MEASURES Such measures can help address urgent situations that warrant immediate relief to environmental abuses. The Commission and Court have the power to insist on such actions, and States have a vested interest in complying with Court and Commission requests.

INSTITUTIONAL REPORTS AND SHADOW REPORTS Reports issued by the Commission and Court are important pressure mechanisms for States to comply with environmental legislation or respond with remedial actions necessary to remunerate victims of abuse. NGOs may find it useful to provide the Commission with information about a given case the Commission may be including in one of its reports to ensure that the eventual report covers the case properly. NGOs may also decide that State reports on the condition of the environment and related human rights abuses are not accurate or do not contain information pertinent to the case in question. In such cases NGOs may draft Shadow Reports to clarify or add information about an environmental case.

AMICI CURIAE The System is ripe to consider the environmental issues in human rights claims. Although this is a new area to explore within the System, the first reactions of the Commission and Court to admitting environmental arguments have been positive. Several amici curiae that stress the links between the environment and human rights have already been favorably admitted and used at the Commission and Court levels. NGOs working on human rights or the environment in the hemisphere should consider submitting amici curiae to the System.

PRESSURE ON STATES The pressure the System exerts on States is important enough to warrant consideration by environmental advocates.

JURISPRUDENCE Gradually introducing petitions that include environmental issues within human rights cases will make the System more apt to protect the environment.

Consideration before Choosing the IAHRS for Environmental Advocacy

The IAHRS may be a very effective tool to address environmental issues in the American Hemisphere. It can even serve to influence other continental jurisprudence, as has been the case with civil and political human rights. However, the System may not always be the most appropriate channel, or a unique channel, for environmental advocacy. These are some questions environmental advocates should ask themselves before choosing the IAHRS to pursue their objectives:

1 To what degree does the case address human rights as understood by the American Convention? If the Commission does not easily identify violations of the human rights contained in the American Convention, the case may not have a future in the System.
2 Can we properly identify a victim and a State that is a member of the

OAS as a responsible party? The identification of victim and responsible State is key to the case. Without these, we may have a very interesting environmental case, but not one for the Commission or the Court.

3 Are the time constraints, secret nature of the case, and possible costs implied a hindrance to the advocacy desired?

4 Has internal (national) recourse been duly exhausted, or does one of the exceptions apply? If not, the State will have a good argument for the Commission to reject the case.

5 Have we defined a proper lobbying strategy?

6 Is litigation the best choice?

7 Is a Commission report useful? Is it enough? Should we produce a Shadow Report?

8 Can we lobby for legislation or for a regional program?

9 Have we properly identified the best forum for this lobby?

10 Have we understood our limitations and defined our objectives? If our objective is not a legal victory (to win a case), what do we expect to gain (report on a case, program, preventive measures, election of a certain judge or commissioner, establish jurisprudence)?

Guidelines for Presenting a Case before the IAHRS[64]

1 Draft a brief and clear description of the facts. Most petitions experienced NGOs present to the Commission are no longer than four pages.

2 Show that the internal legal mechanisms have been exhausted, or show that one of the exceptions to this rule apply.

3 Present all national legislation and procedures taken in a clear and explicative manner. Many petitions assume knowledge of internal procedures and laws of which the Commission may not be aware.

4 Include a chapter on the violations of the rights contained in the Convention with at least one or two paragraphs explaining each violation. Keep in mind that you can present more information and facts on the violations later.

5 Include a final chapter of conclusions stating that the State is obligated by its ratification of the Convention to protect the rights of the Convention.

6 If a victim or witness is in danger, you may request precautionary measures.

7 Direct your complaint to The Executive Secretary of the Commission, Inter-American Commission on Human Rights, 1889 F. Street,

NW, Washington, D.C. 20006; Telephone: (202) 458-6002; Fax: (202) 458-3992

8 Include contact information such as your address, e-mail address, telephone number, fax number.

Results That Can Be Expected

The IAHRS offers multiple inroads to defend against environmental abuses. It also offers the possibility to prevent them. We've seen that the IAHRS is more than a mere courtroom to litigate. States are reluctant to go to court and will seek alternative conflict-resolution mechanisms. Likewise, the System offers a wide variety of possible results from its use. These results range from monitory retribution to new legislation, from education programs to the press, from exposure to regional and international experience in protecting the environment. Knowing what the results may be is the best way to make the most of the System for our advocacy objectives. The IAHRS can be

1 a forum for litigation in favor of environment
2 a way to force States Parties to abide by hemispheric conditions
3 a way to obtain precautionary measures to stop imminent danger to the environment and to people who suffer environmental abuse
4 a channel to gain press coverage in favor of environmental concerns
5 a forum for debate, design, and implementation of more environmentally sustainable national laws and international treaties
6 a way to ensure that States develop appropriate environmental education programs
7 a forum on which to build environmental jurisprudence (history) at the international level
8 an international forum that permits individuals, NGOs, and other civil society actors to defend themselves against States.

Conclusion

While the idea of an Inter-American Human Rights System swarmed with environmental cases may seem far-fetched, certainly there is room to include the environment and environmental issues in human rights advocacy. This practice is already a reality. The intention of this guideline is not to call openly for environmental cases to approach the System. It is not about raining cases on the Commission, which is already overloaded with what are strictly traditional human rights cases. Such a result may in fact work against the introduction of environmental issues into the System. What would be more effective would be the steady and progressive recognition of the system of environmental human rights and the ways human rights can be adversely affected by environmental degradation. This aim will be achieved only by the strategic insertion of cases with a high environmental profile. The environmental advocacy community has an interesting and powerful tool in reach that must be carefully evaluated and strategically employed to achieve meaningful results. At first, small victories may be more useful than large ones; these victories will serve to focus primarily on building jurisprudence, experience, and history. The community must always strive to build awareness and harness useful legal instruments to protect and promote the environment.

NOTES

1. See website for the Center for International Environmental Law (CIEL) at www.ciel.org and for the Center for Human Rights and Environment (CEDHA) at www.cedha.org.ar

2. Paul Gormley, *Human Rights and Environment: The Need for International Cooperation* (Sijthoff and Leyden 1976), first sentence.

3. Richard Falk, *Human Rights and State Sovereignty* (1981), quoted in Michael Kane, The Yale Journal of International Law 18, 1 (Winter 1993).

4. Earthrights International, "Human Rights and Environment" (paper presented to the Centre for Human Rights, United Nations Office, Geneva, January 1997.

5. Quoted in Michael Kane, The Yale Journal of International Law 18, 1 (1993).

6. See Jorge Daniel Taillant, *Environmental Discrimination: Issues and Themes* (CEDHA, 2000).

7. Paul Gormley, *Human Rights and Environment,* 41–42.

8. Allen Boyle and Michael Anderson, *Human Rights Approaches to Environmental Protection* (Oxford University Press, 1996).

9. See, for example, the San Salvador Protocol, Article 11, and the African Convention.

10. Much of the historical information on the Inter-American Human Rights System in this section is largely adapted from César Gaviria (secretary general of the Organization of American States), *Toward a New Vision of the Inter-American Human Rights System,* The Journal of Latin American Affairs (1996).

11. Organization of American States, *Human Rights: How to Present a Petition in the Inter-American System*.

12. The Commission Statute and Regulations, in force as of May 2001, are

available on the OAS website at http://www.cidh.org/Básicos/nuevoreglamento.htm

13. The ratifying countries are Argentina, Bolivia, Colombia, Costa Rica, Chile, Ecuador, Guatemala, Honduras, Nicaragua, Panama, Peru, Surinam, Trinidad and Tobago, Uruguay, and Venezuela.

14. The protected rights of the Convention are the right to juridical personality (to be recognized as a person before the law); the right to life; the right to humane treatment, including the right not to be subjected to cruel, inhuman, or degrading punishment or treatment; freedom from slavery; the right to personal liberty; the right to a fair trial by a competent tribunal; freedom from ex post facto laws; the right to compensation in a case where sentencing is a final judgment through a miscarriage of justice; the right to privacy; freedom of conscience and religion; freedom of thought and expression; the right to reply or to make a correction to inaccurate or offensive statements; the right of assembly; freedom of association; rights of the family; the right to a name; rights of the child; the right to nationality; the right to property; freedom of movement and residence; the right to participate in government; the right to equal protection of the law; the right to judicial protection against acts that violate fundamental rights.

15. The countries that have accepted jurisdiction of the court are Argentina, Barbados, Bolivia, Brazil, Colombia, Costa Rica, Chile, Ecuador, El Salvador, Guatemala, Haiti, Honduras, Mexico, Nicaragua, Panama, Paraguay, Peru, The Dominican Republic, Suriname, Trinidad and Tobago, Uruguay, and Venezuela.

16. General Secretariat of the Organization of American States, *Basic Documents Pertaining to Human Rights in the Inter-American System,* see http://www.cidh.oas.org/basic.htm

17. See Norris Buergenthal and Dinah Shelton, *La Protección de los Derechos Humanos en las Américas* (Instituto Interamericano de Derechos Humanos, 1990): 41–42.

18. Organization of American States, *Human Rights: How to Present a Petition in the Inter-American System.*

19. The definitions of "convention" and "declaration" as well as the analysis of the system with respect to each is taken from an unpublished draft manual on the Inter-American Human Rights System prepared by the Center for Justice and International Law (CEJIL).

20. The recently in force San Salvador Protocol has broadened the spectrum.

21. See Articles 18 and 19 of the Statute of the Inter-American Commission.

22. Organization of American States, *Human Rights: How to Present a Petition in the Inter-American System.*

23. See American Convention, Articles 52–54.

24. See www.cedha.org.ar (Documents on Line or Amicus Briefs section).

25. Rio Declaration, supra at note 20. As explained in greater detail in annex 1, the precautionary principle was first introduced explicitly into international law in the North Sea Ministerial Conference and was included in the Final Declaration of the Second International North Sea Conference in 1987. The principle was repeated at the Third North Sea Conference in 1990, and the principle was

eventually included in the 1992 Convention for the Protection of the Marine Environment of the North-East Atlantic (the OSPAR Convention). Declaration of the Third International Conference on Protection of the North Sea, 7–8 March 1990, reprinted in First Yearbook of Intl. Envtl. L., 1990, 658, 662–73; see Convention for the Protection of the Marine Environment of the North-East Atlantic, Article 2(2)(a), 22 September 1992, reprinted in 32 ILM 1069 (1993), entered into force 25 March 1998.

26. When the court applies such measures they are referred to as interim measures.

27. Organization of American States, *Human Rights: How to Present a Petition in the Inter-American System.*

28. When petitioners contend that they are unable to prove the exhaustion of local remedies, it is up to the government against which the petition has been lodged to demonstrate to the commission that the remedies under domestic law have not previously been exhausted (Article 37, Statute of the Commission).

29. See Article 32, Statute of the Commission.

30. Petitions may be filed against any Member State of the OAS, although the procedure, possible remedies, and court jurisdiction depend on whether or not the State is party to the Convention and has accepted court jurisdiction.

31. See Article 35, Statute of the Commission.

32. See Article 43, Statute of the Commission.

33. See Article 44.1, Statute of the Commission.

34. See Article 44.2, Statute of the Commission.

35. See Article 44.3, Statute of the Commission.

36. See Article 53, Statute of the Commission.

37. See www.cidh.org

38. See Article 46, *Rules of Procedure of the Court.*

39. See Awas Tingni and Wichi cases at CEDHA website (available in Spanish and English): www.cedha.org.ar (in amicus brief section).

40. United Nations, General Assembly, Resolution 217 A(III), Article 3, *Universal Declaration of Human Rights* (hereinafter Universal Declaration) 10 December 1948; OAS Resolution 30, Document OEA/Ser. IV/I.4, rev, Article 1, *American Declaration on the Rights and Duties of Man* (hereinafter American Declaration), adopted by the Ninth International Conference of American States, 30 March–2 May 1948, 1965; *American Convention,* supra note 4, at Article 4; ICCPR, supra note 31, at Article 6; ICESCR, supra note 32, at Article 6; CRC, supra note 34, at Article 6.

41. Universal Declaration, supra note 35, at Article 7; American Declaration, supra note 35, at Article 2; American Convention, supra note 4, at Article 24; ICCPR, supra note 31, at Articles 3 and 26; ICESCR, supra note 32, at Article 3; CERD, supra note 33, at Article 3.

42. Universal Declaration, supra note 35, at Article 8; American Convention, supra note 4, at Article 25; ICCPR, supra note 31, at Article 2.3.

43. Universal Declaration, supra note 35, at Article 13; American Declaration, supra note 35, at Article 8; American Convention, supra note 4, at Article 22; ICCPR, supra note 31, at Article 12.1; CERD, supra note 33, at Article 5.d.i.

44. Universal Declaration, supra note 35, at Article 17; American Declaration, supra note 35, at Article 23; American Convention, supra note 4, at Article 21; CERD, supra note 33, at Article 5.d.v.

45. Universal Declaration, supra note 35, at Article 18; American Declaration, supra note 35, at Article 3; American Convention, supra note 4, at Article 12; ICCPR, supra note 31, at Article 18.1; CERD, supra note 33, at Article 5.d.vii; CRC, supra note 34, at Article 14.1.

46. Universal Declaration, supra note 35, at Article 27; American Declaration, supra note 35, at Article 13; ICESCR, supra note 32, at Articles 15.1 and 15.2.

47. ICCPR, supra note 31, at Articles 1, 2, and 3; ICESCR, supra note 32, at Article 1.

48. Universal Declaration, supra note 35, at Articles 1 and 2; ICCPR, supra note 31, at Articles 2.1 and 26; ICESCR, supra note 32, at Article 2; CERD, supra note 33, at Article 1.

49. ICESCR, supra note 32, at Article 12.1; CRC, supra note 34, at Article 24.

50. ICESCR, supra note 32, at Article 12.1.b. Protocol of San Salvador, Article 11.

51. American Declaration, supra note 35, at Article 9; American Convention, supra note 4, at Article 11; ICCPR, supra note 33, at Article 17; CRC, supra note 34, at Article 16.

52. ICCPR, supra note 31, at Article 27; CRC, supra note 34, at Article 30.

53. CRC, at Article 8.

54. The recently in force San Salvador Protocol has broadened the spectrum.

55. See "Amicus Curiae for Awas Tingni" for reinterpretation of the right to life; www.cedha.org.ar in amicus curiae section. Also for reinterpretation of the right to participate see "Wichis Amicus Brief" at same site.

56. Signatory countries are Argentina, Bolivia, Brazil, Colombia, Costa Rica, Dominican Republic, Ecuador, El Salvador, Guatemala, Haiti, Mexico, Nicaragua, Panama, Paraguay, Peru, Suriname, Uruguay, and Venezuela.

57. These countries are Brazil, Colombia, Costa Rica, Ecuador, El Salvador, Guatemala, Mexico, Panama, Paraguay, Peru, Suriname, and Uruguay.

58. San Salvador Protocol, Preamble.

59. San Salvador Protocol, Article 7(e).

60. See amicus briefs on Awas Tingni and Wichis at www.cedha.org.ar

61. See San Salvador Protocol, Article 19(6), Means of Protection.

62. See San Salvador Protocol, Article 19(2), Means of Protection.

63. See San Salvador Protocol, Article 19(7), Means of Protection.

64. Taken from an unpublished draft manual on the Inter-American Human Rights system prepared by the Center for Justice and International Law (CEJIL).

9

Sharing Common Ground

A Cautionary Tale on the Rights of Indigenous Peoples and the Protection of Biological Diversity

Annecoos Wiersema

THERE IS AN AGELESS HISTORY of biological harmony between indigenous peoples and their environment, a history going back uncounted thousands of years. This benign balance was grounded in use, spirituality, and long-term survival. As such, it transcends industrialized peoples' constant need to find justifications for the protection of that environment. The relationship of indigenous peoples with their environment has traditionally incorporated a holistic view of nature and placed humans within that nature, not separated them from it. Historically, indigenous peoples have not recognized individual ownership of parcels of land, embracing instead a communitarian approach, nor have they allowed a level of use of plants or animals that would destroy the ecosystem or any part of it. Indeed, whenever environmental degradation occurs, be it clear-cutting, burning of forests, or extractive exploitation of indigenous lands, there is an immediate and accompanying unraveling of the social fabric of the indigenous people, a deterioration followed by irreparable social collapse.

Today, with widespread eradication of indigenous peoples a dire and ongoing reality, the decline of cultural diversity is a fact. Simultaneously, the extinction of species is occurring on an increasing scale and at an accelerating rate. Species are disappearing as a result of habitat loss, direct taking for markets, pollution, and disruption of ecosystems due to introduced species. It is therefore no surprise that the claims of indigenous peoples for recognition of their rights to land, to cultural integrity, and to self-determination are increasingly being tied to efforts to halt the tragic rate of species extinction. As both cultural and biological diversity are under fire as never before, the record of mutually successful coexistence between indigenous peoples and their natural surroundings has been highlighted, particularly in international fora.[1]

The harmony between nature and indigenous people today, however, is rarely intact. It has been threatened from the time colonization began to the time of our modern global market economy, where little remains unaffected by the market. Old relationships with land and nature have, at best, been frayed, and have, at worst, disintegrated. Those who claim rights for indigenous peoples and those who call for the protection of species are involved in distinct struggles. The International Alliance of the Indigenous/Tribal Peoples of the Tropical Forests (IAIP) has noted that a constructive and useful interpretation of the Biodiversity Convention can arise only from the context of indigenous rights as a whole. Particular note should be made of the rights of indigenous peoples to self-determination, collective rights, control of our territories, access to our resources, recognition of our political and legal institutions and control of traditional knowledge.[2] The World Wide Fund for Nature (WWF) "encourages and supports ecologically sound development activities, particularly those that link conservation and human needs. WWF may choose not to support, and may actively oppose, activities it judges unsustainable from the standpoint of species or ecosystems, or which are inconsistent with WWF policies on endangered or threatened species or with international agreements protecting wildlife and other natural resources, even if those activities are carried out by indigenous communities."[3] These two quotations emphasize the basic fact that each side will always view the other's interests with an eye to furthering its own position. And, as each claim gains more attention from the international community,[4] each can reinforce its position by demonstrating a need to be present and to participate in discussions touching on the other.

There are times, however, when conflict may arise between the two goals. This article, therefore, sounds a warning note and identifies some areas of potential difference in the hope of directing attention toward lasting solutions. These differences should not deter either party from making common cause; clearly, the survival of both cultural diversity and biological treasure is inextricably linked. This, then, is a cautionary tale, not a plea to take sides, but an appeal to look with a cold eye before we leap.

The Convention on Biological Diversity[5] is one international forum where discussion about the simultaneous relationship between the protection of indigenous peoples' rights and the conservation of biodiversity has begun, with the role of indigenous peoples expressly recognized.[6] The Convention has, however, been treated warily by both groups, in part because the breadth of its language gives scope to so many possibilities without clear direction and in part because the Convention resoundingly reinforces the rights of the nation-state. The internationalization of indigenous peoples' demands for recognition of their legal rights and of conservationists' attempts to develop legal protections for nature has in both cases been repeatedly hampered by State claims for sovereignty, and by the role of the State as implementer and enforcer of protection mechanisms for both parties. The project of both indigenous peoples and conservationists has tended to push for a blurring of the boundaries of the State, to limit its rights, and to check its authority. The Convention on Biological Diversity may, in its express emphasis on State sovereignty, recognize this pressure on sovereignty, but, as we shall see, it has not yielded any ground.

As such, the Convention's provisions do not conclusively resolve the difficulties, which arise from linking indigenous peoples' interests with those of conservationists. In some cases, it exacerbates them. Yet in spite of, or perhaps because of, this lack of resolution, the Convention's provisions provide the backdrop for many debates about how best to protect both cultural and biological diversity. The article begins, therefore, with a brief overview of the Convention's themes and main provisions before considering three issues of concern to both indigenous peoples and conservationists, which reveal themselves in the shadow of the Convention. First, the relationship of intellectual property rights and biotechnology to the protection of both cultural and biological diversity affects both calls for indigenous peoples' rights and conservation efforts. Where indigenous peoples have already suffered the disruptive effects of assimilation policies and the market economy, they may increasingly wish to open up their ancient knowledge to this economy. Here, conflicts with conservation goals may arise, which are discussed in the section on the convention, intellectual property, and indigenous peoples. Second, the definition of indigenous peoples and the appropriateness of seeking to define indigenous peoples in a manner that maintains a close link with conservation is discussed in the section on defining indigenous peoples. Third, the range of rights that can or should be claimed under the banner of sovereignty, whether of a nation-state or of a group claiming self-determination rights, is considered under sovereignty and self-determination.

The 1992 Convention on Biological Diversity

The Convention on Biological Diversity is not the first Convention to deal with the protection of species,[7] nor is it the first to recognize the need for an ecosystem approach to the protection of species.[8] But the Convention does have some important claims to originality. It was the first international legal instrument to adopt the new battle cry of biological diversity, and it was the first international treaty that attempted to deal comprehensively with protection, serving as a framework convention not only to future protocols, but also de facto to some of the more specific treaties that already existed.[9] As such, the premises of the Convention and its focus are vital for an understanding of the direction of international, national, and subnational attempts to protect the natural world.

The Convention begins on a groundbreaking note as the first binding international instrument to recognize and refer to the intrinsic value of biological diversity as a justification for its protection.[10] It states that it was "Conscious of the intrinsic value of biological diversity and of the ecological, genetic, social, economic, scientific, educational, cultural, recreational and aesthetic values of biological diversity and its components."[11] While intrinsic value is separated from the other values listed and appears to stand alone, it is nevertheless buttressed by values that speak more directly to instrumental concerns.[12] Only biological *diversity* is granted intrinsic value, leaving its components, including species and habitats, to rely on these instrumental justifications. Although much literature assumes that multiple reasons for protection may coexist, it is arguable that each time instrumental values are added to a list of reasons for protection, these will tend to subsume the more intangible, often motivating, reasons for seeking to protect species.[13] Thus the Convention's recognition of intrinsic value in its Preamble will not in itself prevent the intrinsic value of diversity from being overtaken by the emphasis on use of its components that runs throughout the substance of the Convention.[14]

The Preamble also reflects another notable feature of the Convention, the reassertion of all States' sovereign rights over their own biological resources,[15] reiterated again in Article 3.[16] While it may not be easy for a State to assert sovereignty over an entire species,[17] it can certainly do so over the local population of that species. This principle has, therefore, a clear effect in practice on any decisions over uses of land, which directly or indirectly destroy ecosystems, such as logging and mining. It also ensures that decisions taken by a State regarding national priorities cannot be questioned in the international arena. This recognition of the sovereign rights of nation-states is repeatedly reinforced throughout the Convention.[18] One of the most important aspects of the Convention, access to genetic resources, is left entirely to the determination of national governments and is subject to national legislation.[19] Significantly, the negotiating parties chose in the Preamble to refer to the conservation of biological diversity as a "common *concern* of humankind,"[20] thus rejecting the more contentious approach of the United Nations Convention on the Law of the Sea which had adopted the concept of "common heritage."[21]

This reaffirmation of sovereignty over resources is not unusual in an international agreement, particularly in an international environmental agreement. The right to the use and exploitation of a State's own natural resources was expressed in the international arena as early as 1952.[22] In the early 1970s, declarations of the United Nations General Assembly, predominantly supported by newly liberated States, sought the establishment of a New International Economic Order, which included among its guiding principles the "full, permanent sovereignty of every State over its natural resources and all economic activities."[23] This same principle is now routinely repeated in a wide range of international treaties and forms the basis for the only provision common to both the International Covenant on Civil and Political Rights[24] and the International Covenant on Economic, Social and Cultural Rights.[25] Article 3 of the Convention on Biological Diversity follows the exact wording of Principle 21 of the Stockholm Declaration of 1972,[26] a principle widely accepted as reflecting customary international law,[27] and the only principle repeated, with only slight modification, in the Rio Declaration of 1992.[28]

Other aspects of the Preamble set the stage for the substantive provisions of the Convention. A reference in the Preamble to the traditional knowledge of "indigenous and local communities"[29] is reiterated in Article 8(j), discussed further below, and the provisions on equitable sharing of benefits arising from the use of such knowledge run throughout the Convention. Indeed, the objectives of the Convention are listed in Article 1 as "the conservation of biological diversity, the sustainable use of its components, and the fair and equitable sharing of the benefits arising out of the utilization of genetic resources."[30] Although the need for equitable sharing can certainly be applied to indigenous peoples, this aspect of the Convention is more a reflection of political compromise between developed and developing countries than a reflection of true interest in protecting indigenous peoples' interests.[31] When stressing the importance of and the need to promote international, regional, and global cooperation among States, intergovernmental organizations and the nongovernmental sector,[32] the Preamble does not even mention indigenous peoples or communities.

Biological diversity is defined broadly to include "*inter alia,* terrestrial, marine and other aquatic ecosystems and the ecological complexes of which they are part; this includes diversity within species, between species and of ecosystems."[33] Article 8 clearly reinforces this ecosystem-based approach to protection by providing for the in situ conservation of biological diversity, including a requirement to establish "a system of protected areas or areas where special measures need to be taken to conserve biological diversity."[34] The Convention defines "Biological Resources" to include "genetic resources, organisms or parts thereof, populations, or any other biotic component of ecosystems with actual or potential use or value for humanity."[35] This broad coverage fits with the core of the Convention in its emphasis on economic incentive measures[36] and the enhancement of biotechnology as a source of such incentives.

Article 15 provides that, while authority to determine access to genetic resources rests with national governments,[37] these governments should endeavor to create conditions to facilitate access to genetic resources for environmentally sound uses by other Contracting Parties.[38] Such access must be on mutually agreed upon terms,[39] and be in accordance with the principles of fair and equitable sharing of "benefits arising from the commercial and other utilization of genetic resources."[40]

Subsequent articles deal with access to and transfer of technology;[41] exchange of information, including indigenous and traditional knowledge;[42] technical and scientific cooperation, including the use of indigenous and traditional technologies;[43] and the handling of biotechnology and distribution of its benefits.[44] Provision for new and additional financial resources to be made available from developed country Parties to developing country Parties is made in Article 20, and implementation by developing country Parties of the commitments under the Convention is linked to the provision of these resources.[45]

The emphasis in these key aspects of the Convention is on the use of biological resources, the dissemination of knowledge coming from both developed and developing countries, and the equitable sharing of profits arising from such use and dissemination. Although, at first blush, indigenous peoples' ability to share in these benefits is clearly established in the Convention, it is up to each State to set the legislation, which will ensure their ability. In addition, the Convention does not leave much room for maneuvering away from narrow reliance on enhancing commercial values to further the protection of biological diversity.

The Convention, Intellectual Property, and Indigenous Peoples

The provisions outlined above reflect a belief throughout the Convention that the protection of biological diversity can best be ensured by increasing economic incentives for States and populations where the bulk of that biological diversity is found. Where biotechnology can find a use for a plant, and where some profits from the resulting product are passed back to the community that lives with or near that plant, so the argument goes, that community will have an incentive to protect the source of its newfound income. In addition, the knowledge on the part of locals and governments that applications can be derived from still-unknown natural resources gives added force to calls for protection of as yet uncounted components of biological diversity. And, since the destruction of one part of an ecosystem will have unforeseen impacts on other parts of that ecosystem, this approach should ensure the protection of whole ecosystems.

Since indigenous peoples have deep experience and knowledge about human uses of plants, that knowledge will, initially at least, play a vital role in attempts to develop biotechnology. This knowledge must, therefore, be rewarded to fulfill the promise of economic incentives. Article 8(j) provides the main source of protection for indigenous peoples from exploitation:

> Subject to its national legislation [each Contracting Party shall, as far as possible and appropriate], respect, preserve and maintain knowledge, innovations and practices of indigenous and local communities embodying traditional lifestyles relevant for the conservation and sustainable use of biological diversity and promote their wider application with the approval and involvement of the holders of such knowledge, innovations and practices and encourage the equitable sharing of the benefits arising from the utilization of such knowledge, innovations and practices.[46]

The article does at least recognize the need for the equitable sharing of any and all benefits that technological developments may bring when based on traditional knowledge, innovations, and practices. The reliance on the State, however, to ensure respect for traditional knowledge, has been criticized by IAIP.[47] Also taken to task by IAIP is the position of Article 8(j) that emphasizes in situ conservation, given that many indigenous peoples are as concerned about the State using its coercive powers to remove them from an area to be preserved as a nature reserve as they are about the State removing them from their land for the purposes of resource exploitation.[48] Article 15 vests the right to determine access to genetic resources in the State, and only the prior informed consent of the Contracting Party is expressly required. Indigenous peoples have good cause to fear the integrity of the State in which they reside, since examples of government exploitation of resources that damages indigenous peoples abound.[49] With history as a guide, indigenous peoples' calls for rights at the international level are all about autonomy and protection from the nation-state. In the absence of a strong review process to which indigenous peoples have access, reliance on the State for just compensation of the use of traditional knowledge may do little to strengthen indigenous peoples' international legal rights.

Even the most well-intentioned government will face difficulties in implementing the Convention's requirements. One means of ensuring that benefit sharing will occur and that the economic incentives will work is to vest property rights in the original owners of the knowledge, which leads to biotechnological discoveries. This vestment would take the form of intellectual property rights. Yet how such an approach might work for indigenous knowledge is far from clear. The granting of patents, the most likely form of intellectual property right to be granted in this context, generally requires four criteria to be fulfilled: that the process or product be an invention, that it be new, that it involve an inventive step, and that it have industrial applicability, in other words, be useful.[50] These requirements rarely fit either traditional use or knowledge of indigenous peoples.[51] Indeed, the requirements of a patent are far more likely to correspond with the product of biotechnology, and since patents provide exclusive monopoly rights, indigenous peoples can then be left both without benefit from the original source of the biotechnology and without the right to use the plant in the manner in which it has always been used.[52] The notion that such technologies must be shared as specified in Article 16 of the Convention is, for Northern corporations, highly contentious, and largely explains the failure of the United States to ratify the Convention on Biological Diversity. IAIP is concerned that Article 17(2) of the Convention, "which promotes 'exchange of results of technical, scientific and socioeconomic research, as well as information on training and surveyed programmes, specialized knowledge, indigenous and traditional knowledge' could be interpreted as providing open access to indigenous knowledge which does not receive the same protection as either states or large companies."[53]

The solution for IAIP is to call for strengthened protection of their knowledge, perhaps through a sui generis system of intellectual property rights, and to ensure control over the development and manipulation of this knowledge.[54] However, this approach to the protection of biological diversity is extremely problematic. The sole reliance on economic incentives to justify the protection of biological diversity suffers from a failure to recognize other values, including the other values listed in the first paragraph of the Preamble. This overreliance threatens to override these other values. Where a newly valuable plant can be commercially cultivated, perhaps to the destruction of a whole ecosystem, there is little to ensure that the economic incentives will not encourage a deadening monoculture. The emphasis on biotechnology and economic incentives represents a modification of both traditional knowledge and of species and their diversity. Such modification leaves them subject to the vagaries of the global economy, with no assurance that they will remain sufficiently highly valued to ensure their protection, especially alongside a newly lucrative crop.

Nor is the strengthening of intellectual property rights a problem-free solution for the protection of indigenous peoples. Where indigenous peoples are induced into a cash economy, their reliance on that cash economy has nearly always had a detrimental effect on their traditional lifestyle and their social cohesion. As such groups become more dependent on cash to feed and clothe themselves, their survival becomes dependent on the marketability of their resources, a marketability subject to geographical and political tempests beyond their control. The granting of property rights in aspects of individual species is also directly contrary to the collective and holistic approach to the environment, which originally gave rise to the indigenous peoples' sustainable coexistence with the land.

Where indigenous peoples live in a manner that depends on the integrity of whole ecosystems, such problems do not arise since there are other values that ensure that economic values do not become singularly decisive. Thus, ensuring that individual species remain outside of the market can benefit both indigenous peoples and conservation. Yet, the difficulties for indigenous people to remain outside of a cash economy may lead to tensions between the two goals. The root of these tensions will become evident in the discussion that follows.

Defining Indigenous Peoples—Traditions vs Autonomy

The level of protection of traditional knowledge is not the only aspect of the Convention on Biological Diversity and Article 8(j), which is contentious for indigenous peoples. In referring to "indigenous and local communities," the Convention ignores the generally accepted term "indigenous peoples."[55] This is more than merely a semantic oversight, however. Since "indigenous peoples" does not enjoy a uniformly agreed-upon definition, it is equally not automatically restricted by territorial or traditional continuity. The use of the term "indigenous peoples" in ILO Convention 169 reflected an important shift from the term "populations" in ILO Convention 107, agreed in 1957, and was significant enough to warrant a disclaimer in Article 1.[56] In addition, the scope of the ILO Convention, including both indigenous peoples and tribal peoples, ensures that the Convention applies in all regions of the world.[57] The Biodiversity Convention fails to incorporate the notion of tribal peoples, even as it adds local communities, communities that may well have no connection whatever with the land in the way that indigenous peoples are generally understood to have. Of equal concern to both conservationists and indigenous groups alike is the fact that these local communities can be people with an economic interest in extractive industries, having moved there in search of work. Without the indigenous tie to land, culture, and community, there will be far less pull on them to avoid irrevocably destroying the land and its resources.

The question of definition is, therefore, extremely important in considering the connection between environmental protection and indigenous peoples. International instruments do not agree on a definition of indigenous peoples, and the United Nations Draft Declaration leaves the issue unmentioned.[58] Yet many of those seeking to bring the interests of indigenous peoples and those of conservationists closer together speak of indigenous peoples in a manner that often reads like a de facto definition: "Often called the guardians or caretakers of the earth, indigenous people share a profound attachment to and stewardship of their environment, which encompasses many of the world's most valuable and vulnerable ecosystems. . . . In order to survive for millennia on these fragile environments, native people have developed a holistic knowledge of their land and resources that many contemporary societies lack. Where most of humankind tends to seek dominion over the natural world, the approach of indigenous people is the very essence of sustainable development."[59] Statements such as these hide as much as they reveal. For indigenous peoples, the view that they have traditionally maintained a spiritual, communitarian, and holistic relationship with the land and environment is not contested. What is contested, however, is the notion that that relationship should be fixed to the past and not allowed to change, adapt, or adjust to new circumstances. That aspect of the Biodiversity Convention that narrows, rather than broadens, the scope of indigenous communities by including the term "embodying traditional lifestyles" is as contentious as the recognition of local communities.[60] An important aspect of the claims of indigenous peoples to self-determination is to allow them to adapt as they wish to the changing world around them.[61] As Lawrence Rosen, a lawyer and an anthropologist, points out, "[a]s Westerners think about indigenous peoples, they may, with the best of intentions, tend to freeze such groups at a particular moment in time or to create a climate in which certain 'natural' processes will not be disrupted by outside influences."[62]

If the mutually beneficial links between indigenous people's rights and conservationists' goals are to be maintained and strengthened, the solution cannot simply be to recognize and accept this adaptation. Even without development that completely eradicates habitats and some ecosystems, modernization is generally in tension with the interests of biological diversity protection. In some areas, the failure to adhere to traditional taboos on the killing of certain animals and the use of modern weapons is resulting in scientists finding empty forests and the imminent threat of extinction of several species.[63] The pressures on indigenous peoples from new people attracted by logging, mining, or plantations, as well as the opening up of forests by logging roads, is resulting in these peoples hunting to feed themselves, either directly or through sale at local markets.[64] The conservationists' links with indigenous peoples are based on the strong assumption that indigenous peoples, if left unmolested by the global economy and by national priorities emphasizing development, will continue to maintain a sustainable and time-honored relationship with the land.[65] Yet, although the conservation movement is slow to pick up the cues, this ideal is today more myth than reality.[66]

Is it possible, then, to redefine the concept of indigenous peoples so that it will be more frequently compatible with conservation goals? This would require the phrase to be limited to those who remain untouched by modern society. There are several reasons why attempting to define away the problem in this way, using the concept of "indigenous peoples," is not the solution. First, such an attempt would result in a top-down, patronizing definition of indigenous peoples, which ignores the importance of self-definition within all indigenous claims for self-determination.[67] Second, defining the term narrowly has the effect of penalizing groups, which have already been decimated by both coercive and noncoercive assimilationist policies. Third, a narrow definition of indigenous peoples as those peoples who retain their traditions without alteration would have the result of preventing any level of assimilation in the future, even where such assimilation would ensure the survival of the group as a whole, or benefit a significant number of individuals in the group.[68]

Yet this problem of definition need not stop us in our tracks. Rather than attempting to find a unified approach to indigenous peoples,[69] or a single, strict definition, we might follow a more contextual approach. This approach would rely on the circumstances to determine the interests to be taken into account in a given situation. A broad application of the term "indigenous people" need not preclude some restrictions being placed on the activities of those indigenous people. How such restrictions might be made palatable will form the basis of the following discussion. This approach allows for a dialogue between the two interests, without fixed and limited definitions alienating one party or the other.[70]

Sovereignty and Self-Determination

The difficulty of ensuring that a contextual approach would not result in permission to destroy the environment is one that may come down to a question of rights and obligations in the international arena. The demands for indigenous rights are often framed as demands for self-determination. The existence of a right to self-determination in international law is not uncontested. Even for those who accept such a right exists, there is no clear agreement on what it might include, with one of the more contentious debates centering around the problem of whether a right to self-determination incorporates a right to secession from the original State. However, a right to secession is not demanded by indigenous peoples, and their narrower claims to the right to pursue their own economic, social, and cultural development are therefore less contentious than the phrase "self-determination" might otherwise imply.[71] In international law, as we have seen, the claim to State sovereignty over natural resources is prominent. The claims of indigenous peoples to self-determination, which incorporates a right to make decisions about development, has much in common with these attributes of sovereignty.

We have already seen that the claim of State sovereignty over natural resources is prominent in the Convention on Biological Diversity, which echoes international law. This sovereignty is exercised not only regarding the protection of biological diversity, but also with regard to the rights of indigenous peoples. As IAIP says, the reliance on the State to ensure that indigenous peoples benefit equitably from the use of resources does not foster high optimism among most indigenous peoples,[72] and for good reason. Indeed, indigenous peoples are usually defined by their separation from the rest of the population of the country in whose borders they find themselves. They are not merely populations of a different region, but defined by themselves as *different peoples,* indigenous and tribal peoples.[73] Relying on the jurisdiction of the State too often contradicts this very distinction. More practically, indigenous peoples are almost not represented at all in the governance of their States.

All too often the boundaries of an indigenous people and ecological boundaries do not conform to State boundaries; yet both suffer at the hands of international law's jurisdictional boundaries. Article 3 of the Convention does little more than reassert the accepted principle that a State has sovereignty over its natural resources.[74] Obligations not to destroy the natural world abound, but are not applicable between States unless damage is caused to the biodiversity of *another* State. There is no provision for compensation and responsibility to other States for damage to biological diversity in the Convention, only an exhortation for future cooperation.[75] That the parties rejected the concept of "common heritage" in favor of "common concern" well illustrates this failure. Nevertheless, complete rejection of sovereignty and a strengthening of international obligations enforceable at the international level alone will not ensure protection where the needs of local communities are ignored or not represented.[76] Where indigenous peoples are concerned, a recognition of autonomy may, as we have seen, enhance the possibilities for protection.

Yet the interpretation of sovereignty as entailing absolute rights over natural resources, which rights the indigenous peoples' claims to self-determination reject, often seem to reappear in those very claims to self-determination. Article 30 of the United Nations Draft Declaration on the Rights of Indigenous Peoples is indicative of this approach: "Indigenous peoples have the right to determine and develop priorities and strategies for the development or use of their lands, territories and other resources, including the right to require that States obtain their free and informed consent prior to the approval of any project affecting their lands, territories and other resources, particularly in connection with the development, utilization or exploitation of mineral, water or other resources . . ."[77] The article reflects an underlying presumption that if any destructive development is done, it will be on the initiative of the State. However, the article reserves indigenous peoples' right to develop resources in any manner they choose. There is no guarantee that this development will be ecologically sound, which is less likely once indigenous peoples have been socially fractured by outside forces. Even the most ardent believers in the harmony between indigenous peoples and the protection of biological diversity implicitly recognize that the same principles do not apply where indigenous peoples are living in a desperate state of reliance on a cash economy without adequate access to that cash.[78] The incentive of jobs and of development over which the indigenous people themselves have control is understandably alluring.

Yet, to some extent, this problem is also one of definition, more easily resolved than the search for a definition of indigenous peoples. Rather than attempt to limit the granting of rights to self-definition and self-determination, the better solution would be to question the absolute nature of sovereignty in the same manner that both indigenous peoples and conservationists have been questioning it in recent decades.

If the concept of sovereignty is limited to accept only those practices that do not irrevocably degrade ecosystems, then conservationists can have no qualms about supporting the rights of indigenous peoples to share in those attributes of sovereignty that are echoed in claims to self-determination. A sound relationship between the two could well see a reawakening of interest in traditional activities that are genuinely sustainable within a rich natural environment, and in this renewed interest, a restoration of the group pride that is now so often lacking in the remaining individuals of decimated tribes and indigenous peoples.

For indigenous peoples who balk at such limits on the rights that come with self-determination, there are both pragmatic and theoretical legal responses. The international community does not allow the export of the psychedelic yage vine from the Amazon River Basin, nor of psilocybin mushrooms from the high valleys of Ecuador. Human rights conventions are applied to indigenous peoples and compliance with the obligations of such conventions is expected. In such cases the rights of individuals and the rights of the indigenous group must be both respected and carefully balanced. The result will be a discourse by which both indigenous practices and human rights norms will be affected.

A similar process can occur with regard to the protection of species and ecosystems, ensuring that neither indigenous peoples nor biological diversity is irrevocably destroyed. As general exhortations to protect biological diversity are translated into concrete obligations with local application, this very translation will be influenced by and will influence the activities of indigenous peoples, facilitating a delicate exercise of ensuring compatibility.

More importantly, and equally pragmatic, development paths that result in the destruction of biological diversity will, either immediately or over time, also result in the degradation of the very land over which indigenous peoples claim rights as part of their claims for self-determination. Destruction of this land and the environment on which their existence as an indigenous people depends is not in the long-term interests of indigenous and tribal peoples. Compensation should certainly be available for the costs involved in protecting the environment, but extractive uses of biological diversity and the modification of its components should not provide the source of such compensation, since these uses threaten the very people they purport to help.

The theoretical argument is simply this: where rights are claimed, obligations must follow. First, for every indigenous people that chooses to develop land and cut down a forest, another indigenous people is seeking to maintain its traditional life within that very forest. Encroachment, piecemeal as it may be, harms those self-sustaining communities that wish to remain distinct and separate from the market economy of their State. Land is not a thing inherently divided into owned plots, and indigenous peoples tend toward a communitarian approach to ownership at odds with such division.[79] Land is, rather, a continuous and contiguous whole. Thus, the rights of indigenous peoples must inevitably be limited by the very holistic view of the environment they so often recognize.

Second, where rights are recognized and enforced at an international level, the indigenous peoples assume obligations to live within the legal boundaries of that international sphere. The rights attached to sovereignty are not as unqualified as legal instruments or declarations by States often suggest. As concrete obligations to protect species and habitats are developed to achieve the ultimate goal of protecting biological diversity, these obligations will be applicable to States without their sovereignty being undermined. Such obligations are applicable to the activities of States, individuals, and groups. It follows that they must also be applicable to the activities of indigenous peoples.

Conclusion

We have seen that some of the potential areas of conflict between indigenous peoples and conservationists who seek the protection of biological diversity cut to the very heart of the aims of both groups. For indigenous peoples, the call for rights has arisen in the context of centuries-long oppression and deterioration. Their newfound voice is, much like the newly independent States of the 1960s, being raised in search of autonomy over their future. And, since so much of this oppression is linked to the destruction of land and natural treasure, the survival of both are clearly inextricably linked.

Yet this very history of oppression has disrupted traditions and relationships with the land, even as these relationships form the basis of the conservationists' reliance on indigenous peoples to ensure protection of biological diversity. The result is that projects to economize biodiversity as a means of protecting it may quickly succumb to the pressures of markets, which have so often led to outright obliteration, far removed from any concept of sustainable use. As we saw in the second section, while intellectual property rights may be seen as a way for indigenous peoples to secure more autonomy and compensation for exploitation, they are by no means an assurance of success in protecting biological diversity, giving rise to the first of the three tensions discussed here that arise from efforts to link the rights of indigenous peoples to calls for the protection of biological diversity.

The second tension, discussed in the third section, becomes apparent in any attempt to define away the first tension. To seek to limit the concept of indigenous peoples to those who remain untarnished by the industrialized world is both offensive and naive. Yet failure to limit the rights that indigenous peoples are seeking could result in the choice of development paths that are destructive of species and only hasten the extinction of age-honored cultures, as well as of species. Thus, the proposal here is that the granting of rights themselves not be restricted to particular groups. This gives rise to a third tension, discussed in the fourth part, which can arise when the scope of rights is limited in order to ensure the protection of biological diversity. Here, the similarities between demands for self-determination and the rights pertaining to State sovereignty give rise both to the problem and to the possible solution.

Rights are never absolute. Clearly, where traditional practices are undisturbed, there need be no interference, but where adaptation to the modern world is pursued, some limits must be placed on activities that otherwise threaten species and ecosystems. The common ground that indigenous peoples and species must share can survive only if the protection of biological diversity is a central focus of the choices indigenous peoples make in the exercise of their rights.

NOTES

1. International Alliance of the Indigenous/Tribal Peoples of the Tropical Forests (IAIP), *The Biodiversity Convention—The Concerns of Indigenous Peoples*

(hereinafter IAIP, *The Biodiversity Convention)* 11 (visited 10 October 1999) http://www.gn.apc.org/iaip/IFB/BiodiversityConvention-ip1.htm

2. Worldwide Fund for Nature (WWF), Principle 21, *Statement of Principles: Indigenous Peoples and Conservation,* 1996 (visited 10 October 1999). http://www.panda.org/resources/publications/sustainability/indigenous/principles.html

3. See, for example, Nancy Seufert-Barr, *International Year for the World's Indigenous People, 1993: Seeking a New Partnership,* UN Chron. 30, June 1993, at 40.

4. The United Nations is increasingly addressing the rights of indigenous peoples. The General Assembly proclaimed 1993 the International Year for the World's Indigenous People, and it subsequently launched the International Decade of the World's Indigenous People, 1995–2005. In 1993, the Working Group on Indigenous Populations, first established in 1982, completed the draft of United Nations, Document E/CN.4/Sub.2/1993/29, *Declaration on the Rights of Indigenous Peoples.* See Julian Burger, "Indigenous Peoples and the United Nations," in Cynthia Price Cohen, ed., *The Human Rights of Indigenous Peoples* 3 (1998). The International Labor Organization replaced its assimilationist ILO Convention 107 of 1957 with a new convention in 1989, ILO Convention 169. See *Convention 107 Concerning the Protection and Integration of Indigenous and Other Tribal and Semi-Tribal Populations in Independent Countries* (hereinafter ILO Convention 107) 328 UNTS 247, 26 June 1957; *Convention 169 Concerning Indigenous and Tribal Groups in Independent Countries* (hereinafter ILO Convention 169), 28 ILM 1384, 27 June 1989; Russel Lawrence Barsh, *Revision of ILO Convention 107,* 81 Am. J. Int'l L. 756 (1987); Lee Swepston, *The ILO Indigenous and Tribal Peoples Convention (No. 169),* in The Human Rights of Indigenous Peoples, 17. See generally, Russel Lawrence Barsh, *Indigenous Peoples: An Emerging Object of International Law,* 80 Am. J. Int'l L. 369 (1986); S. James Anaya, Indigenous Peoples in International Law (1996). The increasing international attention being paid to the protection of biological diversity is largely reflected by the adoption of the Convention on Biological Diversity, infra note 5, and the proportion of funding that the global environment facility allocates for programs for biodiversity protection. See infra note 45.

5. Convention on Biological Diversity, 5 June 1992, 31 ILM 818 (1992; hereinafter Biodiversity Convention).

6. Ibid., Preamble, paragraph 12, Article 8(j), Article 17(2), and Article 18(4). The Convention's reference to "indigenous and local communities," as opposed to "indigenous peoples," is discussed below.

7. See, for example, 27 UST 1087, 993 UNTS 243, *The Convention on International Trade in Endangered Species of Wild Fauna and Flora,* 3 March 1979; 19 ILM 15, Convention on the Conservation Migratory Species of Wild Animals, 23 June 1979 (1980). See generally P. van Heijnsbergen, *International Legal Protection of Wild Fauna and Flora* (1997). Simon Lyster, *International Wildlife Law: An Analysis of International Treaties Concerned with the Conservation of Wildlife* (1985).

8. See, for example, Convention on Wetlands of International Importance especially as Waterfowl Habitat, 2 February 1971, 996 UNTS 245.

9. See *Summary of the Fourth Meeting of the Conference of the Parties to the Convention on Biological Diversity,* 4–15 May 1998, 9(96) Earth Negotiations Bulletin, 18 May 1998, at 13, which describes the Convention as an "umbrella" Convention.

10. Lyle Glowka et al, "A Guide to the Convention on Biological Diversity" 9, IUCN Environmental Law and Policy Paper 30, 1994 (hereinafter Guide to the Convention).

11. Biodiversity Convention, supra note 5, Preamble, para 1.

12. Intrinsic value should not be confused with inherent value. Intrinsic value is, like instrumental values, an anthropocentric value in that it relies on an external value, as distinct from inherent value, which refers to the value that entities have in and of themselves. Michael Bowman, "The Nature, Development and Philosophical Foundations of the Biodiversity Concept in International Law," in Michael Bowman and Catherine Redgwell, eds., *International Law and the Conservation of Biological Diversity* 5, 21 (1995, hereinafter *International Law and the Conservation of Biological Diversity*). Inherent value has not yet been addressed by any international legal instrument for the protection of species and ecosystems.

13. See Lawrence H. Tribe, *Ways Not to Think About Plastic Trees: New Foundations for Environmental Law,* 83 Yale L.J. 1315, 1329, 1330–31 (1974). This paradox has been most forcefully argued in the context of placing economic values on the environment or parts of the environment as a means of ensuring protection: "If a price can be put on something, that something can be devalued, sold, and discarded." Edward O. Wilson, *The Diversity of Life* 348 (1992). See also Mark Sagoff, *The Economy of the Earth: Philosophy, Law and the Environment* 97 (1988), and John Foster, *Introduction: Environmental Value and the Scope of Economics,* in Valuing Nature?: Ethics, Economics, and the Environment 1, 11 (1997).

14. See Michael Bowman and Catherine Redgwell, introduction to *International Law and the Conservation of Biological Diversity,* supra note 12, at 1, 4.

15. Biodiversity Convention, supra note 5, Preamble, para 4. See also para 5, which reaffirms that "[s]tates are responsible for conserving their biological diversity and for using their biological resources in a sustainable manner." While this adds a note of obligation to the rights expressed in the previous paragraph, it does not diminish the force of recognizing that each State retains sovereign rights over those resources in their use. See also Article 4, which clarifies the jurisdictional scope of the Convention.

16. Biodiversity Convention, supra note 5, Article 3.

17. See Cyril De Klemm, *Biological Diversity Conservation and the Law* 2 (1993), which queries whether a State can have sovereignty over a species, given that a species is more than the sum of its individual parts.

18. See, for example, the reliance on national legislation to implement the provisions of the Convention. Almost all of the substantive provisions begin with disclaimers, such as the phrases "in accordance with (each Contracting Party's) particular conditions and capabilities" and "as far as possible and appropriate." Biodiversity Convention, supra note 5, Articles 5, 8, 9, 10, 11.

19. Ibid., Article 15(1).

20. For conservation as a common concern of humankind, see ibid., Preamble, para 3 *[emphasis added]*. Françoise Burhenne-Guilmin and Susan Casey-Lefkowitz, *The Convention on Biological Diversity: A Hard Won Global Achievement,* 3 Y.B. Int'l Envtl. L. 43, 47 (1992), observe that the proposition that biological diversity should be considered the common heritage of mankind was rejected early since most components of biological diversity are situated in areas under national jurisdiction.

21. See United Nations, 21 ILM 1261, Articles 136 and 137, Convention on the Law of the Sea, 10 December 1982 (UNCLOS). Patricia W. Birnie and Alan E. Boyle, *International Law and the Environment* 120 (1992). The only other binding international legal instrument referring to the common heritage is the Moon Convention of 1979. While the reference to "common heritage" was contentious in the negotiations for UNCLOS, it is easy to see a common theme in both UNCLOS and the Moon Convention in that they both deal with areas outside the national jurisdiction of any one State. States will undoubtedly be more open to giving up claims on territory or resources over which they previously exercised no control, the global commons, than those over which they have a long history of jurisdictional authority. See Jacob Werksman, *Consolidating Governance of the Global Commons: Insights from the Global Environment Facility,* 6 Y.B. Int'l Envtl. L. 27, 43 (1995).

22. See United Nations, General Assembly, Seventh Session, Resolution 626, Supplement 20, Document A/2361, 1952, at 106.

23. See United Nations, General Assembly, Seventeenth Session, Resolution 1803, Supplement 17, Document A/5217, 1962, which was unanimously adopted. See also United Nations, General Assembly, Sixth Special Session, Resolution 3201, Supplement 1, Document A/9559, 1974, and United Nations, General Assembly, Sixth Special Session, Resolution 3203, Supplement 1, Document A/9559, 1974. These two later resolutions were not adopted unanimously.

24. United Nations, T.S., 999, 171, Article 1(2), International Covenant on Civil and Political Rights, 16 December 1976.

25. United Nations, T.S., 993, 3, Article 1(2), International Covenant on Economic, Social and Cultural Rights, 16 December 1976.

26. See United Nations, Principle 21, 11 ILM 1416, *Declaration of the United Nations Conference on the Human Environment* (hereinafter Stockholm Declaration), 16 June 1972.

27. See Birnie and Boyle, 1992, supra note 21, at 90.

28. See United Nations, 31 ILM 874, Principle 2, Conference on Environment and Development: Rio Declaration on Environment and Development, 14 June 1992. Principle 2 of the Rio Declaration contains the word "development," an addition to the text of Principle 21 of the Stockholm Declaration, supra note 26.

29. Biodiversity Convention, supra note 5, Preamble, para 12.

30. Ibid., Article 1. The division between sustainable use and conservation has been criticized by some as ignoring the scientific view that conservation often incorporates sustainable use. However, for the purposes of a legal instrument, the distinction allows for more precision in defining the times when sustainable use

will not be appropriate, and emphasizing that use must be sustainable. The advantage of a distinction is reflected in Article 8 on in situ conservation, which refers in certain parts only to conservation (see Article 8(a)). Conservation is deliberately not defined in the Convention, while sustainable use is defined only very broadly (see Article 2). Alan E. Boyle, "The Rio Convention on Biological Diversity," in *International Law and the Conservation of Biological Diversity,* supra note 12, at 33, 38.

31. See Guide to the Convention, supra note 10, at 15, which refers to this purpose of the Convention as "the heart of the political agreement upon which the Convention is founded."

32. Biodiversity Convention, supra note 5, Preamble, para 14.

33. Ibid., Article 2. "Ecosystem" is defined to mean "a dynamic complex of plant, animal and micro-organism communities and their non-living environment interacting as a functional unit."

34. Ibid., Article 8(a).

35. Ibid., Article 2. "Genetic material" is defined to mean "any material of plant, animal, microbial or other origin containing functional units of heredity."

36. Ibid., Article 11.

37. Ibid., Article 15(1).

38. Ibid., Article 15(2).

39. Ibid., Article 15(4)(7).

40. Ibid., Article 15(7).

41. Ibid., Article 16.

42. Ibid., Article 17(2).

43. Ibid., Article 18(4)

44. Ibid., Article 19.

45. Ibid., Article 20(4). The Global Environment Facility (GEF) is the funding body for the Convention. See *Financial Resources and Mechanism,* Decision I/2, First Conference of the Parties of the Convention on Biological Diversity (1994); *Financial Resources and Mechanism,* Decision II/6, Second Conference of the Parties of the Convention on Biological Diversity (1995). See also *Additional Guidance to the Financial Mechanism,* Decision III/5, Third Conference of the Parties of the Convention on Biological Diversity (1996); *Guidelines for the Review of the Effectiveness of the Financial Mechanism,* Decision III/7, Third Conference of the Parties of the Convention on Biological Diversity (1996); *Memorandum of Understanding between the Conference of the Parties to the Convention on Biological Diversity and the Council of the Global Environment Facility,* Decision III/8, Third Conference of the Parties of the Convention on Biological Diversity (1996). As of December 1998, the cost of the GEF's programs related to biodiversity was US$848,702 million, 39.4 percent of the total cost of all GEF programs. See Global Environment Facility, *GEF Programs, Operational Report on GEF Programs,* December 1998, 2–21 (visited 11 October 1999) http://www.gefweb.org/OPREPORT/opers.htm

46. Biodiversity Convention, supra note 5, Article 8(j). Interpretation and implementation of Article 8(j) has given rise to a Workshop on Traditional Knowledge and Biological Diversity. See *Summary of the Workshop on Traditional*

Knowledge and Biological Diversity: 24–28 November 1997, 9(75) Earth Negotiations Bulletin, 1 December 1997. At the Fourth Conference of the parties, the parties established an ad hoc, open-ended intersessional working group on Article 8(j) and related provisions. *Implementation of Article 8(j) and Related Provisions,* Decision IV/9, Fourth Conference of the Parties of the Convention on Biological Diversity (1998). See *Summary of the Fourth Meeting of the Conference of the Parties to the Convention on Biological Diversity: 4–15 May 1998,* 9(96) Earth Negotiations Bulletin, 18 May 1998, at 6–8. Observers, including representatives of indigenous groups, were excluded from the negotiation of the draft text of decision IV/9. Ibid., at 7.

47. IAIP, *The Biodiversity Convention,* supra note 1, at 5.

48. Ibid., at 6. See also Benedict Kingsbury, *"Indigenous Peoples" in International Law: A Constructivist Approach to the Asian Controversy,* 92 Am. J. Int'l L. 414, 440 (1998).

49. For one example, oil development in the rain forests of the Amazonian indigenous peoples of Ecuador, particularly the Huaorani, see Adriana Fabra, "Indigenous Peoples, Environmental Degradation, and Human Rights: a Case Study," in Alan E. Boyle and Michael R. Anderson, eds., *Human Rights Approaches to Environmental Protection* 245 (1996). See also http://www.forests.org (visited 13 October 1999); this website gathers news stories concerning forests from around the world.

50. Ian Walden, "Intellectual Property Rights and Biodiversity," in *International Law and the Conservation of Biological Diversity,* supra note 12, at 171, 173.

51. See generally ibid. See also W. Lesser, *Sustainable Use of Genetic Resources under the Convention on Biological Diversity: Exploring Access and Benefit Sharing Issues* 113–135 (1997). See also Fourth Conference of the Parties of the Convention on Biological Diversity, Decision IV/9, Preamble, paras 6 and 7, *Implementation of Article 8(j) and Related Provisions,* 1998.

52. See Vandana Shiva and Radha Holla-Bhar, "Piracy by Patent: The Case of the Neem Tree," in Mander and Goldsmith, eds., *The Case against the Global Economy and for a Turn toward the Local* 146 (1996), hereinafter *The Case against the Global Economy.*

53. IAIP, *The Biodiversity Convention,* supra note 1, at 7.

54. IAIP, *Charter of the Indigenous and Tribal Peoples of Tropical Forests,* Article 44 (visited 14 October 1999) http://www.gn.apc.org/iaip/chart/char1.html#SCRL8

55. See ILO Convention 169, supra note 4. IAIP, *The Biodiversity Convention,* supra note 1, at 6.

56. "The use of the term 'peoples' in this Convention shall not be construed as having any implications as regards the rights which may attach to the term under international law." ILO Convention 169, supra note 4, Article 1(3).

57. Kingsbury, supra note 48, at 420.

58. See United Nations Draft Declaration on the Rights of Indigenous Peoples, supra note 4.

59. Nancy Seufert-Barr, *The Development Dilemma: Sustaining Resources, Improving Livelihoods,* United Nations Chron., June 1993, at 45.

60. The IAIP is concerned that the phrase might be interpreted to apply only to indigenous peoples "who are isolated, fossilised in some cultural time-warp living in a never changing present. . . . Our concern is that the term 'traditional' is being used to exclude anyone who has adapted their lifestyle to reflect the contemporary and continuing colonial situation in which we find ourselves." IAIP, *The Biodiversity Convention,* supra note 1, at 6.

61. Ibid.

62. Lawrence Rosen, *The Right to be Different: Indigenous Peoples and the Quest for a Unified Theory,* 107 Yale L. J. 227, 252 (1997). Rosen reviews Will Kymlicka, *Multicultural Citizenship: A Liberal Theory of Minority Rights* (1995) and S. James Anaya, *Indigenous Peoples in International Law* (1996). See also Kingsbury, supra note 48, at 440; John Woodliffe, "Biodiversity and Indigenous Peoples," in *International Law and the Conservation of Biological Diversity,* supra note 12, at 255, 269. Woodliffe takes up the anthropologist Darrel Posey's caution that we must avoid the patronizing myth that indigenous people "live in perfect harmony with nature and therefore should stay there and never change."

63. See John Carey, *Where Have All the Animals Gone?* Int'l Wildlife, November/December 1999, at 13. Donald G. McNeil Jr., *The Great Ape Massacre,* N.Y. Times (Sunday Magazine), 9 May 1999, at 56.

64. Ibid., at 18.

65. "In the tropical forest countries . . . large segments of the population are immediately dependent upon local biological resources. This is especially true of the forest peoples and the rural poor . . . *When traditional community structures are still intact,* these uses are *generally* sustainable" *[emphasis added].* Heffa Schücking and Patrick Anderson, "Voices Unheard and Unheeded," in Shiva et al, eds., *Biodiversity: Social and Ecological Perspectives* 13, 27 (1991; hereinafter *Biodiversity*).

66. See Carey, supra note 63, at 17.

67. Andrew Gray, "The Impact of Biodiversity Conservation on Indigenous Peoples," in *Biodiversity,* supra note 65, at 59, 73. Gray argues that top-down approaches are unacceptable and that dialogue and initiatives regarding indigenous peoples and the protection of biodiversity need to treat indigenous peoples with respect, otherwise there will be nothing to gain for either group. See also ILO Convention 169, supra note 4, Article 1(2), and Kingsbury, supra note 48, at 440–41.

68. "The appropriation by non-natives of the imagined ecological superiority of native peoples is not only historically misleading, but may also serve to justify policies that force natives to choose between specific types of economic development and maintaining their legal protections as native peoples." Rosen, supra note 62, at 255.

69. Ibid., generally.

70. "Enthusiasm for the local and the historical can undercut desirable arrangements for taking some decisions at other levels to protect other deserving interests, and for valuing innovative and hybrid forms that do not qualify as traditional." Kingsbury, supra note 48, at 436.

71. See ibid., at 439.

72. IAIP, *The Biodiversity Convention,* supra note 1, at 5.

73. IAIP dislikes the term "indigenous . . . communities" in the Biodiversity Convention precisely because it does not recognize indigenous peoples as peoples. IAIP, *The Biodiversity Convention,* supra note 1, at 6.

74. See supra notes 22 through 28, accompanying text.

75. Biodiversity Convention, supra note 5, Article 5.

76. See Richard Falk, *Environmental Protection in an Era of Globalization,* 6 Y.B. Int'l Envtl. L. 3, 10–11 (1995). Falk reconsiders his conclusions of twenty-five years ago that increased centralization would be necessary for stronger environmental protection. See generally, *The Case against the Global Economy,* supra note 52.

77. United Nations, Draft Declaration on the Rights of Indigenous Peoples, supra note 4.

78. See Schücking and Anderson, supra note 65.

79. See Rosen, supra note 62, at 251.

10

The Mayagna Indigenous Community of Awas Tingni and Its Effort to Gain Recognition of Traditional Lands

The Community's Case before the Human Rights Institutions of the Organization of American States

S. James Anaya

SINCE AT LEAST 1992 the indigenous community of Awas Tingni, Nicaragua, has been petitioning the government of that country to gain formal recognition of its traditional lands. Awas Tingni is one of numerous ethnically Mayagna, or Sumo,[1] indigenous communities in the isolated Atlantic Coast region of Nicaragua.[2] Like most of the indigenous communities of the Atlantic Coast, Awas Tingni is still today without formal government recognition of its traditional lands in the form of a land title or other official document. Nonetheless, community members demonstrate a sense of territoriality in relation to a certain area that is defined by the community's traditional land and resource tenure, and they have continued to resist incursions by outsiders into that area.

Not having been resolved by Nicaraguan government officials at the domestic level, Awas Tingni's land claim has been taken up by the human rights institutions of the Organization of American States (OAS). For the first time, the OAS Inter-American Commission on Human Rights has sided with an indigenous community in its grievance over land rights and taken the extraordinary step of submitting that grievance to the OAS Inter-American Court on Human Rights. The Inter-American Court has the authority to issue decisions that are legally binding on OAS Member States. The outcome of the case will establish an international legal precedent regarding the extent of a country's obligation to recognize and protect indigenous traditional land and resource tenure. Recognizing the importance of the case, a broad coalition of indigenous organizations and communities of Nicaragua, including communities with land claims that overlap that of Awas Tingni, have submitted an *amicus curiae* (friend of the court) brief in support of the proposition that Nicaragua generally has acted contrary to the land rights of indigenous communities and that it is obligated to put in place and execute a mechanism to demarcate and title indigenous communal lands.[3] Given the potential impact of the case beyond Nicaragua, indigenous, environmental, and human rights organizations from outside that country also have submitted or are in the process of submitting to the Court *amicus curiae* briefs.[4]

The concerns of Awas Tingni over land tenure security had intensified when transnational companies began entering the community's claimed lands, with the permission of the Nicaraguan government, to inventory the valuable tropical forest resources and plan for large-scale logging. In December of 1993 the Nicaraguan government, through its Ministry of Environment and Natural Resources (MARENA), granted a concession to the Dominican-owned company Maderas y Derivados de Nicaragua, S. A. (MADENSA) for logging on approximately 43,000 hectares of land, most of which is within the area claimed by Awas Tingni on the basis of traditional land tenure. Under pressure from the World Wildlife Fund (WWF), a major international environmental organization, the government agreed to suspend the concession until an agreement could be negotiated with the Awas Tingni community and adequate environmental controls could be established.

WWF funded and helped develop a project of the University of Iowa College of Law (the Iowa Project) to assist the community in negotiations with the government and MADENSA. The community enthusiastically accepted the offer of assistance and, with the counsel of the group of attorneys and a forestry expert assembled by the Iowa Project, proceeded to negotiate a trilateral agreement with MARENA and MADENSA for sustainable timber harvesting within the 43,000-hectare area. The agreement, which was signed in May 1994, provided for economic benefits to the community and, furthermore, committed the government to a process by which it would definitively identify and title the community's traditional lands.[5] Additionally, under the agreement the government agreed not to take any action that would prejudice or undermine the community's land claim.[6]

The government's commitment to a process of land titling in favor of Awas Tingni, however, proved illusory. Even as the government was formalizing this commitment as part of a written agreement, it was engaged in discussions with a second logging company, Sol del Caribe, S.A. (SOLCARSA), a Korean-owned firm, which was soliciting the government for a concession to log an area of 63,000 hectares of land adjacent to the MADENSA management area. By the time Awas Tingni community leaders learned of the SOLCARSA initiative in July of 1995, the government had already granted SOLCARSA an exploration license and had given preliminary approval of the concession. Through the community's Nicaraguan attorney who was contracted as part of the Iowa Project, Awas Tingni protested the SOLCARSA initiative, arguing that most of the area sought by SOLCARSA was also part of the community's traditional territory.

A period of time passed with no response by the government to the community's written protest. Awas Tingni leaders and community members became increasingly alarmed by the presence of SOLCARSA agents who were conducting an inventory of the timber resources within lands used by the community for agriculture and for subsistence hunting and gathering. When it became apparent that the government was determined to go ahead and grant SOLCARSA the concession under the assumption that the lands in question were entirely state-owned lands, the community decided to take legal action. Awas Tingni filed an action for *amparo* (emergency relief) within the Nicaraguan judicial system, alleging violations of the relevant provisions of Nicaraguan law that affirm in general terms rights of indigenous communities over traditional communal lands.[7] When that effort failed the community petitioned the OAS Inter-American Commission on Human Rights, under the complaint procedure provided in the American Convention on Human Rights, to which Nicaragua is a party.[8] In these and related legal actions the community has been represented by attorneys working under the auspices of the Iowa Project, and later also under the auspices of the Indian Law Resource Center, a United States–based organization that provides legal assistance to indigenous peoples in several countries throughout the hemisphere.

The petition to the Inter-American Commission alleged violations of the right to property, the right to cultural integrity, and other rights that are affirmed in the American Convention on Human Rights and other international instruments, and it requested that the Commission assist the community in its effort to stop the concession to SOLCARSA and to achieve secure land tenure. The full text of the petition, which is the basis for ongoing proceedings within the OAS Human Rights System, is reproduced in appendix 1.

An important component of the legal actions taken by Awas Tingni at the national and international levels is the data that have been compiled in maps and a related ethnographic study. The initial terms of reference for the WWF–funded Iowa Project included assisting Awas Tingni to compile the data to support its claim to traditional lands, with the expectation that this data would be the basis of discussions with the government that in turn would lead to titling or other official recognition of Awas Tingni lands. The data instead became the basis of contentious legal proceedings that have reached the highest level of adjudication within the Inter-American Human Rights System.

In its early phases the Iowa Project established a cooperative relationship with Harvard's Weatherhead Center for International Affairs in order to assist Awas Tingni to document the historical, ethnographic, and geographic data relevant to its land claim. Theodore Macdonald, an anthropologist from Harvard's Weatherhead Center, spent several weeks at the community conducting research in collaboration with a specially selected team of community members. Prior to Dr. Macdonald's arrival at the community or the establishment of the Iowa Project, community leaders had sketched a map of the Awas Tingni traditional lands without any outside assistance. With this sketched map as an initial point of reference, Dr. Macdonald worked with the community researchers to document the Awas Tingni's historical and continuing land tenure patterns. Using a simple handheld electronic device, a Magellan Geographical Positioning System (GPS), the community researchers located relevant geographic coordinates, which were to be the basis for the production of a map illustrating Awas Tingni historical land tenure.[9]

At the time the Awas Tingni community discovered the plans for the SOLCARSA concession in mid-1995, the research just described was ongoing. After Awas Tingni filed its complaint to the Inter-American Commission on Human Rights in October of 1995, a preliminary ethnographic report and accompanying map in support of the community's land claim was completed. The map was generated by computer using the data compiled by the community researchers and Dr. Macdonald. Awas Tingni subsequently amended the map to include a line designating the land, within the community's historical use area, that the community proposed to be recognized by the government as Awas Tingni communal land.

The preliminary report and map were submitted to the Inter-American Commission and to relevant Nicaraguan government agencies, including MARENA and the regional governing body of the North Atlantic Autonomous Region.[10] Along with the submission of the preliminary report and map, Awas Tingni in early 1996 again raised to the government its concern over the SOLCARSA concession and proposed that consideration of the concession be suspended pending resolution of the community's land claim or an agreement with the community.[11]

Ignoring the community's submissions and proposal, the government nonetheless proceeded with its plans and formally granted the concession to SOLCARSA on 13 March 1996. In response to the mounting threat of logging under the SOLCARSA concession against the wishes of the Awas Tingni community, community leaders developed yet another map. This map, which was sketched by hand, details the land and resource tenure patterns of the community within the concession area, and it also was submitted to the Inter-American Commission on Human Rights and relevant government agencies. In defending itself before the Inter-American Commission, the Nicaraguan government maintained the position that the amount of land claimed by Awas Tingni was excessive, although the government never contested the data presented by the community, illustrated by maps, of historical and continuing land tenure. Faced with this data at a hearing before the Inter-American Commission at its headquarters in Washington, D.C., in October 1997, representatives of the Nicaraguan government conceded that at least part of the land within the SOLCARSA concession area was Awas Tingni communal land to which the community was legally entitled.

While the case was proceeding at the international level before the Inter-American Commission on Human Rights, the SOLCARSA concession became the subject of an additional legal proceeding within the Nicaraguan judicial system. At the request of the Awas Tingni community, and with the assistance of the Iowa Project/Indian Law Resource Center attorneys, two members of the Regional Council of the North Atlantic Autonomous Region filed with the Nicaraguan Supreme Court another *amparo* action, again demanding that SOLCARSA's concession be revoked. Remarkably, this *amparo* action was successful. The Nicaraguan Supreme Court declared the SOLCARSA concession unconstitutional in February 1997, on the ground that the Regional Council had not approved the concession as required by Article 181 of the Political Constitution of Nicaragua. More than a year later, and after yet another legal action that demanded execution of the Supreme Court's February 1997 ruling, the government agency MARENA notified SOLCARSA that its concession had been made null.

The nullification of the SOLCARSA concession was a notable success for the Awas Tingni community and for other indigenous communities and sectors of Nicaraguan civil society who opposed the concession. Still, the underlying land tenure issue remained unresolved. Awas Tingni, like the majority of other indigenous communities of the Atlantic coast, continued to lack official demarcation of its traditional territory or other official, specific recognition of traditional land and resource tenure.

A few weeks after MARENA's grudging nullification of the SOLCARSA concession, the Inter-American Commission on Human Rights decided to submit the case to the OAS Inter-American Court of Human Rights for its review. Although the SOLCARSA concession had been canceled, the Inter-American Commission was dissatisfied with the continued lack of action by the Nicaraguan government to demarcate and otherwise secure Awas Tingni traditional lands.

In its complaint of June 1998 to the Inter-American Court, the Inter-American Commission charged Nicaragua with essentially the same violations of international human rights law that were articulated by Awas Tingni in its initial petition to the Commission, which is reproduced in appendix 1. Relying on the ethnographic research and mapping described above, the Inter-American Commission requested that the Inter-American Court order Nicaragua to provide monetary compensation to Awas Tingni for the infringement of its territorial rights and to establish and implement a procedure that will result in the prompt demarcation and specific recognition of Awas Tingni communal lands, in accordance with the community's traditional land tenure patterns.

Nicaragua attempted to have the case dismissed on the grounds that Awas Tingni had failed to exhaust all available domestic remedies. On 1 February 2000, the Inter-American Court unanimously ruled against Nicaragua's preliminary objections and held the case admissible.[12] A hearing and ruling on the merits of the case are expected some time this year.

This case involves an effort by an indigenous community to defend and transmit to future generations its traditional land tenure system in relation to a specific territory. Documentation and mapping of traditional land tenure are not ends in themselves, but are tools in aid of a strategy to achieve security for that land tenure. The strategy is grounded on the active demand that States recognize and take the steps necessary to secure indigenous lands, and that they do so in accordance with an assessment of traditional land tenure patterns and not on the basis of broad government discretion. The community of Awas Tingni has made such a demand against Nicaragua, and that demand, having been validated by the Inter-American Commission on Human Rights, is now before the Inter-American Court of Human Rights, one of the world's few international judicial organs with the authority to render decisions that are binding upon States. A ruling by the Inter-American Court on the merits of the Awas Tingni case will, one way or another, affect government perceptions throughout the Hemisphere, and probably beyond, about the strength of future similar demands.

NOTES

1. The people of Awas Tingni prefer to call themselves *Mayagna* as opposed to *Sumo,* a commonly used designation. They regard the latter term as one imposed by outsiders.

2. The Atlantic Coast region of Nicaragua is generally understood to include roughly the eastern third of the country. The geographically isolated region has a unique history and cultural milieu, being home to the Miskito, Mayagna (Sumo), and Rama Indians and to a substantial Black Creole population. For a demography and history of the Atlantic Coast region, see Carlos M. Vilas, *Del colonialismo a la autonomía: modernización capitalista y revolución social en la costa atlántica* (Managua: Editorial Nueva Nicaragua, 1990), 19–127.

3. See Memorial de Amicus Curiae, Presentado por Comunidades, Organizaciones, y Representantes Indígenas de Nicaragua, en el Caso de la Comunidad Mayagna (Sumo) de Awas Tingni, CIDH—Caso No. 11.555 (available at http://www.indianlaw.org/at_amicus_curiae_esp.html). Also included as appendix 1 of this publication.

4. See Amicus Curiae, presented by the International Human Rights Law Group and the Center for International Environmental Law in the Case of the Mayagna Community of Awas Tingni; Case 11.555 is available at http://www.cedha.org.ar/ in documents on line.

5. See Convenio de Aprovechamiento Forestal entre la Comunidad de Awas Tingni; Maderas y Derivados de Nicaragua, S.A.; y el Ministerio del Ambiente y los Recursos Naturales, 15 de mayo de 1994. The process leading to this agreement and the agreement's content are summarized in S. James Anaya and S. Todd Crider, *Indigenous Peoples, The Environment, and Commercial Forestry in Developing Countries: The Case of Awas Tingni, Nicaragua,* Human Rights Quarterly, 18 (2), May 1996, 345.

6. Article 3.2 of the agreement states: "MARENA promises to facilitate the definition of the communal lands and not to undermine the territorial aspirations

of the Community . . . Such definition of lands should be carried out according to the historical rights of the Community and within the relevant legal framework" (translation from Spanish).

7. The relevant provisions of the Political Constitution of Nicaragua and the Statute of Autonomy for the Atlantic Coast Regions of Nicaragua are discussed in Awas Tingni's Petition to the Inter-American Commission on Human Rights (see appendix 1).

8. For a discussion of this complaint procedure and its relevance to indigenous peoples, see S. James Anaya, *Indigenous Peoples in International Law* (New York and Oxford: Oxford University Press, 1996), 166–70 and notes.

9. The ethnographic research and mapping in relation to Awas Tingni's land claim is described in S. James Anaya and Theodore Macdonald, *Demarcating Indigenous Territories in Nicaragua: The Case of Awas Tingni,* Cultural Survival Quarterly, 19 (3), Fall 1995, 69, 72–73; *Territorio Awas Tingni,* Cultural Survival Quarterly, 20 (1), Spring 1996, 73.

10. The Atlantic Coast of Nicaragua is divided into two geopolitical regions: the North Atlantic Autonomous Region and the South Atlantic Autonomous Region.

11. The community submitted written proposals for a memorandum of understanding to the MARENA and to the Ministry of Foreign Relations, which is in charge of representing the government in the proceedings before the OAS institutions. The community submitted a separate proposal, with the ethnographic study and maps, to the regional council of the North Atlantic Autonomous region. In its "Solicitud de la Comunidad de Awas Tingni al Consejo Regional Autónoma Norte para el Reconocimiento y Demarcación de las Tierras Ancestrales de la Comunidad," the community asked that the council impede the granting of the concession pending resolution of the land tenure issue and, to resolve the issue, the community proposed the following procedure:

1. An evaluation of the ethnographic study presented by Awas Tingni (Annex B) and the elaboration of a supplementary study if the Council found it necessary.
2. A process of agreement on the land limits of their community lands between Awas Tingni and the neighboring communities.
3. An identification of the State lands on the area, if any exist.
4. On the basis of points 1, 2, and 3 and the relevant legal criteria, the delimitation of Awas Tingni communal lands.

12. See *Caso de al Comunidad Mayagna (Sumo) Awas Tingni, Excepciones Preliminares,* Sentence 1 February 2000, IHR Court.

Appendix 1

Inter-American Commission on Human Rights
Organization of American States

Petition

by

THE MAYAGNA INDIAN COMMUNITY OF AWAS TINGNI and JAIME CASTILLO FELIPE, on his own behalf and on behalf of the Community of Awas Tingni,

against

NICARAGUA

(Editors' note: The following is the actual Petition in its original format without editing or content variation.)

I. Introduction

1. This petition is submitted by the MAYAGNA INDIAN COMMUNITY OF AWAS TINGNI and its leader, JAIME CASTILLO FELIPE, against NICARAGUA based on Nicaragua's failure to take steps necessary to secure the land rights of Awas Tingni and other indigenous communities in Nicaragua's Atlantic Coast region. Nicaragua's acts and omissions in this regard constitute violations of the American Convention on Human Rights (the "American Convention"), the American Declaration of the Rights and Duties of Man (the "American Declaration") and other provisions of international human rights law.

2. Through its government officials, Nicaragua has allowed to emerge a pervasive condition under which the enjoyment of indigenous land rights is generally threatened. Adding to this environment of government neglect, the Nicaraguan Ministry of Environment and Natural Resources (commonly referred to by its Spanish acronym "MARENA") is about to grant to a Korean-owned company a long-term concession for timber harvesting on Awas Tingni lands in disregard of the Community's property and other rights. The government already has granted the company permission to enter the Community's lands and to undertake preliminary work toward the planned timber exploitation, and the company is con-

structing nearby a timber processing plant. Communications of protest to the responsible government officials have gone unanswered, and efforts at a judicial resolution have not been fruitful.

3. Significantly, this Petition arises in the aftermath of conditions affecting the indigenous communities of Nicaragua's Atlantic Coast that attracted the attention of this Commission in the early 1980s. In response to complaints of human rights abuses against the indigenous peoples of the Atlantic Coast, the Commission conducted an investigation which included an on-site visit and published its findings in its *Report on the Situation of a Segment of the Nicaraguan Population of Miskito Origin* (hereinafter "*Miskito Report*").[1] Among the problems identified by the Commission in its report was that of unsecured land tenure for the Miskito and other indigenous groups of the region. The Commission recommended that the government take steps to remedy this problem. However, over a decade later, the land rights of Awas Tingni and other indigenous communities remain vulnerable to violations in the persistent absence of effective government protections.

4. The Community of Awas Tingni and Mr. Castillo seek the Commission's assistance in reversing the acts and omissions of the Nicaraguan government that violate their rights and in safeguarding their rights in the future. The Commission's involvement is particularly important since, as set forth below, the government of Nicaragua appears willing to respond, if at all, only when pressure is exerted by the international community.

II. Jurisdiction

5. The Inter-American Commission on Human Rights has competence to receive and act on this petition in accordance with articles 44–51 of the American Convention, to which Nicaragua is a party, and article 19 of the Commission's Statute.

III. The Petitioners

6. THE MAYAGNA INDIAN COMMUNITY OF AWAS TINGNI (the "Community" or "Awas Tingni") is one of the "communities of the Atlantic Coast" region recognized by the Political Constitution of Nicaragua under its articles 5, 8, 11, 49, 89, 90, 91, 121, 180, and 181, and by the Statute of Autonomy of the Atlantic Coast Regions of Nicaragua, Law No. 28 of 1987. The term "Mayagna" refers to the larger indigenous ethno-linguistic group of which Awas Tingni and its members form a part.[2] The Community is organized and functions under a traditional, customary leadership structure that is common to other Mayagna communities and that is recognized by the Nicaraguan Constitution, arts. 89, 180, and the Statute of Autonomy, art. 11(4). The Community's principal village is on the Wawa River, within the municipality of Waspam, Northern Atlantic Autonomous Region, Nicaragua.

7. JAIME CASTILLO FELIPE, a citizen of Nicaragua and an indigenous Mayagna, is the "Síndico" of Awas Tingni. In accordance with longstanding tradition among the indigenous communities of the Atlantic Coast, the Síndico is Awas Tingni's principal leader. In addition to serving as the Community's Síndico, Mr. Castillo's occupations include farming and seasonal wage labor. His address is Community of Awas Tingni, Waspam, Northern Atlantic Autonomous Region, Nicaragua. In submitting this petition, Mr. Castillo acts both individually and on behalf of the Community.

8. For the purposes of this petition and all related proceedings, the legal representative of the Community and Mr. Castillo is THE UNIVERSITY OF IOWA COLLEGE OF LAW, CLINICAL LAW PROGRAMS, an institution of The University of Iowa which is chartered by the State of Iowa, located at 386 Boyd Law Building, Iowa City, Iowa 52242. See appendices 1 and 1-A hereto. The Petitioners' counsel of record, to whom all notices and correspondence should be sent, is S. JAMES ANAYA of The University of Iowa College of Law, Clinical Law Programs. Mr. Anaya, an attorney and professor of law, is a United States citizen domiciled in Iowa City, Iowa and is a member of the bars of the State of New Mexico and the United States Supreme Court.

9. Also assisting the Community as legal counsel are MARIA LUISA ACOSTA CASTELLÓN, attorney, a citizen of Nicaragua, with domicile and address at casa 21-B del Asentamiento José Martí del Bo. Santa Rosa, Bluefields, Región Autónoma Atlántico Sur, Nicaragua; SIMPSON THACHER & BARTLETT (a partnership which includes professional corporations), a United States law firm with its principal offices located at 425 Lexington Avenue, New York, New York 10017–3954; and the INDIAN LAW RESOURCE CENTER, a non-profit legal advocacy organization with an office at 601 E Street Southeast, Washington, D.C. 20003.

IV. Facts

Awas Tingni and Its Lands

10. The Community of Awas Tingni has a population of approximately 150 families, or about 650 individuals. Community members converse among themselves almost exclusively in the Mayagna language, although most also speak at least some Spanish. The principal village of the Community is located in an isolated forested area approximately a hundred kilometers inland from Nicaragua's northeastern Atlantic or Caribbean coast.

11. The Community's leadership is comprised of a governing counsel which includes, in addition to the Síndico, the vice-Síndico ("Suplente del Síndico"), the Judge of the People ("Juez del Pueblo"), and the Guardian of the Forest ("Responsable de Bosque"). The members of the governing council are elected by and answer directly to the Community at large, which meets regularly in an assembly open to all adult members of the Community.

12. Community members subsist primarily from itinerant agriculture, hunting and fishing. These activities are carried out within Awas Tingni's ancestral territory according to a traditional system of land tenure that is linked to the Community's socio-political organization.

13. Awas Tingni's ancestral territory includes land that members of the Community have traditionally used and occupied, and over which the Community's dominance has exceeded that of other groups, within the customary system of territorial distribution historically functioning among the indigenous communities of the Atlantic coast region. Within the system of land tenure common to Atlantic Coast communities, Awas Tingni holds its lands collectively while individual Community members and families enjoy subsidiary rights of use and occupancy.

14. The Community's possession of its territory, or communal lands, extends as far back in time as the earliest moments in the history of the Mayagna that can be recounted by Community elders. Beyond providing a means of sustenance for Community members, Awas Tingni's communal land base comprises a crucial aspect of the Community's existence, continuity and culture.

General Legal Recognition of Indigenous Land Rights

15. The Political Constitution of Nicaragua adopted in 1985 contains progressive provisions recognizing the rights of indigenous communities to their traditional communal lands.[3] Two years after the Constitution was adopted, the Nicaraguan National Assembly supplemented the legal protections for indigenous land rights and, more generally, exalted the rights of the Atlantic Coast peoples by enacting the Statute of Autonomy for the Atlantic Coast Regions of Nicaragua, Law No. 28 of 1987.

16. Amendments of the Constitution early this year further strengthened the juridical status and rights of indigenous communities. These developments in Nicaraguan law coincide with recently articulated international standards that affirm the rights of indigenous communities to the lands they traditionally have used and occupied, rights that exist independently of formal land title.[4] However, the protection promised indigenous land rights under Nicaraguan law has largely failed to translate into reality for Awas Tingni and most of the other indigenous communities of the Atlantic Coast.

The Lack of Specific Recognition and Adequate Protection of Indigenous Lands

17. Despite the constitutional and statutory provisions upholding indigenous land rights in general terms, the Nicaraguan government has taken no definitive steps toward demarcating indigenous lands or otherwise providing formal recognition of specific indigenous lands. The Nicaraguan Institute for Agrarian Reform ("INRA"), and other government agencies that are competent to address indigenous land tenure have failed to establish procedures to fill this void. Thus,

like the vast majority of indigenous communities of Nicaragua's Atlantic Coast, Awas Tingni lacks specific government recognition of the boundaries of its territorial rights.

18. With insecure territorial boundaries comes precarious land tenure, and, as a result, Awas Tingni and other coastal communities are vulnerable to the rush by outsiders, often uncontrolled, to acquire land with the region and to exploit its natural resources. Contemporary concerns over land rights among indigenous communities already are threatening to erupt into social unrest and even violence.

19. The Community of Awas Tingni has made a good faith effort to resolve these land tenure issues with the Nicaraguan government. Community leaders and representatives have on numerous occasions contacted government agencies, including INRA, in an attempt to have the existence and geographic extent of Awas Tingni communal lands certified. In each case, government officials have failed to take action, claiming instead that recognition of the Community's property rights must be preceded by a "coordinated effort" by all relevant government agencies to resolve the larger problem of land tenure in the Atlantic Coast region.

20. Tellingly, over ten years after the Commission's publication of the *Miskito Report*—in which the Commission recognized the dimensions of the land tenure crisis in the Atlantic Coast and admonished the Nicaraguan government to take action—the government has failed to conduct any such "coordinated effort" to resolve the issue of land tenure. On the contrary, government agencies, particularly MARENA, have repeatedly acted in disregard of indigenous land rights in general and in defiance of the Community's land rights in particular.

21. Exacerbating the problem, Nicaragua's approach to the issue of land tenure in the Atlantic Coast region quite clearly is animated by the government's interest in securing its *own* property interest in the resource-rich region. Under the Nicaraguan Civil Code, all lands not titled to private owners belong to the state. Accordingly, the government apparently has assumed that, because the Community's lands are not "privately held" under a formal title, the government is entitled to exploit the natural resources located on those lands. In taking this position, the government overlooks the fact that the Nicaraguan Civil Code is superseded to the extent that the Nicaraguan Constitution recognizes rights appurtenant to indigenous communal lands, rights that do not depend on the existence of a formal title but that instead may be founded entirely on traditional patterns of use and occupancy. See infra note 7.

The Natural Resources Ministry (MARENA) and Its Disregard for Awas Tingni Land Rights

22. The Community of Awas Tingni has been particularly affected by the government's persistent disregard for indigenous land rights. Especially at fault is MARENA, the government institution in charge of overseeing environmental protection and natural resource development in Nicaragua. The principal officials within MARENA who are responsible for acts against the Community in-

clude MILTON CALDERA CARDENAL, the Minister of MARENA; ROBERTO ARAQUISTAIN, the Director of MARENA's forest services; and ALEJANDRO LAÌNEZ, the Director of the forest service unit in charge of forestry on state lands.

The Maderas y Derivados de Nicaragua, S.A. Concesión

23. In late 1993 or early 1994, MARENA secretly granted a concession to Maderas y Derivados de Nicaragua, S.A., a joint Nicaraguan-Dominican company, for lumbering on 43,000 hectares of lands, most of which were within lands claimed by the Community. MARENA eventually suspended the concession, but only after the Community learned of the concession and protested through attorneys it had retained with funding from the World Wildlife Fund (the "WWF"), an international non-governmental organization, and after the WWF itself pressured MARENA.

24. A period of subsequent negotiations led to a trilateral agreement signed by the Community, the company, and MARENA (the "Trilateral Agreement"). Under the Trilateral Agreement, harvesting of timber in the 43,000 hectare area was to proceed under specified environmental safeguards and annual planning procedures that would involve the Community. MARENA provisionally recognized the Community's right to the timber in the area and agreed to assist the Community in the following terms: "MARENA promises to facilitate the definition of the communal lands *and not to undermine the territorial aspirations of the Community* . . . Such definition of lands should be carried out according to the historical rights of the Community and within the relevant juridical framework."[5]

The Korean Timber Concession

25. MARENA's commitment to promote the Community's land rights according to the application of legal standards proved to be illusory. Shortly after executing the Trilateral Agreement, MARENA turned its attention to another segment of Awas Tingni's communal lands, repeating its pattern of surreptitious dealings exclusive of the Community.

26. At various times from May 1994 through the present, MARENA has issued permits allowing a second timber company, Sol del Caribe, S.A., ("SOLCARSA"), a subsidiary of the Korean conglomerate Kumkyung Co., Ltd., to enter Awas Tingni communal lands to explore the forest for its commercial potential, to conduct an inventory of timber resources, and to engage in work in preparation for tree cutting operations.

27. Members of the Community became increasingly alarmed when they observed an ever greater presence of SOLCARSA agents with the Community's lands in July and August of 1995. In early September 1995, undersigned counsel Anaya, while traveling from the major coastal town of Puerto Cabezas to Awas Tingni, met and talked at length with a forestry engineer employed by SOLCARSA. The engineer said he was on his way to rejoin a team of other SOLCARSA agents engaged in forest inventory in preparation for large scale tree harvesting.

28. Reliable sources within the government state that MARENA is about to execute an agreement granting SOLCARSA a long-term timber concession in an area adjacent to the lands subject to the Maderas y Derivados de Nicaragua, S.A. concession described above. In July 1995, MARENA's delegate for the Northern Atlantic Autonomous Region, James Gordon, confirmed that the process of government approval of the SOLCARSA concession was in its final stages. Further, in early September 1995, MARENA and other government sources told undersigned counsel Acosta and Anaya that MARENA had already approved the management plan developed by SOLCARSA for its intended forest exploitation.

29. In anticipation of its operations, SOLCARSA has established a permanent office in Puerto Cabezas, the capital of the Northern Atlantic Autonomous Region. The office is located in a hotel owned by another MARENA official, Rodolfo Jenski, and it is headed by foreign nationals from the Korean parent company. Additionally, SOLCARSA is constructing a large timber processing plant in the area.

30. The management plan developed by SOLCARSA and approved by MARENA is for timber cutting in an area approximately 61,000 hectares, the greater part of which is within Awas Tingni's communal lands. Within the area targeted for timber operations under the management plan is the site of the old principal village of the Community, Tuburus. Some Community members today maintain primary residences in Tuburus, while others have secondary shelters and agricultural plots there. Additionally, Community members continue to use this site (as well as others throughout the area of the management plan) for multiple purposes, including hunting, fishing, and itinerant (swidden) agriculture. Places that have major religious significance to the Community, including burial grounds, are located within the area targeted for timber harvesting. Domesticated palm and fruit tree plantations within the area further mark the Community's historical and continuing patterns of territorial domain.

31. Totally ignoring its previous commitment to assist Awas Tingni in securing its land rights and "not to undermine the Community's territorial aspirations" (*see supra* at ¶182; 24), the government has permitted SOLCARSA to enter Awas Tingni land and is now poised to grant the Korean company a timber concession without ever having consulted with the Community. Throughout the negotiations with SOLCARSA, the government has taken no account of the Community's property and use rights in its communal lands and forest resources and has disregarded the hunting, fishing and other activities crucial to the subsistence and cultural survival of the Community and its members.

Failed Efforts to Prevent the Korean Timber Concession and to Reverse Government Malfeasance

32. The Community has attempted, without success, to prevent the responsible government officials from granting a timber concession to SOLCARSA. On

July 10, 1995, after the Community learned of SOLCARSA's plans, attorneys acting on behalf of Awas Tingni raised the Community's concerns in a meeting with James Gordon, MARENA's regional delegate. Mr. Gordon responded first by laughing and then by stating that the Community had no "title" to the concession area.

33. The next day, by letter dated July 11, 1995, the Community petitioned Minister Caldera of MARENA not to go forward with the timber concession in the absence of consultation and agreement with members of the Community. In this letter (a copy of which is attached as Exhibit A) the Community explained the basis for its claim that the area of the planned concession, or a substantial part of it, belongs to the Community and stressed its desire to find a negotiated solution to the problem. Neither Minister Caldera nor any other MARENA official responded to this letter.

34. As a result of the government's apparent unwillingness to negotiate with the Community, on September 11, 1995, the Community and Mr. Castillo, along with other Community leaders, submitted a petition for amparo to the Court of Appeals of Matagalpa, Nicaragua (a copy of which is attached as Exhibit B). Under Nicaraguan law, an amparo action is initiated in the relevant court of appeals for a determination on admissibility; if deemed admissible, the action is then considered by the Nicaraguan Supreme Court of Justice for a ruling on the merits.

35. Under existing practice in Nicaragua, an amparo action must be filed in person. The Court of Appeals of Matagalpa, which has jurisdiction over Awas Tingni, is located in the city of Matagalpa, a city outside the Atlantic Coast region that is at least a full day's travel from the Community even when commercial air transportation is used. The Community incurred the substantial travel and other costs required for its leaders and Nicaraguan counsel, Maria Luisa Acosta, to go to Matagalpa to file the amparo petition. By the amparo action, the Community sought a court order that would require the responsible MARENA officials to:

1. Abstain from granting the concession to SOLCARSA;
2. Direct the agents of SOLCARSA to leave Awas Tingni's communal lands where they currently are engaged in tasks in preparation for the start of timber exploitation operations;
3. Initiate a process of dialogue and negotiation with the Community of Awas Tingni if the company continues to be interested in forestry development in the Community's lands;
4. Provide any other remedy that the Honorable Court may deem just. (Translation from Spanish)

36. On or about September 18, 1995, the Court of Appeals ruled that the petition is inadmissible. In accordance with its practice, the Court of Appeals would not provide the Community's counsel, Ms. Acosta, with any information by telephone or mail concerning its decision, other than to communicate that an order had been rendered. Thus, Ms. Acosta was forced to travel again to Matagalpa to obtain a copy of the order rejecting the petition (a copy of which is attached as Exhibit C).

37. In ruling that the amparo petition is inadmissible, the Court of Appeals observed that the Nicaraguan law precludes such petitions where the petitioners have tacitly or actually consented to the government action being challenged. In addition, the Court of Appeals found that tacit consent may be inferred from the petitioner's failure to present the petition within thirty days of the petitioner's knowledge of the contested government action. The Court of Appeals held that, as evidenced by the July 11, 1995 letter from the Community to Minister Caldera, the Community had knowledge of MARENA's negotiations with SOLCARSA before that date, which was more than thirty days prior to filing the petition on September 11, 1995. Accordingly, the Court of Appeals reasoned that the Community must have "consented" to the Korean timber concession. Exhibit C.

38. The error in the appellate court's reasoning is immediately apparent. Plainly, the Community's July 11, 1995 letter *protesting* certain actions taken by the Nicaraguan government (including MARENA's negotiations with SOLCARSA) cannot logically serve as the basis for a finding that the Community has *consented* to those very actions. Indeed, this recent decision by the Court of Appeals is further evidence that the Nicaraguan government is at all levels unwilling to protect the Community's rights or to take seriously its obligations under either domestic or international law.

39. On September 21, 1995, Ms. Acosta filed a petition for a writ of mandamus ("recurso de hecho") in the Nicaraguan Supreme Court of Justice (a copy of which is attached as Exhibit D) seeking review of the September 18, 1995 decision by the Court of Appeals. There is no apparent time limit within which the Supreme Court is required to rule on this application, which remains *sub judice.*

V. Violations of International Human Rights Law

40. By its acts and omissions described above, the Nicaraguan government has failed to satisfy its obligations under both the American Convention on Human Rights and the American Declaration on the Rights and Duties of Man, as well as under other provisions of international human rights law.

The Right to Effective Measures to Secure Property

41. The Nicaraguan government has failed to demarcate the communal lands of Awas Tingni and other indigenous communities or to otherwise take effective measures to secure the Community's property rights in those lands. This failure constitutes a violation of articles 1, 2 and 21 of the American Convention, which together establish a right to such effective measures. Articles 1 and 2 obligate states to take the measures necessary to implement the rights affirmed in the American Convention, and among these rights is the right to property set forth in article 21.[6]

42. Awas Tingni's traditional possession of its communal lands, including the waters and forests within those lands, is a form of property recognized under both

Nicaraguan and international law.[7] Therefore, the obligation of Nicaragua to take effective measures to secure the rights in the American Convention, including property rights, extends to the land rights of Awas Tingni and other indigenous communities.

43. The Commission has articulated the nature and scope of this obligation and corresponding right in its recent Draft of the Inter-American Declaration of the Rights of Indigenous Peoples ("Draft Declaration"):

> Indigenous peoples have the right to the recognition of their property and ownership rights with respect to lands and territories they have historically occupied, as well as to the use of those to which they have historically had access for their traditional activities and livelihood . . . Where property and user rights of indigenous peoples arise from rights existing prior to the creation of those States, *the States shall recognize the titles of indigenous peoples relative thereto as permanent, exclusive, inalienable, imprescriptible and indefeasible* . . . The rights of the indigenous peoples to existing natural resources on their lands must be especially protected . . . *States shall give maximum priority to the demarcation of properties and areas of indigenous use.*[8]

44. Notably, the Commission's recent articulation of indigenous land rights is fully consistent with contemporary international standards, which recognize traditional patterns of use and occupancy by indigenous groups as giving rise to property rights that states are bound to respect. The contemporary international consensus concerning indigenous land rights is reflected in International Labor Organization Convention (No. 169) on Indigenous and Tribal Peoples in Independent Countries ("ILO Convention No. 169"). Article 14(1) of Convention No. 169 states: "The rights of ownership and possession of the peoples concerned over the lands which they traditionally occupy shall be recognized. In addition, measures shall be taken in appropriate cases to safeguard the right of the peoples concerned to use lands not exclusively occupied by them, but to which they have traditionally had access for their subsistence and traditional activities." Convention No. 169 further provides that: "Governments shall take steps as necessary to identify the lands which the peoples concerned traditionally occupy, and to guarantee effective protection of their rights of ownership and possession."[9]

45. As set forth with particularity above, the Nicaraguan government has utterly failed to fulfill its obligations under the American Convention to take effective measures to secure the property rights of Awas Tingni and other indigenous communities. But the government's acts and omissions go well beyond passive neglect. The government has actively violated the right to property affirmed in article 21 of the American Convention by granting SOLCARSA permission to enter Awas Tingni lands and to conduct work in preparation for lumbering without the Community's consent. Additionally, the imminent granting of a concession to SOLCARSA for large scale timber exploitation threatens further and more egregious violations of the Community's right to property and of the derivative rights of its members.

The Right to Cultural Integrity

46. Related to the obligation of Nicaragua to serve indigenous land rights is Nicaragua's more general obligation to protect the integrity of indigenous cultures. In its 1983 *Miskito Report,* the Commission found that the indigenous groups of Nicaragua's Atlantic Coast are entitled to "special legal protections" for the preservation of their cultures and that these protections should cover "the aspects linked to productive organization, which includes, among other things, the issue of ancestral and communal lands."[10]

47. The Commission cited the cultural rights guaranteed by article 27 of the International Covenant on Civil and Political Rights, stressing that Nicaragua's obligations as a party to that human rights treaty could not be overlooked in considering the situation of its indigenous population. Article 27 provides: "In those States in which ethnic, religious or linguistic minorities exist, persons belonging to such minorities shall not be denied the right, in community with other members of their group, to enjoy their own culture, to profess and practice their own religion, or to use their own language." The United States Human Rights Committee has confirmed that, where indigenous groups are concerned, traditional land tenure is an aspect of the enjoyment of culture protected by article 27 of the Covenant.[11]

48. In its recent Draft Declaration, this Commission once again articulated the obligation of states to respect the cultural integrity of indigenous peoples, expressly linking land rights to the very survival of indigenous cultures:

> States shall respect the cultural integrity of indigenous peoples, their development in their respective habitats and their historical and archeological heritage, which are important to the identity of the members of their groups and their ethnic survival . . . Indigenous peoples are entitled to restitution and respect of property of which they have been dispossessed, or compensation in accordance with international law.[12]

49. Accordingly, Nicaragua's failure to secure indigenous land rights also constitutes a violation of a broader obligation to secure indigenous cultural integrity, an obligation that the Commission previously has admonished Nicaragua to fulfill. Nicaragua's failure in this regard is particularly significant. As detailed above, the cultural identity of the Awas Tingni people is inextricably tied to the communal lands that have been used and occupied by the Community since its inception. The government's actions and omissions threaten to cause Awas Tingni to become dispossessed of its communal lands, and dispossessing the Community of those lands is tantamount to destroying the Community's culture.

The Right to Religion

50. An important element of the Community's culture implicated in this case is its religion. As specified above, the lands in question include burial sites and other

areas of religious significance to the Community and its members. Thus, the government's actions and omissions, which threaten to break the link between the Community and its ancestral lands, also threaten violations of the right to freely exercise religion, a right guaranteed by article 12 of the American Convention, as well as by article 27 of the International Covenant on Civil and Political Rights.

51. The Commission's Draft Declaration acknowledges the link between land and indigenous people's religious practices and, furthermore, reflects the contemporary international consensus imposing relevant affirmative obligations upon states: "Indigenous peoples have the right to liberty of conscience, freedom of religion and spiritual practice for indigenous communities and their members . . . In collaboration with the indigenous peoples concerned, the States shall adopt effective measures to ensure that their sacred sites, including burial sites, are preserved, respected and protected."[13]

The Right to Equality before the Law

52. The Community of Awas Tingni and its members are being denied equal protection of the law, in violation of article 24 of the American Convention and article II of the American Declaration. The people of Awas Tingni and other indigenous communities are being denied legal protections that are ordinarily available to other Nicaraguan citizens with respect to their property rights. This kind of discriminatory treatment of indigenous people's property rights in connection with ancestral lands has occurred over centuries, and the reversal of this pattern of discrimination has since the early 1970s been an express goal of the international community including the Inter-American system for the protection of human rights.[14]

The Right to Participate in Government

53. The government's failure to consult even minimally with the Community or its leaders, in considering and moving toward final approval of the timber concession to SOLCARSA, violates the right of the Community and its members to effectively participate in government decisions affecting them. Article 23(1)(a) of the American Convention affirms the right of every citizen "to take part in the conduct of government affairs, directly or through freely chosen representatives."

54. The implications of this right where indigenous communities are concerned are expressed in the Commission's Draft Declaration, which states: "Indigenous populations have the right to participate without discrimination . . . in all decision-making, at all levels, with regard to matters that might affect their rights, lives and destiny. They may do so through representatives elected by them in accordance with their own procedures."[15]

55. As specified in ILO Convention No. 169, the right of indigenous peoples to participate in the decision-making affecting them applies particularly with regard to the management of their lands and resources. According to article 7(1) of the Convention:

> The peoples concerned shall have the right to decide their own priorities for the process of development as it affects their lives, beliefs, institutions, and spiritual well-being and lands they occupy or otherwise use, and to exercise control, to the extent possible, over their own economic, social and cultural development. In addition, they shall participate in the formulation, implementation and evaluation of plans and programmes for national and regional development which may affect them directly.[16]

The Right to Petition and a Prompt Response

56. Finally, in not responding to the Community's July 11, 1995 letter petition to Minister Caldera of MARENA to suspend consideration of the timber concession to SOLCARSA, the government violated article XXIV of the American Declaration, which affirms "the right to submit respectful petitions to any competent authority . . . and the right to obtain a prompt decision thereon."

VI. Exhaustion of Domestic Remedies

57. The requirement that domestic remedies be exhausted has been satisfied. Article 46(2)(a) of the American Convention establishes an exception to this requirement which applies where, as here, "the domestic legislation of the State concerned does not afford due process of law for protection of the right or rights that have allegedly been violated." The Nicaraguan legal system does not provide due process of law for the complete vindication of rights asserted in this Petition. In particular, there is no administrative or judicial procedure to compel the governmental action that is required to provide specific official recognition of the boundaries of the communal lands of the Awas Tingni and other indigenous communities and to take whatever other measures are necessary to regularize indigenous land tenure in accordance with applicable legal standards.

58. Even if the Community were required to exhaust less formal procedures to secure its rights, however, the Community has done so and has been unable to accomplish its objectives. As set forth above, the Community has had numerous contacts with the responsible government agencies, including INRA and MARENA, all of which have proved fruitless. *See supra* at ¶¶ 19–33.

59. The Nicaraguan government may contend in response in this Petition that the requirement to exhaust domestic remedies has not yet been satisfied since the amparo action has not been finally adjudicated by the Nicaraguan Supreme Court of Justice. This argument should be rejected. *First,* under governing Nicaraguan law and institutional practice, the amparo action, even if successful, will

not result in judicial order to compel the type of coordinated action among relevant government institutions that is required to fully vindicate Awas Tingni's land rights. At most, the amparo petition will result in an order enjoining MARENA officials from granting a timber concession to SOLCARSA. Such an order, while welcome, would not reach the heart of the problem addressed here—namely, the need for affirmative government measures to effectively secure indigenous lands rights in the midst of a generally unsecured land tenure situation. *Second,* in light of the September 18, 1995 decision by the Nicaraguan Court of Appeals rejecting the amparo action (*see supra* at ¶ 37), the Community is unable to rely on the Nicaraguan judiciary as a means of resolving even the narrow issue of the SOLCARSA timber concession. Under "generally recognized principles of international law," which are incorporated into the admissibility standards governing petitions to the Commission, *see* American Convention, art. 46(2), the Petitioners need not exhaust procedures that are likely to be ineffective.[17]

60. Even if the amparo action were considered in some way determinative of the exhaustion of domestic remedies in this case, it should not prevent this Petition from being lodged with the Commission at this time. Under the applicable Nicaraguan law, the amparo action has fewer than sixty days to run its course once it is accepted as admissible, and ordinarily admissibility is to be determined within three days of filing. By the time the Commission is likely to consider the merits of this case, either the Supreme Judicial Court will have upheld the appellate court decision rejecting the amparo action or the action otherwise will or should have been fully resolved.[18] If, on the other hand, the Supreme Judicial Court does not rule on the lower court's admissibility decision within one or two weeks of the filing of this petition, and the amparo action remains pending for some time after that, the Commission should then consider the delay to be unwarranted under the circumstances. With such an unwarranted delay, 46(c) of the American Convention would come into play, which deems judicial proceedings inconsequential for the purpose of exhausting domestic remedies where "there has been unwarranted delay in rendering a final judgment."

VII. Timeliness

61. This Petition is timely: It alleges ongoing and threatened further violations, and the last attempts at obtaining redress for these violations through domestic procedures occurred within the last six months.

VIII. Absence of Parallel International Proceedings

62. The subject of this petition is not pending in any other international proceeding for settlement.

IX. Requested Relief

63. By reason of the foregoing, the Community of Awas Tingni and Jaime Castillo respectfully request that the Commission place itself at the disposal of the

parties to mediate a friendly settlement of the disputes described herein, as authorized by article 48(f) of the American Convention and article 45 of the Regulations of the Inter-American Commission.

64. Alternatively, if no friendly settlement is reached, the Community of Awas Tingni and Jaime Castillo respectfully request that the Commission prepare a report setting forth all of the facts and applicable law, declaring the Nicaragua is in violation of its obligations under international law, and recommending that Nicaragua:

1. establish and institute a procedure under domestic law, acceptable to the indigenous communities concerned, that will result in the prompt demarcation and official recognition of the territory of Awas Tingni and other indigenous communities;
2. suspend consideration of all government timber and other natural resource concessions within the communal lands of Awas Tingni and other indigenous communities until the land tenure issues affecting indigenous communities have been resolved, or unless a specific written agreement has been reached between the government and the indigenous community affected by the proposed concession;
3. suspend all activity relative to the planned timber concession to SOLCARSA until a suitable arrangement is negotiated between the government and the Community; and
4. engage in dialogue with the Community to determine whether and under what circumstances the proposed timber concession to SOLCARSA may go forward.

X. Request for Provisional Measures

65. In order to avoid the irreparable damage that would result from the planned timber concession to SOLCARSA or from other such concessions, the Community of Awas Tingni and Jaime Castillo respectfully request that the Commission institute provisional measures as appropriate under article 29 of the Regulations of the Inter-American Commission. The irreparable damage that the people of Awas Tingni will suffer, if SOLCARSA is allowed to further establish a foothold on Awas Tingni lands and begin logging operations, is uncertain only in the magnitude of its severity. The long history of encroachment onto indigenous lands establishes that, once commenced, such encroachment and its negative consequences for indigenous cultures are extremely difficult, if not impossible, to reverse.

66. The Community and Mr. Castillo respectfully request that the provisional measures include, at a minimum, the recommendations specified in paragraph 64(c) & (d) above. Additionally, the Petitioners request the Commission immediately request of the government full clarification of all pending concessionary proposals, agreements and plans with respect to the exploitation of any natural resources within the area of Awas Tingni, in order to establish the foundation for friendly settlement efforts.

Date: October 2, 1995
Respectfully submitted,

By: ______________________________

S. James Anaya
John S. Allen
THE UNIVERSITY OF IOWA COLLEGE
OF LAW, CLINICAL LAW PROGRAMS
386 Boyd Law Building
Iowa City, Iowa 52242
(319) 335–9023

Attorneys for Petitioners
THE MAYAGNA INDIAN
COMMUNITY OF AWAS TINGNI
and JAIME CASTILLO, on his
own behalf and on behalf
of the Community of Awas Tingni
MARIA LUISA ACOSTA CASTELLÒN
Attorney at Law
(Nicaraguan Co-Counsel)
casa 21-B del Asentamiento Jose
Martí del Bo. Santa Rosa
Bluefields, Región Autónoma Atlàntico Sur
Nicaragua
011–505–82 387

NOTES

1. OEA/Ser.L/V/II.62, doc. 10, rev. 3 (1983).

2. While "Mayagna" is the preferred term among those who comprise the group, the term "Sumo" is more commonly used by outsiders.

3. See infra note 7.

4. See infra note 9 and text.

5. Convenio de Aprovechamiento Forestal entre la Comunidad de Awas Tingni; Maderas y Derivados de Nicaragua, S. A.; y el Ministerio del Ambiente y los Recursos Naturales, 15 de mayo de 1994, article 3.2 (translation from Spanish, *emphasis added*).

6. Complementing the right to property established by American Convention is the right to residence and movement set forth in article VIII of the American Declaration, which provides that "[e]very person has the right to fix his residence within the territory of the state of which he is a national, to move about freely within such territory, and not to leave it except by his own will."

7. Notably, Nicaraguan law is consistent with the protections offered by international human rights law, see infra, at paragraph 44. Article 5 of the Political Constitution of Nicaragua affirms: "El Estado reconoce la existencia de los pueblos indígenas, que gozan de los derechos, deberes y garantías consignados en la Constitución, y en especial los de mantener . . . las formas comunales de sus tierras y el goce, uso y disfrute de las mismas, todo conforme la ley."

Similarly, article 89 of the Constitution states: "El Estado reconoce las formas comunales de propiedad de las tierras de las Comunidades [indígenas] de la Costa Atlántica. Igualmente reconoce el goce, uso y disfrute de las aguas y bosques de sus tierras comunales."

The communal property incorporated into the Nicaraguan legal system by the Constitution is defined in article 36 of the Statute of Autonomy for the Atlantic Coast regions of the Country, Law No. 28, as follows: "La propiedad communal la constituye las tierras, aguas y bosques que han pertenecido tradicionalmente a las comunidades [indígenas] de la Costa Atlántica."

8. Draft of the Inter-American Declaration on the Rights of Indigenous Peoples, article XVIII(2), (3), (4), and (8), approved by the IACHR at the 1278th session held on 18 September 1995, OEA/Ser/L/V/II.90, doc. 9, rev. 1 (1995) (hereinafter IACHR Draft Declaration)*[emphasis added]*.

9. International Labor Organization Convention (No. 169) on Indigenous and Tribal Peoples in Independent Countries, article 14(2). Although Nicaragua has not yet ratified Convention No. 169, the core elements of its land rights provisions represent newly developing customary international law. See S. James Anaya, *Indigenous Peoples in International Law* (Oxford University Press, 1996); S. James Anaya, *Indigenous Rights Norms in the Contemporary International Law*, 8 (No. 2) Ariz. J. Int'l & Comp. L. 1, 8–15, 27–29 (1991). See also Raidza Torres, *The Rights of Indigenous Peoples: The Emerging International Norm*, 16 Yale J. Int'l. L. 127, 160–1 (1991).

> In its 1983 *Miskito Report*, the Commission stated that is was "not in a position to decide on the strict legal validity of the claim of Indian communities to their ancestral lands," although it did recognize land claims in Nicaragua as a problem whose resolution "would represent a valuable precedent." OEA/Ser. L/V/II.62, at 127. However, in light of developments in Nicaraguan and international law and the Commission's own activities since the 1983 report promoting indigenous rights, the legal entitlement of indigenous communities to rights of property in connection with their traditional communal lands can no longer be in question.

10. OEA/Ser.L/V/II.62, doc. 10, rev. 3, at 81. The commission reiterated this position in promoting steps by the government of Brazil to secure the territorial rights of the Yanomami Indians. Case No. 7615 (Brazil), IACHR, OEA/Ser.L/V/II.66, doc. 10, rev.1, at 24, 31 (1985).

11. In *Ominayak, Chief of the Lubicon Band v. Canada*, Communication No. 267/1984, U.N. Doc. A/45/40, Annex 9(A) (1990), the U.N. Human Rights Committee construed the cultural rights guarantees of article 27 of the International Covenant to extend to "economic and social activities" upon which the

Lubicon Lake Band of Cree Indians relied as a group. Thus, the Committee found that Canada, a signatory to the International Covenant on Civil and Political Rights, had violated article 27 by allowing the provincial government of Alberta to grant leases for oil and gas exploration and for timber development within the aboriginal territory of the Band. Ibid., at 27.

12. IACHR Draft Declaration, supra note 8, article VII(1) and (2).

13. IACHR Draft Declaration, supra note 8, article X(1) and (3).

14. See the 1972 resolution of the Inter-American Commission on Human Rights identifying long-standing patterns of discrimination against indigenous peoples and stating that "special protection for indigenous populations constitutes a sacred commitment of the states." IACHR, OEA/Ser.P.AG/doc.305/73, rev. 1, at 90–91 (1973).

15. IACHR Draft Declaration, supra note 8, article XV(2).

16. *[Emphasis added]* Notably, ILO Convention No. 169 makes clear that governments have a duty to consult with indigenous peoples in connection with natural resource development even when the government retains ownership of the resources. Article 15(2) of the Convention states:

> In cases in which the State retains the ownership of mineral sub-surface resources or rights to other resources pertaining to lands, governments shall establish or maintain procedures through which they shall consult with these peoples, with a view to ascertaining whether and to what degree their interests would be prejudiced, before undertaking or permitting any programmes for the exploration or exploitation of such resources pertaining to their lands.

17. See Hurst Hannum, "Implementing Human Rights: An Overview of Strategies and Procedures," in *Guide To International Human Rights Practice* 19, 26 (Hurst Hannum, ed., 2d ed. 1992).

18. Indeed, applying a similar rule requiring exhaustion of domestic remedies, the European Commission of Human Rights has allowed petitions to be lodged in the face of such contingencies. This practice was upheld by the European Court of Human Rights in *The Matznetter Case,* Eur. Court H.R. Ser. A., at 25, 33 (Judgment of November 10, 1969).

Appendix 2

Amici Curiae

AWAS TINGNI MAYAGNA (SUMO) INDIGENOUS COMMUNITY

v.

THE REPUBLIC OF NICARAGUA

presented by

The International Human Rights Law Group (IHRLG)

and

The Center for International Environmental Law (CIEL)

(Editors' note: The following is the actual Amici Curiae presented to the Inter-American Court on Human Rights. It has been left in its original format without editing or content variation.)

Honorable Inter-American Court on Human Rights:

Romina Picolotti, in representation of the International Human Rights Law Group (IHRLG), address at 1200 18th Street, NW, Suite 602, Washington D.C., 20036; and Owen J. Lynch, in representation of the Center for International Environmental Law (CIEL), address at 1361 Connecticut Avenue, NW, Suite 300, Washington D.C., 20036, respectfully present the following amicus brief on the case of *Awas Tingni Mayagna (Sumo) Indigenous Community v. The Republic of Nicaragua*:

Request to Be Considered Amici Curiae

The amicus curiae brief is primarily a common law institution although countries with Romano-Germanic law traditions use it. Professor W. Michael Reisman of Yale Law School has succinctly stated the value of amicus briefs in correspondence with the Registrar of the International Court of Justice.

> In common law countries, the amicus curiae brief has been an institution which has provided useful information to courts, permitted private parties

who were not litigating to inform the court of their views and the probable effects the outcome might have on them and, overall, has served as a means for integrating and buttressing the authority and conflict-resolving capacities of domestic tribunals.[1]

Consistent with the custom of the Inter-American Court on Human Rights of accepting amicus briefs, we wish to request that the honorable Court admit this Amici Curiae in support of the international human rights of the Mayagna (Sumo) Indigenous Community of Awas Tingni.

Interests of the Amici Curiae

The IHRLG is a non-profit human rights organization comprised of legal professionals engaged in human rights advocacy, litigation and training around the world. Founded in 1978, the IHRLG has worked in more than 80 countries in 5 continents. Our mission is to support and help empower advocates to expand the scope of human rights protection and to promote broad participation in strengthening human rights standards and procedures at the national, regional, and international levels. Presently, the IHRLG has a civil society-strengthening program in the Atlantic Coast of Nicaragua, with two offices, one in Puerto Cabezas and the other in Bluefields.

CIEL is a public interest environmental law organization founded in 1989 to focus the energy and experience of the United States' public interest environmental law movement on reforming international environmental law and institutions, and on forging stronger and more meaningful connections between the top-down diplomatic approach of international law and the bottom-up participatory approach that has been the hallmark of the public interest environmental law movement. CIEL is part of a growing movement, and an informal network, of civil society institutions from various parts of the world that are committed to promoting public interest law and sustainable development.

As non-governmental organizations dedicated to the promotion and protection of human and environmental rights, we have closely followed the legal proceedings and discussion on the recognition and demarcation of indigenous territorial rights, and have taken a special interest in the Awas Tingni Mayagna (Sumo) case.

The forthcoming decision in this case will be of major importance for the development of the human rights of indigenous peoples as well as international human rights and environmental law. The case is poised to set a precedent on the commitment of the Inter-American human rights system to protect the human rights of indigenous peoples in an effective and adequate manner. It is worth noting that nearly 30 million indigenous people are citizens of Organization of American States (OAS) member states, yet the Inter-American Human Rights Court has rarely had the opportunity to rightfully and emphatically define and defend indigenous peoples rights.[2]

We approach the Court in the status of Amici Curiae, in support of efforts to encourage an enlightened and proactive role by the Inter-American human rights system in the defense of indigenous peoples' rights and to promote constructive linkages between human rights and environmental laws in defense of the Awas Tingni Mayagna and other indigenous peoples.

Petitum

With the anticipation that this contribution might assist the Court to reach a just decision for the parties involved with the Awas Tingni Mayagna (Sumo) case, we respectfully request that the Honorable Court:

1. admit the International Human Rights Law Group (IHRLG) and the Center for International Environmental Law (CIEL) as Amici Curiae for this case

2. attach this amicus to the case file; and,

3. adopt the views set forth in this brief.

The Importance of the Awas Tingni Case for the Development of the Inter-American Human Rights System

This case presents an important opportunity for Nicaragua and the Inter-American Human Rights system to promote national and regional interests by fostering an appropriate balance between human rights and environmental and economic interests. Nicaragua's forests represent important long-term national assets with potential benefits for all Nicaraguans. Forests stabilize and invigorate Nicaragua's ecology,[3] provide rich troves of genetic diversity (for pharmaceutical and agricultural products), produce lumber, and provide homes for indigenous peoples. The true value of forestlands to Nicaragua is in jeopardy if the court does not grant an adequate and effective protection to the Awas Tingni community. Multinational corporations or others who will not suffer the effects of deforestation can too easily buy logging concessions. Without means for accounting for the true environmental costs of logging, Nicaragua will find it difficult to capitalize on the value these forests represent.

The Awas Tingni case presents a landmark opportunity for the evolution of the Inter-American Human Rights System. The decision of the Inter-American Court will potentially have great impact on the development of hemispheric indigenous rights and on the promotion and protection of environmental human rights. The Awas Tingni case provides the Inter-American Court on Human Rights with its first opportunity to rule on a case concerning the legal recognition and demarcation of the property rights of indigenous peoples, an issue of major regional and international concern.

The Inter-American Human Rights System requires clarity and the development of existing jurisprudence on indigenous peoples, specifically as concerns:

- Terminology Used to Address Indigenous Peoples;
- Need for Special Legal Protection for Indigenous Peoples

Summary of the Argument

In analyzing the Awas Tingni case, we have focused on Nicaragua's international obligations. We have anchored our observations on standards and rules applicable to human rights, indigenous peoples, and the environment. These rules and standards are mandated in universal and/or regional international agreements freely entered into by Nicaragua and by general principles in international human rights and environmental law.

The central contention of this brief is that the Inter-American Human Rights System can adequately and effectively protect the rights of indigenous peoples, including the Mayagna (Sumo) people of Awas Tingni. The Inter-American Court, being the highest organ of the Inter-American Human Rights System, has an affirmative duty to interpret the American Convention on Human Rights[4] according to its object and purpose, i.e., the international protection of the basic rights of human beings. The historical, contemporary and severe discrimination faced by indigenous peoples requires the development and enforcement of special legal protection to ensure their enjoyment of basic human rights. In the case of Awas Tingni, the *sole* way of achieving this special protection is by interpreting the American Convention in a way that: a) integrates Nicaragua's international obligations under the American Convention with other international instruments freely entered into by Nicaragua; and, b) includes indigenous concepts.[5]

Further, this brief argues that the intrinsic connections between land, environment, life, religion, identity, and culture, are so deeply rooted, that it is not possible to provide an effective and adequate protection of a single right, such as the right to property, without considering other rights such as the right to life, identity, culture and religion. In the case of indigenous peoples the above mentioned rights are inextricably woven into geo-spatial and cultural dynamics, and cannot be considered as isolated matters without undermining the special nature of indigenous circumstances. Recognition of these unique rights also has important implications for ensuring that indigenous stewardship of Nicaragua forest resources continues and is legally supported in ways that are culturally and economically appropriate.

Structure of the Amicus Curiae

Part I of this brief identifies the terminology used by the Inter-American Human Rights System to address indigenous peoples and recommends that the Inter American Court rely on the definitions developed by the United Nations Working Group on Indigenous Populations and on the Draft Inter-American Declaration on the Rights of Indigenous Peoples. Part II asserts that in the case of indigenous peoples the purpose of the American Convention is served by special protection, and argues that the need for a special protection in the case of indigenous peoples mandates the application of Article 29 of the American Convention. Finally, it describes the content of this special protection in the case of Awas Tingni. Part II (i) sketches the international obligations assumed by Nicaragua beyond the American Convention and provides a list of correlative rights relevant to the Awas Tingni case that should be integrated in the interpretation of the American Convention. Part II (ii) argues that the applicability of Article 29 requires that the Court take into account the contemporary development of indigenous concepts. This necessarily includes the indigenous concept of collective rights in the Awas Tingni case.

Part III conceptualizes collective rights including: i. the right to property, ii. the right to life, iii. the right to a healthy environment including the applicability of environmental economics and the internalization of environmental costs, iv. the right to culture, and v. the right to participate in government. The brief also provides an annex containing a short comparative domestic overview of recent legal developments on the recognition of indigenous community-based property rights in Canada, Australia and the Philippines.

I. Terminology Used to Address Indigenous Peoples

On different occasions, the Inter-American Commission has used a variety of terms to refer to indigenous peoples: minorities,[6] ethnic minorities,[7] ethnic group,[8] peoples,[9] tribes,[10] indigenous cultures,[11] and population.[12] The Commission has not explained why it has preferred a term over the others.[13]

In choosing a terminology to address indigenous peoples, it is important that this Honorable Court select terms that preserve the right of these communities to decide who belongs to them, without external interference. The terminology used by the following definition not only fulfills this requirement, but also reflects the collective characteristic of indigenous peoples' rights. For these reasons, we strongly encourage this Honorable Court to adopt the following definition developed by the leading United Nations study on indigenous populations:[14]

> Indigenous *communities, peoples and nations* are those which, having a historical continuity with pre-invasion and pre-colonial societies that developed on their territories, consider themselves distinct from other sectors of the societies now prevailing in those territories, or parts of them. They form at present non dominant sectors of society and are determined to preserve, develop and transmit to future generations their ancestral territories, and their ethnic identity, as the basis of their continued existence as peoples, in accordance with their own cultural patterns, social institutions and legal systems. *[emphasis added]*

This definition, which this brief adopts, is the product of many years of discourse in which indigenous peoples from throughout the world have actively participated.[15] It is consistent with the Draft Inter-American Declaration on the Rights of Indigenous Peoples, which defines indigenous peoples as:

those who embody historical continuity with societies which existed prior to the conquest and settlement of their territories by Europeans. (alternative 1) [, as well as peoples brought involuntarily to the New World who freed themselves and re-established the cultures from which they have been torn] (alternative 2) [, as well as tribal peoples whose social, cultural and economic conditions distinguish them from other sections of the national community, and whose status is regulated wholly or partially by their own customs or traditions or by special laws or regulations.]"[16]

II. Need for Special Legal Protection for Indigenous Peoples

Article 31 (1) of the Vienna Convention on the Law of Treaties provides that: "A treaty shall be interpreted in good faith in accordance with the ordinary meaning to be given to the terms of the treaty in their context and in the light of its object and purpose."

What then, is the purpose of the American Convention? The Honorable Court in the Gallardo case concluded that, "The Convention has a purpose—the international protection of the basic rights of human beings . . ."[17] Thus, in the present case, the purpose of the American Convention is served by providing international protection of the basic rights of indigenous peoples. The continuous and severe discrimination faced by indigenous peoples requires deep reflection on how to ensure that this protection is adequate and effective. The prevention of discrimination, on the one hand, and the implementation of special protections, on the other, are merely two aspects of the same problem: that of fully ensuring equal rights to all persons.[18]

The term "special protection" contains within it the principle of non-discrimination, the *rationale* being the principle of "juridical equality."[19] This is understood to be a measure of justice that provides for reasonably equal treatment to everyone in the same circumstances. Applying the principle of "juridical equality" requires that factual inequalities be recognized in order for law to address them and achieve justice. In other words, the special circumstances faced by indigenous peoples throughout the Americas and worldwide require special legal treatment in order to render justice.[20]

The IACHR has consistently advocated for special protection of indigenous peoples in reports as well as in its resolutions.[21] Already in 1971, citing Article 2 of the American Declaration, the IACHR found that indigenous peoples were entitled to special legal protection because they suffered severe discrimination. The Commission called upon the OAS member states "to implement the recommendations made by the Inter-American Charter of Social Guarantees which deals with the protection of indigenous peoples."[22] A year later, the IACHR adopted a resolution that stated that "for historical reasons and because of moral and humanitarian principles, special protection for indigenous populations constitutes a sacred commitment of the states."[23] Subsequently in referring to the Miskitos,[24] Yanomamis,[25] Mapuches,[26] and the indigenous peoples of Ecuador,[27] the IACHR reiterated the need for a special protection.

The indigenous nature of the Awas Tingni case requires that this Honorable Court implement special protection. Without special protection, the essential preconditions for the enjoyment of other rights do not exist and the purpose of the American Convention will not be served.

Even though the best way of achieving special protection is by the development and application of specific law,[28] Article 29 of the American Convention can already support special legal protection for the indigenous peoples of Awas Tingni. In order to do this, the American Convention should be interpreted to:

i. integrate Nicaragua's international obligations under the American Convention with other international instruments freely entered into by Nicaragua; and,

ii. take into account the contemporary development of concepts that encompass indigenous values such as the concept of collective rights.

As explained *ut supra*, there is an urgent and unpostponable need for special protection in the case of indigenous peoples to provide minimum legal guarantees for the enjoyment of their basic human rights. The current absence of specific law in the Inter-American system to provide for this special protection requires that Article 29 be applied. In other words, the affirmative duty of the Inter-American Court to interpret the American Convention according to its object and purpose mandate application in this case of Article 29 of the American Convention. The application of Article 29 is *mandatory* in order to protect the indigenous peoples of Awas Tingni in an adequate and effective manner.

i. Integration of Nicaragua's International Obligations under the American Convention with Other International Instruments—Applicability of Article 29b. of the American Convention

The American Convention allows for the integration of different instruments that codify international human rights law. On this matter, this Honorable Court in its consultative opinion number one stated:

> A certain tendency to integrate the regional and universal systems for the protection of human rights can be perceived in the Convention. The Preamble recognizes that the principles on which the treaty is based are also proclaimed in the Universal Declaration of Human Rights and that "they have been reaffirmed and refined in other international instruments, worldwide as well as regional in scope." Several provisions of the Convention likewise refer to other international treaties or to international law, without speaking of any regional restrictions. (See, e.g., Convention, Arts. 22, 26, 27 and 29.) Special mention should be made in this connection of Article 29,[29] which contains rules governing the interpretation of the Convention, and which clearly indicates an intention not to restrict the protection of human rights to determinations that depend on the source of the obligations . . ."[30]

It is particularly important to emphasize the special relevance that Article 29b. has to the Awas Tingni case. The indigenous nature of this case requires that the Court consider the utilization of other international human rights instruments in its analysis in order to provide adequate and effective protection to Mayagna (Sumo) people. Since the adoption of the American Convention, specific rights in international law pertaining to indigenous peoples have been developed. Article 29b. allows the Court to integrate other international instruments that Nicaragua has voluntarily signed and ratified, and which bind Nicaragua to their content, to protect indigenous peoples.

In addition to the American Convention, as a United Nations member state Nicaragua is obliged by articles 55 and 56 of the United Nations Charter to respect and promote the principles of equal rights and self-determination of peoples and the observance of human rights and fundamental freedoms for all without distinction as to race, sex, language, or religion. These clauses mark the modern foundation of international human rights law, and the International Court of Justice has confirmed their mandatory character.[31]

While these articles do not define "human rights and fundamental freedoms," the 1948 Universal Declaration of Human Rights is today recognized as being declaratory and interpretive of the obligations of United Nations member states under the Charter. Further, by virtue of being a member of the Organizations of American States, Nicaragua is obliged to uphold the basic rights and guarantees proclaimed in the 1948 American Declaration of the Rights and Duties of Man (American Declaration).[32]

In addition to these constitutive instruments and declarations, Nicaragua has ratified the International Covenant on Civil and Political Rights (ICCPR);[33] the International Covenant on Economic, Social and Cultural Rights (ICESCR);[34] the International Convention on the Elimination of all form of Racial Discrimination (CERD);[35] the Convention on the Rights of the Child (CRC).[36] By ratifying these instruments, Nicaragua assumed a solemn duty toward other States Parties and toward its own citizens to respect and ensure the free exercise of rights guaranteed in these treaties.

The international instruments mentioned *supra* enshrine the international obligation of Nicaragua to ensure and respect, among others, the following rights:

- right to life;[37]
- right to equality before the law;[38]
- right to an effective judicial remedy;[39]
- right to residence and movement;[40]
- right to own property alone as well as in association;[41]
- right to religious freedom and worship;[42]
- right to the benefits of culture;[43]
- right to self determination;[44]
- right to be free from discrimination;[45]
- right to health;[46]

- right to a clean environment;[47]
- right to be free from interference with one's home;[48]
- right of minorities;[49] and,
- right to identity.[50]

These rights are directly implicated in the case of Awas Tingni and should be considered by this Honorable Court when interpreting the American Convention according to Article 29. As discussed below, relationships between indigenous peoples and their land and other natural resources cannot be reduced to a matter of property rights. The Mayagna (Sumo) peoples have repeatedly expressed the importance of their land for their survival, as well as its intrinsic connection to the preservation of their culture, religion and identity. Thus any analysis of the property rights of the Mayagna (Sumo), and any violation thereof, necessarily includes the rights mentioned *ut supra.*

ii. Applicability of Article 29 to Take into Account Contemporary Development of International Laws that Accommodate Indigenous Values

Article 29 of the American Convention wisely articulates a mechanism that allows the American Convention to adapt itself to the evolution of international law, including the adoption of new concepts and trends.

Judge Rodolfo E. Piza Escalante summarizes:

> 2. *In this regard, in my opinion, both the principles of interpretation established in the Vienna Convention on the Law of Treaties, and those stemming from Article 29 of the American Convention, correctly understood above all in the light of the law on human rights, serve as a basis for the application of criteria of interpretation and even of integration that are principles, ends, and established for the greatest protection of the rights established.* The Court has utilized these criteria in one way or another. [See for example OC-1/82 (paras. 24–25, 41); OC-2/82 (paras. 27 ff., sp. 27, 29, 30–31); OC-3/83 (paras. 50, 57, 61, 65–66), as well as my separate opinion in the case, Gallardo et al. (para. 21).] *These criteria also point to the need to interpret and integrate each standard of the Convention by utilizing* the adjacent, underlying or overlying principles in other international instruments, in the country's own internal regulations and in *the trends in effect in the matter of human rights, all of which are to some degree included in the Convention itself by virtue of the aforementioned Article 29,* whose innovating breadth is unmatched in any other international document.
>
> 3. With regard to my separate opinion, *I invoke as of special importance first of all the principle that human rights are progressive and expansive in addition to being requirable. These features require the consequent interpretative approach and, therefore, they impose the need to consider in each instance not only the meaning and scope of the very standards interpreted in their literal text, but also their potential for growth,* in my judgment put in the form of legislated law by Articles 2 and 26 of the American Convention, among other international instruments on the

subject, the first for all rights, and the second in terms of the so-called economic, social and cultural rights . . . This is why the principles of "progressive development" contained in Article 26 of the Convention, although they refer literally to the economic, social, educational, scientific, and cultural standards contained in the Charter of the Organization of American States, should in my judgment be understood to be applicable to any of the "civil and political" rights established in the American Convention, to the extent and in the ways in which they are not reasonably requirable in themselves, and vice versa, that the standards of the Convention itself may be understood to be applicable to the so-called "economic, social and cultural rights," to the degree and in the ways in which they are reasonably requirable in themselves (as occurs, e.g., with the right to strike). In my opinion, this flexible and reciprocal interpretation of the Convention's standards with other international standards on the subject, and even with those of national legislation, is consistent with the "standards of interpretation" of Article 29 thereof, applied in accordance with the aforementioned criteria of principles and ends.[51] *[emphasis added]*

Accordingly, Article 29—which, as expressed *ut supra,* is mandatory in this case—requires the adoption of the trends in effect in international law concerning indigenous peoples. The relevant trend in effect concerning the Awas Tingni case is the concept of collective rights.

III. Collective Rights

Collective rights are thought of *as rights that cannot be exercised but in-groups or rights where right holders are collective agents.* Their collective characteristic is what constitutes their value. Therefore the deprivation of its collectiveness will imply the emptiness of the content of the right, and subsequently, its non-existence.

The first "category" of collective rights are rights that can only be exercised in a group, as is the case with the right to freedom of expression. An individual in isolation cannot realize his or her right to freedom of expression; rather an individual must be able to share ideas with others to fully enjoy this right.

The second "category" are rights in which the rights holders are collective agents. These rights are by nature collective. Therefore the right can only be enjoyed if the group as a whole realizes the right. The right to culture and to community-based property[52] provide an example. These rights cannot be understood absent their presence within a group in which these rights have meaning and through which they are exercised and enjoyed.

Collective rights can be found with every known indigenous community rights system, as is the case of the Awas Tingni community. The intrinsic nature of collective rights has forced a change in the language of international law since they could not be adequately addressed as individual rights. International human rights law has recognized collective rights, in both categories. A consensus has developed during the past decade that indigenous peoples have distinctive community-based collective rights.[53] Agreements signed by the States at the Rio Conference explicitly recognized indigenous peoples' collective rights[54] and provide strong evidence of this emerging consensus. Among these distinctive internationally recognized collective rights are the right to land and other natural resources, cultural integrity, environmental security, and control over their own development.[55]

Even though the American Convention does not expressly use the word "collective," some of the rights that it enshrines are indeed collective. The IACHR in its report on Ecuador recognizes:

> Certain individual rights guaranteed by the American Convention on Human Rights must be enjoyed in community with others, as is the case with the rights to freedom of expression, religion, association and assembly . . . The ability of the individual to realize his or her right both contributes to and is contingent upon the ability of individuals to act as a group. For indigenous peoples, the free exercise of such rights is essential to the enjoyment and perpetuation of their culture.[56]

For the sake of brevity we will only focus, in this case, on the collective characteristic of the right to property and its implications concerning: the right to life, the right to a healthy environment, the right to culture and the right to participate in government.

i. The Collective Perspective of the Right to Property—Article 21 of the American Convention

Specifically concerning indigenous peoples, the right to property has a collective perspective. As the U.N Special Rapporteur on human rights of indigenous peoples affirmed:

> In summary, each of these examples underscores a number of elements that are unique to indigenous peoples: (1) a profound relationship between indigenous peoples and their lands, territories and resources exists; (2) that this relationship has various social, cultural, spiritual, economic, and political dimensions and responsibilities; (3) that the collective dimension of this relationship is significant; and (4) that the inter-generational aspect of such a relationship is also crucial to indigenous peoples identity, survival and cultural viability.[57]

The indigenous right to property is a community-based right that derives from long-term relationships between indigenous peoples and the natural resources that sustain them. In the case of Awas Tingni, the Mayagna Sumo community has a system of communal property in which the land belongs collectively to the community.[58]

Particularly in the case of Nicaragua, it must be noted that the collective right of the Mayagna Sumo peoples, to own on a community basis the rights to land they have traditionally occupied, is expressly recognized in Articles 5 and 89 of the Nicaraguan Constitution.

Article 5 of the Nicaragua Constitution reads: "The State recognizes the existence of indigenous peoples, who enjoy the rights, obligations and guarantees recognized in the Constitution, especially those that maintain and develop their identity and culture . . . *so as to maintain the communal forms, enjoyment, use and benefit of their lands,* all in conformity with the law . . ." *[emphasis added]*

Article 89 of the Nicaragua Constitution reads: ". . . The State recognizes the communal forms of property of the Atlantic Coast Communities' lands; it also recognizes the enjoyment, use and benefit of the waters and forests of their communal lands . . ." *[emphasis added]*

The definition of communal land is provided by article 36 of the Autonomy Statute of Nicaraguan Atlantic Coast Autonomous Region: "Article 36: Communal property is the land, water and forest that have traditionally pertained to the [indigenous] communities of the Atlantic Coast."

As noted *ut supra,* Nicaragua's internal laws in this case expand the concept of right to property express in Article 21 of the American Convention. Article 29 of the American Convention in this case requires that this Honorable Court integrate Nicaragua's domestic legislation in the interpretation of Article 21. This Honorable Court, therefore, should recognize the collective right to property of the indigenous peoples of Awas Tingni.

A sentence by this Honorable Court mandating the legal demarcation and documentation of indigenous community-based rights in Awas Tingni will not only establish an important legal precedent on the collective rights of indigenous peoples in Nicaragua; it would also provide a legal foundation for fostering goodwill between indigenous communities and governments throughout the Americas. It would provide indigenous communities with state-sanctioned authority to prevent migration and unsustainable commercial activities within their ancestral domains. Technical assistance to improve and develop organizational capacities and support sustainable management would, along with expanded credit programs, complement such a move.

ii. The Collective Perspective of the Right to Life—Article 4 of the American Convention

Understanding the contextual complexities of indigenous peoples and their relationships to their land and other natural resources is essential for promoting their legal interests and well being. This requires an appreciation of the collective relationship between life and land.

The basis of all substantive legal rights is the right to life. This right is not limited to individual human beings. The United Nations in several resolutions, where it affirmed that not only all individuals but all peoples have an inherent right to life, has recognized the collective dimension of the right to life.[59] Safeguarding this fundamental right is an essential condition for enjoying the entire range of civil and political rights.[60]

Wisely, the President of this Honorable Court affirmed: "This brings to the fore the safeguard of the right to life of all persons as well as *human collectivities, with special attention to the requirement of survival* (as a component of the right to life) *of vulnerable groups* (*e.g.*, the dispossessed and deprived, disabled or handicapped persons, children and the elderly, ethnic minorities, *indigenous populations,* migrant workers . . .)"[61] *[emphasis added]*

Actions taken by indigenous leaders to defend their cultural patrimony and heritage have focused on the need to protect traditional territories. Displacement from ancestral domains and damage to the local environment invariably harms the cultural integrity and well being of indigenous peoples, and often leads to physical harm and the loss of life.[62] Therefore any analysis of Awas Tingni community-based property right pursuant to Article 21 requires consideration of the right to life—Article 4.

In the case of *Bernard Ominayak & The Lubicon Lake Band v. Canada,*[63] the applicants alleged that the government of the province of Alberta had deprived the Lake Lubicon Indians of their means of subsistence and their right to self-determination by selling oil and gas concessions on their lands. The H.R. Committee found that historical inequities and certain more recent developments, including oil and gas exploration, were threatening the way of *life [emphasis added]* of the Lake Lubicon Band and were thus violating minority rights, contrary to Article 27 of the ICCPR.[64]

The threat to the right to life in its collective and individual dimension of the Mayagna Sumo peoples is real and concrete.[65] This threat remains permanent, like Damocles' sword, if the State fails to take positive, adequate and effective measures to protect indigenous territories and rights. Experience repeatedly shows that the failure of States to protect indigenous rights, including the authorization of incursions by external forces into indigenous territories, has hastened the extinction of the indigenous peoples and communities. The overwhelming evidence of these hostile state-sanctioned incursions, and the consequent extinction of indigenous peoples, has driven scholars of indigenous communities and other concerned parties to refer to the problem as being genocidal in nature.[66]

As incursions into indigenous territories increase, the symbiotic tie between culture, land and life for the Awas Tingni community becomes more and more self-evident. Consequently a violation of the community-based property rights of Awas Tingni will necessary imply a violation of the right to life consecrated in Article 4 of the American Convention.

iii. The Right to a Healthy Environment as Corollary of the Right to Life

The right to life entails negative as well as positive obligations. Thus the right to life implies the negative obligation not to practice any act that will result in the arbitrary deprivation of human life and the positive obligations to take all appropriate measures to protect and preserve human life. The European Commission of Human Rights recognizes that Article 2 of the European Convention of Human

Rights imposed on states the positive obligation *de prendre des mesures adéquate pour protéger la vie.*[67] Further, the Human Rights Committee stated regarding Article 6 of the UN Covenant on Civil and Political Rights that states are required "to take positive measures to ensure the right to life, including steps to reduce the infant mortality rate, prevent industrial accidents, *and protect the environment.*"[68] *[emphasis added]* From this perspective, the right to a healthy environment appears as a corollary to the right to life.

In the realm of international law, the right to a healthy environment is found in several environmental agreements[69] as well as in human rights instruments. Hence, the ICESCR includes a right to a clean environment.[70] The term "healthy environment" was also incorporated in the 1988 Additional Protocol to the American Convention on Human Rights.[71] The Hague Declaration of 1989 was one of the most important international statements before the United Nations Conference on Environment and Sustainable Development (UNCED) that connected environmental degradation to human rights issues. It declared that environmental harm threatens "the right to live in dignity in a viable global environment."[72]

Interest in and support for recognizing a right to healthy environment has continued to develop momentum since the UNCED. A major development was publication of the 1994 Final Report on Human Rights and the Environment, of the Commission on Human Rights Sub-commission on Prevention of Discrimination and Protection of Minorities, more generally known as the "Ksentini 1994 Report." That document discussed the legal foundations of a right to a satisfactory environment.[73]

A right to a healthy environment is also included in the United Nations Environment Programme's 1993 Proposal for a Basic Law on Environmental Protection and the Promotion of Sustainable Development. It includes within its "Governing Principles" the "... right of present and future generations to enjoy a healthy environment and decent quality of life ..."[74] The Draft Principles on Human Rights and the Environment (which is attached to the 1994 Ksenti Report states that " [a]ll persons have the right to a safe and healthy working environment."[75] The IUCN draft Covenant on Environment and Development requires that "Parties undertake to achieve progressively the full realization of the right of everyone to an environment and a level of development adequate for their health, well-being and dignity."[76] The IUCN draft also avers that "[a]ll persons have a duty to protect and preserve the environment ... ,"[77] thus recognizing that the right to good environment entails both a right for everyone to benefit from the environment as well as obligation for all to manage it sustainably. It is also noteworthy that a right to environment has been included in many national constitutions around the world.[78]

The distinctive nature of indigenous peoples' relationship to the environment within their ancestral domains is captured in the proposed American Declaration on the Rights of Indigenous Peoples, which in its preamble, recognizes "the respect for the environment accorded by the cultures of indigenous peoples of the

Americas." It explicitly acknowledges "the special relationship" between indigenous peoples and the environment, lands, resources and territories on which they live. The preamble also recognizes "that in many indigenous cultures, traditional collective systems for control and use of land and territory and resources, including bodies of water and coastal areas, are a necessary condition for their survival, social organization, development and their individual and collective well-being . . ."

In the same vein, the draft United Nations Declaration on the Rights of Indigenous Peoples, provides in Article 25 that: "Indigenous peoples have the right to maintain and strengthen their distinctive spiritual and material relationship with the lands territories, waters and coastal seas and other resources which they have traditionally owned or otherwise occupied or used, and to uphold their responsibilities to future generations in this regard."

As the president of this honorable Court noted, "The right to a healthy environment has individual and a collective dimensions—being at a time an "individual" and a "collective" right—in so far as its *subjects or beneficiaries* are concerned. Its "social" dimension becomes manifest in so far as its *implementation* is concerned (given the complexity of the legal relations involved). And it clearly appears in its "collective" dimension in so far as *object* of protection is concerned *(a bien commun,* the *human environment).*"[79]

Despite stylistic variations, each articulation contains an identifiable core: that the human right to a healthy environment concerns affording each person as well as a given human collectivity a right to an environment that supports physical and spiritual well being and development. The type of environment suggested in several of the instruments is one which is ecologically sound, an imprecise term, but which would likely proscribe the degradation of forests and the depletion of biodiversity which would coincide with externally controlled timber extraction activities within the ancestral domain of Mayagna (Sumo) people.

In sum, the right to life, which has a corollary the right to a healthy environment, imposes the positive obligation to Nicaragua, in this case, to take adequate measures to protect the environment of the Awas Tingni community. The degradation of forest and the depletion of bio-diversity, by timber companies with the acquiescence of the Nicaraguan state, is in direct conflict with the international legal obligations of the state.

iv. The Right to a Healthy Environment and the Right to Equal Protection—Article 24 of the American Convention

The right to a healthy environment is intimately connected with the notion of juridical equality that contains within it, the principle of non-discrimination. As Kiss noted,

> *il contribue à établir une égalité entre citoyens ou, du moins, à atténuer les inégalités dans leurs conditions matérielles. On sait que les inégalités entre humains de condi-*

tions sociales différentes sont accentuées par la dégradation de l'énvironnement: les moyens matériels dont disposent les mieux nantis leur permettent d'échapper à l'air pollués, aux milieux dégradés et de se créer un cadre de vie sain et équilibré, alors que les plus démunis n'ont guère de telles possibilités et doivent accepter de vivre dans des agglomérations devenues inhumaines, voire des bidonvilles, et de supporter les pollutions.

L'exigence d'un environnement sain et équilibré devient ainsi en même temps un moyen de mettre en oeuvre d'autres doits reconnues à la personne humaine.

Mais, par ses objectifs miemes, le droit à l environnement apporte aussi une dimension supplémentaire aux droits de l'homme dans leur ensemble.[80]

In the case of indigenous peoples, the concept of environmental discrimination takes on special relevance. While governments approve the activities of industries that conduct oil exploration, mining operations, timber exploitation, in communities that are predominantly indigenous, without regards of their proximity to or impact on areas that are populated exclusively or predominantly by indigenous peoples. Specifically in the case of Awas Tingni, the Nicaraguan government has proven to be resistant to enforcing laws and unwilling to protect indigenous communities from environmental degradation. As explained in this brief the symbiotic tie between life, land, environment and culture, of indigenous peoples, implicates that the degradation of the environment threatens the very survival and culture of indigenous peoples. Indigenous peoples suffer disproportionately the failure of the state to act to protect the environment adversely affected as a result of unregulated or uncontrolled industrial exploitation of indigenous natural resources.

The recognition by this honorable Court, of the obligation of the Nicaraguan state to protect the environment of the Awas Tingni community and its correlative right to a healthy environment, will provide the minimal legal guaranties for the enjoyment of their basic human rights, assuring the applicability or juridical equality.

Applicability of Environmental Economics—Internalizing Environmental Costs

Economic activities that preserve the regenerative capacities of renewable resources contribute to sustainable development. Economists treat environmental costs in two ways. The first, and most widespread, view sees costs flowing from environmental destruction as *external* to short-term economic calculations. Individual natural resource extractors do not face the full negative impacts of that ecological decay when no meaningful regulation or procedure forces them to confront it.[81] Ecological costs are difficult to measure for those who do not have to cope directly with them, and they are typically left out of cost-benefit calculations. The long-term effect of externalizing ecological costs is that commercial transactions do not reflect their true ecological costs, impoverishing natural resource sellers who receive too little benefit to offset the ecological costs.

The opposite approach, *internalization*, incorporates ecological costs into economic decision-making through appropriate social, economic and regulatory mechanisms. With perfect internalization, economic decisions keep more of the value of ecological resources in the country that enjoys them. The challenge is to find and nurture appropriate social and legal systems that recognize and protect the true value of natural resources. Absent such systems, entrepreneurs have strong incentives to rig economic transactions so that they benefit while society pays in externalized ecological (and later economic) costs.

In analyzing sustainability, four types of capital can be identified: human-made capital (e.g., factories, cash), natural capital (forests, water, air, soil, etc.), human capital (education, skills, etc.), and social capital (churches, schools, NGOs, private business, government agencies, etc.[82] Without appropriate ways of valuing ecological costs (appropriate uses of social capital), commerce that depletes natural capital will not lead to sustainable development.

Economists have long identified secure property rights as important. Such rights are disrupted when "significant externalities (such as environmental impacts) from resource extraction that have not been internalized through established property rights."[83]

Appropriate property rights protection is an important tool for internalizing environmental costs and promoting sustainable development, providing individuals and groups incentives to manage resources for maximum long-term social and economic benefit.[84] As to the present controversy, this requires the identification and invocation of social and legal rules that help internalize the costs of deforestation before timber concessions are granted.

An essential problem for developing nations is that they are susceptible to short-term economic coercion in the form of pressures to grant concessions to extract and destroy valuable natural resources, like forests. Governments need to build into their natural resource planning systems checks on this vulnerability.

Local forest-dependent people, such as the Mayagna (Sumo) of Awas Tingni, are best positioned to identify the environmental and social costs of deforestation within their ancestral domains.[85] In this light, demarcation and legal recognition of the territorial rights of the Mayagna (Sumo) of Awas Tingni represents an obligation of the Nicaraguan government and an opportunity. Recognition of ancestral domain rights at Awas Tingni will provide the Mayagna (Sumo) with state-sanctioned incentives for long-term sustainable management and can help Nicaragua capitalize on indigenous peoples' social, cultural and economic attachment to their natural resource base.

Without meaningful cultural and institutional checks on overexploitation, Nicaragua and other nations in the Americas are likely to find their natural resources mined at prices that represent only a fraction of the real long-term costs for sustaining economic, ecological and demographic stability. Without meaningful social structures that encourage responsible commerce (commerce that accounts for environmental costs), commerce will lead to systematic environmental decay and long-term impoverishment. In other words, "humans and a diversity of biological organisms can live together in relative harmony when the appropriate system is used."[86]

What is good for Awas Tingni can be good for Nicaragua, if Nicaragua finds ways to accommodate indigenous values and social structures in government policy on the one hand, and the people of Awas Tingni remain stewards of the forest and other natural resources within their indigenous territory on the other.

Sustainable development requires that economic choices take place within social and legal environments that encourage full environmental cost accounting. These social and legal environments can and should operate at the level of the village or town, the nation, and the international arena (including the Inter-American system of nations). This is consistent with the principle of subsidiarity that promotes a preference for the lowest level of decision-making where a decision can best be managed. Recognizing the territorial rights of the Mayagna (Sumo) people of Awas Tingni will help ensure that economic choices will be made in the context of meaningful and culturally appropriate social structures that more fully value and steward natural resources.

.

.

.

iii. The Collective Perspective and the Right to Culture

The Declaration of the Principles of International Cultural Cooperation provides in Article 1 that: "each culture has a dignity and value which must be respected and preserved . . . all cultures form part of the common heritage belonging to mankind."[87]

The right to culture is protected in a range of international instruments that Nicaragua has signed and ratified. Hence, the American Declaration of the Rights and Duties of Man,[88] the Universal Declaration on Human Rights and the International Covenant on Economic Social, and Cultural Rights, recognize the right of every human being to take part in cultural life.[89] In addition, the International Covenant on Civil and Political Rights[90] recognizes the rights of minorities to enjoy their own culture. The International Convention on the Rights of the Child, expressly recognizes this same right—for children.

The International Labour Organization (ILO) Convention No. 169,[91] concerning Indigenous and Tribal Peoples in Independent Countries requires governments to guarantee respect for the integrity of indigenous peoples,[92] including "the full realization of the social, economic and cultural rights of these peoples with respect for their social and cultural identity. . . ."[93] Further Nicaragua has signed the Additional Protocol to the American Convention on Economic, Social and Cultural Rights, which establishes similar guarantees, but has yet to enter into effect.[94]

In addition, the Inter-American Commission on Human Rights Draft Inter-American Declaration on the Rights of Indigenous Peoples ("IADRIP")[95] identifies "property" as an aspect of cultural integrity.[96] Property in this context is understood to include traditional lands, including sacred forests and other sites, which are recognized as vital to the maintenance of cultural integrity, as well as lands required by communities to promote their livelihood and development.

Recognition, respect, and conservation of indigenous territorial rights is essential to the cultural survival of indigenous peoples, including the Awas Tingni. Land, forests and other natural resources provide a geo-spatial habitat where indigenous peoples develop their cultures, their relations with nature, their arts, their beliefs, their histories, and their own perspective of history.[97] Indigenous peoples maintain special ties with the natural resources within their traditional areas, and manifest an intricate dependence upon these resources.

The Special Rapporteur of the UN Sub-Commission on Prevention of Discrimination and Protection of Minorities concludes:

> It is essential to know and understand the deeply spiritual special relationship between indigenous peoples and their land as basic to their existence as such and to all their beliefs, customs, traditions and culture. For such peoples, the land is not merely a possession and a means of production. The entire relationship between the spiritual life of indigenous peoples and Mother Earth, and their land, has a great many deep-seated implications. Their land is not a commodity that can be acquired, but a material element to be enjoyed freely.[98]

The United Nations Human Rights Committee recognizes that in the context of indigenous communities, "traditional land tenure is an aspect of the enjoyment of culture protected under Article 27 of the ICCPR."[99]

Further the Inter-American Commission in its report on Ecuador[100] reflects: "The principle efforts in the struggles carried forward by the Indigenous Nationalities have concentrated on the recuperation and defense of their territories. Historically defended, we consider that these constitute the material sustenance which makes possible our present and future development, and which is additionally the foundation of our historical evolution and the permanent reference of our wisdom and our system of knowledge."[101]

In its General Comment on minority rights, the United Nations Human Rights Committee observed that "*culture manifests itself in many forms, including a particular way of life associated with the use of land resources, especially in the case of indigenous people. . . .*"[102] *[emphasis added]* In the case of *Bernard Ominayak & The Lubicon Lake Band v. Canada,*[103] the H.R. Committee found that historical inequities and certain more recent developments, including oil and gas exploration, were threatening the *culture [emphasis added]* of the Lake Lubicon Band and were thus violating minority rights, contrary to Article 27 of the ICCPR.[104]

As the foregoing excerpts from various international laws demonstrate, Nicaragua has an affirmative obligation to protect the cultural survival of indigenous peoples. Accordingly, the Awas Tingni community has a right to culture. This Honorable Court in light of Article 29 of the American Convention must recognize this right and its correlative international obligation. The symbiotic relationship between land and culture in the case of indigenous peoples requires that, to guarantee the right to culture of the Awas Tingni community, the State of Nicaragua shall take positive measures to identify, recognize and ensure the enjoyment of the Mayagna Sumo ancestral domains. Failure to do so could imply a violation of the right to culture of the Awas Tingni and, consequently, that Nicaragua has incurred an international responsibility.

.

.

.

v. The Collective Perspective and the Right to Participate in Government—Article 23 of the American Convention

Article 23 of the American Convention articulates the right to participate in government. More recent international instruments, including ones focused more on environmental and developmental issues, such as Agenda 21,[105] the Desertification Convention[106] and the Beijing Declaration,[107] make clear that participatory partnerships involving both state and non-state actors, including indigenous communities such as the Awas Tingni, are developing rapidly as a means for facilitating more equitable access and sustainable use of natural resources. One of the first major international documents to make public participation a central developmental objective, including the achievement of equitable socio-economic development, was the 1986 United Nations General Assembly "Declaration on the Right to Development." Its preamble states, *inter alia:* "Recognizing that development is a comprehensive economic, social, cultural and political process, which aims at the constant improvement of the well-being of the entire population and of all individuals on the basis of their active, free and meaningful participation in development and in the fair distribution of benefits arising there from . . . ."[108]

Article 1 of the Declaration, which defines the "right to development," recognizes universal public participation as essential for the expression of the right. It asserts that: "The right to development is an inalienable human right by virtue of which every human person and all peoples are entitled to participate in, contribute to, and enjoy social, cultural and political development, in which all human rights and fundamental freedoms can be fully realized."[109]

The role of public participation as a necessary means for achieving sustainable development was first clearly identified in 1987 in *Our Common Future,* which is also known as the Brundtland Commission Report. It found that: "In the specific context of the development and environment crisis of the 1980s, which current national and international political and economic institutions have not and perhaps cannot overcome, the pursuit of sustainable development requires: *[inter alia]* . . . a political system that secures effective citizen participation in decision making."[110]

The Brundtland Commission identified "effective participation" as a *sine qua non* for achieving sustainable development. It refers particularly to the significance of participation in promoting sustainable development by specific groups of the public, including indigenous peoples[111] and NGOs.[112]

Although the UNCED and related instruments do not refer to "participation" as a right,[113] they indicate that it is vital for achieving sustainable development. They also acknowledge that international laws regarding sustainable development have a central role to play in promoting participation on all levels. Principle 27 of the Rio Declaration, for example, provides that: "States and people shall cooperate in good faith in a spirit of partnership in the fulfillment of the Principles embodied in this Declaration and in the further development of international law in the field of sustainable development."[114]

The preamble to the Rio Declaration[115] recognizes a right to participation by establishing a "new and equitable global partnership" which will be realized through new levels of co-operation among states and with non-state actors, namely ". . . key sectors of societies and people."[116] This new form of co-operation is the right to participation.

In light of the application of Article 29 of the American Convention to this case, the right to participate in government—consecrated in Article 23—should be integrated with the evolution of international law in this matter. As such the Awas Tingni community has a right to participate in decisions concerning the exploitation of their natural resources. The right to participate, however, was not complied with by the Government of Nicaragua when it granted a timber concession that overlapped with the indigenous territory of Awas Tingni. The timber concession was granted without consulting the indigenous community and without assuring that the local people would be able to continue benefiting from natural resources within their ancestral domain. In light of the failure to comply with international laws on participation, there is an urgent need to ensure that the Government of Nicaragua is officially informed of where the indigenous territory of the Awas Tingni is located and to recognize the community-based property rights of the Awas Tingni. No other remedy will ensure that the mistakes of the recent past will not be perpetrated anew.

Conclusion

The basic human rights of indigenous peoples in the Americas have long been neglected. This case presents an unprecedented opportunity for the Inter-American Court to establish a important legal precedent by which the human rights of indigenous peoples can be recognized and protected.

The Inter-American Human Rights System can adequately and effectively protect indigenous peoples by a meaningful interpretation of the American Convention. In the case at hand, a proper analysis of the American Convention on indigenous peoples rights should consider the "symbiotic tie" between the life-land-culture-environment of the Awas Tingni community. It does not suffice that the Court understand that the non-demarcation of indigenous land by the State constitutes a violation of Article 21 of the Convention. The Court must go further considering among others violations to the right to life, to a healthy environment, to culture, to identity, to participate in government, and to freedom of religion.

Historically, indigenous peoples have demanded the recognition by non-indigenous societies of the spiritual, social, cultural, economic and political significance of their lands, territories and other natural resources. This is necessary for the continued survival and vitality of their societies. Addressing the circumstances of indigenous peoples in a different conceptual framework, due to their deeply rooted relationships to lands, territories and resources is essential. Indigenous peoples have urged the world community to assign a clear positive value to these distinct relationships,[117] and they have long awaited an appropriate and just response.

This Court has a unique opportunity to begin to address indigenous peoples' human and environmental rights, recognizing the special relationship indigenous peoples have with their land and resources, and in so doing protecting and promoting the basic human rights of indigenous peoples in an adequate and effective manner.

This brief has identified an array of international human rights and environmental laws, as well as legal and economic concepts, that support the petition of the Inter-American Commission on behalf of the people of Awas Tingni. The Inter-American Court in its wisdom will use this information in ways that it deems most appropriate. The international human rights and environmental communities trust that the final decision will equitably balance the interests at stake and render a decision that promote the well-being of Nicaragua and all of its citizens, especially those who have long endured discrimination and injustice.

Respectfully,

Romina Picolotti
Owen Lynch
International Human Rights Center
for International Environmental Law
Law Group

ANNEX

Contemporary Comparative Insights from Canada, Australia and the Philippines

Comparative domestic developments over the past decade concerning the legal demarcation and recognition of indigenous rights to land and other natural resources make clear that the relief requested in this case is not an isolated, atypical, unprecedented or far-reaching request. Rather, the complaint by the Inter-American Commission on behalf of the Awas Tingni Mayagna (Sumo) indigenous community is very much in accord with the ongoing development of domestic legal standards for recognizing native title and other indigenous rights. The leading countries in terms of domestic laws and jurisprudence may be Australia, Canada and the Philippines. A brief summary of major laws and jurisprudence in these three countries follows.

Canada

The Canadian Constitution Act of 1982 recognizes "Aboriginal and Treaty Rights" in section 35 and its "Charter of Rights and Freedoms" contains several sections regarding indigenous rights. Even before the Constitution Act of 1982 was promulgated, the Supreme Court of Canada (SCC) issued its famous Calder decision.[118] In Calder, the SCC recognized for the first time the continuous existence of an "aboriginal (Indian) title." The case originated in the province of British Columbia (BC) where no treaties with any First Nations existed. Further SCC decisions in Guerin and Sparrow expanded on Calder's recognition of aboriginal rights.[119]

Since 1973 a Canadian "Comprehensive Land Claims Process" (CLCP) has been in place to address legal issues concerning indigenous territorial rights in traditionally occupied areas that are not covered by treaties. The CLCP has been used to negotiate "comprehensive land claim settlements" that include indigenous land and self-determination rights as well as political reforms, particularly in Canada's northern territories.

Current Canadian comprehensive land claim settlements negotiated between Canadian Federal and Provincial Governments and Indian First Nations, as well as other indigenous (Inuit and Metis) groups, recognize a wide range of rights to land and other natural resources, self-government, environmental protections, etc. Early versions of land claim settlements, starting with the James Bay and Northern Quebec Agreement of 1975, the Northeastern Quebec Agreement of 1978, and the Inuvialuit Final Agreement of 1984, include environmental protections. This has been broadened in more recent agreements to address the concept of sustainable development, e.g., Yukon Umbrella Final Agreement (1990), Nunavut Final Agreement and Nunavut Self-Governing Territory (1993).[120]

The latest agreement of this kind is the "Nisga'a Settlement" in British Columbia. This long awaited land claims and self-government treaty was signed on August 4, 1998 for an area that until then was NOT covered by any treaty.[121] More than a dozen major 'regional agreements' exist in Canada and many more are under negotiation. Up to 75 percent of the entire country may soon be under some form of joint indigenous-government agreement. Canadian regional treaties vary and illustrate the general point that different solutions in this field work for different peoples.[122]

Since 1996 there are also new SCC decisions concerning indigenous land and self-determination rights. These decisions concern the interpretation of aboriginal title and aboriginal rights, the validity of indigenous titles, land selection, indigenous self-administration and environmental management, and the fiduciary duties of the state towards indigenous groups. Indian groups are even commonly referred to in Canada as 'First Nations.'

In 1997 the SCC decided the Delgamuukw case[123] and it could now be considered the leading case in Canada on aboriginal title. The court decided that Aboriginal title conceptually falls in-between the rights associated with an inalienable fee simple and those rights traditionally integral to Aboriginal cultures.[124] Chief Justice Lamer held that "*aboriginal title encompasses the right to exclusive use and occupation of the land* held pursuant to that title for a variety of purposes, which need not be aspects of those aboriginal practices, customs, and traditions which are integral to distinctive aboriginal cultures."[125] *[emphasis added]* The Chief Justice emphasizes that the source of this Aboriginal title manifests from the "common law principle that occupation is proof of possession in law."[126] The Court elaborated some important characteristics associated with this new concept of indigenous title: the exclusive right to use the land is not restricted to activities congruent with traditional Aboriginal practices, the land is held communally and is inalienable, and can only be sold or surrendered to the Crown.[127]

The 1996 five volume Report of the indigenous/non-indigenous "Royal Commission on Aboriginal Peoples" (RCAP) is likely to provide the future basis for interpreting and recognizing indigenous (Indian, Inuit and Metis) rights in Canada (see Report of the Royal Commission on Aboriginal Peoples (RCAP) Canada Communication Group, Ottawa 1996, vol. I–V). The RCAP calls for a new partnership between the Canadian government and First Nations. It provides that First Nations shall receive an equal status, but at the same time shall be regarded as different groups" (id., vol. II, part 1, 176). The sovereignty of the Canadian State is understood as the territorial power of peoples, in equality and co-existence. Indigenous, Provincial and the Federal governments are required to work at the same level (id., vol. II, part 1, 240). The rights of indigenous people living outside their traditional territories are given special consideration.

Australia

The High Court of Australia (HCA) has held that native title rights are rights *'sui generis'* because of the special cultural and spiritual connection of aboriginal people to their ancestral domains. The primary prerequisite for gaining legal recognition of ancestral-domain rights is proof of traditional and continuous connections to the area.

Australian jurisprudence concerning native title emanates from a decision rendered on 3 June 1992 *Mabo v. Queensland* in which the High Court of Australia (HCA) upheld the claims of indigenous peoples from Murray Island in the Torres Strait. The HCA ruled that Australia was not *terra nullius* ('empty territory belonging to no one') when settled by the British in 1788. Rather, it was occupied by mainland Aboriginal and Torres Strait Islander people who had their own laws and customs and whose 'native title' to land survived the Crown's annexation of Australia.[128] The position of the HCA in Mabo (1) was reaffirmed in Mabo (2) which held that section 10 of Australia's Federal Racial Discrimination Act of 1975 (No. 52 of 1975) constitutes a Federal 'safety net' against State or Territory legislation that would otherwise extinguish native title rights.[129]

Legally recognized native title rights in Australia are often for hunting, fishing and/or gathering rights, but they can be much more than that. Mabo (2) makes clear that traditional aboriginal rights and customs define the content of native title. Thus indigenous rights to land and natural resources are legally acknowledged to vary from region to region.[130]

Australia's Native Title Act (NTA) of 1993 came into effect on 1 January 1994. This legislation is a direct result of the Mabo (2) decision and provides the first nationally valid mechanism to clarify native title claims. The NTA established a National Native Title Tribunal (NNTT). It also validated state laws that provided for recognition of native title. Procedures and standards for future native title agreements were introduced. A Land Fund was established for those indigenous people who cannot take advantage of the NTA, e.g., they have already lost their traditional connection to their ancestral domain because of involuntary removal.

Pursuant to the NTA, a diverse array of negotiated Native Title Agreements and Land Use and Resource Agreements exist in Australia today. This is encouraging for the negotiation of future indigenous/non-indigenous agreements.

State governments in Australia are also providing for legal recognition of native title. In 1996, the Cape York Land Use (Heads of)Agreement (CYA) was signed by the Peninsular Regional Council of the Aboriginal and Torres Strait Islander Commission (ATSIS), the Cape York Land Council, the Cattlemen's Union of Australia as well as the Australian Conservation Foundation of Nature and The Wilderness Society.[131] The parties committed themselves to the development of "a management regime for ecologically, socially and culturally sustainable land use on the Cape York Peninsular." A final agreement could be registered with the NNTT under section 21 of the NTA. One reason why the CYA is so important is that it strives for government participation and legitimization, as it is now common in Canadian "comprehensive land claim settlements."[132] Another reason is that the CYA represents a first step on the way towards comprehensive Australian regional agreements, in which central stakeholders of the resource industry, environmental as well as indigenous groups agree upon different kinds of land use. This way, each party is assured of being benefited from any agreement.

Regional agreements are defined as a concept of equitable and direct negotiations between Indigenous Peoples, governments and other stakeholders in a region to recognize the rights of indigenous peoples and to protect them in a contemporary legal system. A regional agreement is a way to organize policies, politics, administration and/or public services for or by indigenous peoples in a defined territory of land or land and sea.[133]

The Philippines

The Republic of the Philippines has long relied on a fictitious colonial legal concept, known as the Regalian Doctrine, to justify its claim to State ownership over indigenous lands and resources. After Corazon Aquino became president in 1986 following a "peoples' power revolution" the Philippine Department of Environment and Natural Resources (DENR) became more responsive to and supportive of upland communities, including indigenous communities. The DENR began authenticating and demarcating the perimeters of ancestral domain claims in the early 1990s, and a large-scale community-based forest management program was launched. By 30 June 1998, nearly nine percent of the country's total land mass, or over 2.7 million ha, including many mountain areas, was officially covered by Certificates of Ancestral Domain Claims (CADCs), and even more areas were covered by different types of tenure instruments under various community forestry programs.

Legislative efforts to convert the ancestral claims into ancestral titles received a culminated in October 1997 when the Philippines Congress passed the Indigenous Peoples Rights Act (IPRA).[134] The IPRA establishes a legal presumption that areas inhabited by indigenous peoples are "owned" by them and constitute "not only the physical environment but the total environment including spiritual and cultural bonds."[135] More specifically, ancestral domains are defined to include "lands, forests, pasture . . . hunting grounds, burial grounds, worship areas [and] bodies of water."[136] Ancestral-domain rights include rights of ownership, development and priority setting, regulation of entry by outsiders, conflict resolution, transfer and redemption,[137] and "the right to participate fully . . . at all levels of decision making in matters which may affect their rights."[138]

NOTES

1. I.C.J., Pleadings, Legal Consequences for States of the Continued Presence of South Africa, in Namibia Notwithstanding Security Council Resol. 276 (1970), Vol. II, at 636–37.

2. To date, the court has had only one opportunity to rule in a case concerning indigenous rights. I/A Court H.R., Aloeboetoe et al, Case, Judgement of 10 September 1993, Reparation Phase. The Court specifically ruled on the issue of indigenous customary law.

3. The catastrophic mudslides associated with recent hurricanes illustrate the vulnerability of denuded lands to environmental stresses.

4. American Convention on Human Rights, 22 November 1969, O.A.S. Treaty Ser. No. 36, 1144 U.N.T.S. 123 [hereinafter American Convention] (entered into force July 18, 1978).

5. American Convention, supra note 4, at Article 29. It is worth noticing the relevance of Article 29 of the American Convention as a legal foundation for these ways of interpretation.

6. Inter-American Commission on Human Rights, Report on the Situation of Human Rights of a Segment of the Nicaraguan Population of Miskito Origin, O.A.S. Doc. OEA/Ser.L/V/II.62, doc. 10, rev. 3 (November 29, 1993).

7. Inter-American Commission on Human Rights, Annual Report 1979–1980 [hereinafter Annual Report], OEA/Ser/V/II. 50, doc. 13, rev. 1.

8. Ibid.

9. Ibid.

10. Inter-American Commission on Human Rights, Ten Years of Activities, 1974–1981, Gen. Sec. O.A.S., Washington, D.C., 1982, case 1802.

11. Annual Report, supra note 7.

12. See Inter-American Commission on Human Rights, Report on the Situation of Human Rights of a Segment of the Nicaraguan Population of Miskito Origin, O.A.S. Doc. OEA/Ser.L/V/II. 62, doc. 10, rev. 3 (November 29, 1993). See also Inter-American Commission on Human Rights, Third Report on the Situation of Human Rights in the Republic of Guatemala, OEA/Ser/L/V/II.66, doc. 16 (October 3, 1985).

13. For the sake of brevity we will not reproduce here the ongoing discussion surrounding these terms.

14. Jose R. Martinez Cobo, Study of the Problem of Discrimination Against Indigenous Populations, at 29, U.N. Doc. E/CN.4/Sub.2/1986/7/Add.4, U.N. Sales No. E.86.XIV.3 (1987) *[emphasis added]*. With this definition, the study attempts to distinguish indigenous populations from other minority groups. See discussion of the U.N. Working Group on Indigenous Populations (U.N. Working Group), Part III. D.2.

15. See Closing Statement of Professor Erica-Irene A. Daes, Chairperson of the Working Group, Discrimination Against Indigenous Peoples, Report of the Working Group on Indigenous Populations on its Ninth Session, U.N. Com-

mission on Human Rights, Sub-Commission on Prevention of Discrimination and Protection of Minorities, 43d Sess., Agenda Item 15, at 51, U.N. Doc. E/CN.4/Sub.2/40/rev.1 (1991):

> The Working Group atmosphere during the last session was like a true and democratic assembly, in which Government representatives, Indigenous People's representatives, representatives of the specialized agencies, members of the Working Group, scholars and other individuals openly and freely exchanged their views. In this assembly pluralism, freedom of opinion and expression and the principles of equality and non-discrimination have prevailed throughout the session.

See also Independent Commission on International Humanitarian Issues, Indigenous Peoples: A Global Quest for Justice 8 (1987) (summary statement); Russel L. Barsh, *Indigenous Peoples: An Emerging Object of International Law,* 80 Am. J. Int'l L. 369, 381–83 (1986) (containing an insider's view, for "public" consumption, of many of the Working Group sessions during the 1980s); Raidza Torres, *The Rights of Indigenous Populations: The Emerging International Norm,* 16 Yale J. Int'l L. 127 (1991) (the role of the Working Group in developing an "indigenous norm").

16. Draft of the Inter-American Declaration on the Rights of Indigenous Peoples, Approved by the Inter-American Commission on Human Rights at the 1278th session held on O.A.S. Doc. OEA/Ser/L/V/II.90, doc. 9, rev. 1, September 18, 1995.

17. I/A Court H.R., In the Matter of Viviana Gallardo and Others, Resolution of 15 July 1981, Decision of 13 November 1981, Series A, No. 101/81, para. 16.

18. F. Caportorti, Study on the Rights of Persons belonging to Ethnic, Religious and Linguistic Minorities, para. 585 (United Nations Center for Human Rights 1991).

19. Distinguishable from the principle which called for identical treatment for everyone in every situation.

20. Permanent Court of International Justice, Minority Schools in Albania, Advisory Opinion, 1935 P. C. I.J. (Ser. A/B) No. 64. The P. C. I.J. noted:

> The first is to ensure that a national belonging to racial, religious, or linguistic minorities shall be placed in every respect on a footing of perfect equality with the other national of the State.
>
> The second is to ensure for the minority elements suitable means for the preservation of their racial peculiarities, their traditions, and their national characteristics.
>
> These two requirements are indeed closely interlocked, for there would be no true equality between a majority and a minority if the latter were deprived of its own institutions, and were consequently compelled to renounce that which constitutes the very essence of its being as a minority.

21. For a critique of the way that the IACHR has treated indigenous peoples in its jurisprudence, see Ariel Dulitzky, *Los Pueblos Indigenas: Jurisprudencia del*

Sistema Interamericano de Protección de los Derechos Humanos, Revista IIDH, Vol. 26, 1998.

22. Shelton H. Davis, "Land Rights and Indigenous Peoples The Role of the Inter-American Commission on Human Rights," Cultural Survival Report 29, 1988, iv.

23. Resolution of the IACHR, "On the Problem of Special Protection for Indigenous Populations," OEA/Ser.L/V/II.29, doc. 38, rev. 1972.

24. Report on the Situation of Human Rights of a Segment of the Nicaraguan Population of Miskito Origin, at 127, O.A.S. Doc. OEA/Ser.L/V/II.62, doc. 10, rev. 3 (November 29, 1983).

25. Inter-American Commission on Human Rights, Resolution 12/85, Case 7615, Brazil.

26. Inter-American Commission on Human Rights, Annual Report 1979–1980, O.A.S. Doc. OEA/Ser.L/V/II.50, doc. 13, rev. 1 (IACHR 1980).

27. Inter-American Commission on Human Rights, Report on the Situation of Human Rights in Ecuador, at 91, O.A.S. Doc. OEA/Ser.L/V/II.96 (1997).

28. Which in this case may be an "American Convention on the Human Rights of Indigenous Peoples."

29. American Convention, supra note 4, at Article 29. The document reads as follows:

> No provision of the Convention may be interpreted as:
> a. permitting any State Party, group, or person to suppress the enjoyment or exercise of the rights and freedoms recognized in this Convention or to restrict them to a greater extent than is provided for herein;
> b. restricting the enjoyment or exercise of any right or freedom recognized by virtue of the laws of any State Party or by virtue of another convention to which one of the said states is a party;
> c. precluding other rights or guarantees that are inherent in the human personality or derived from representative democracy as a form of government; or
> d. excluding or limiting the effect that the American Declaration of the Rights and Duties of Man and other international acts of the same nature have.

30. I/A Court H.R., "Other Treaties" Subject to the Consultative Jurisdiction of the Court (Art. 64 of the American Convention on Human Rights), Advisory Opinion OC-1/82 of September 24, 1982, Inter-American Court on Human Rights (Ser. A) No. 1 (1982), para. 41.

31. See Barcelona Traction, Light & Power Co., Ltd. (New Application) *(Belg. v. Spain),* 1970 International Court of Justice 4 (Judgment of February 5), which refers to the "basic rights of the human person." See also Legal Consequences for the States of the Continued Presence of South Africa in Namibia (South Africa) Notwithstanding Security Council Resolutions 276, 1971 International Court of Justice 16, 57 (Advisory Opinion of June 21), which states, in an advisory opinion of the Court, that the "denial [by South Africa] of fundamental human rights is a flagrant violation of the purposes and principles of the Charter."

32. See Interpretation of the American Declaration of the Rights and Duties of Man Within the Framework of Article 64 of the American Convention on Human Rights, 1989 Inter-American Court on Human Rights 49, paras. 43 and 44 (Advisory Opinion of July 14, OC), referred to in the [OAS] Charter: ". . . and that . . . the Charter of the [OAS] . . . cannot be interpreted and applied as far as human rights are concerned without relating its norms, consistent with the practice of the organs of the OAS, to the corresponding provisions of the Declaration."

33. International Covenant on Civil and Political Rights [hereinafter ICCPR], 16 December 1966, G. A. Res. 2200(XXI), 999 U.N.T. S. 277. Nicaragua ratified the ICCPR on 12 March 1980.

34. International Covenant on Economic, Social and Cultural Rights [hereinafter ICESCR], 16 December 1966, G. A. Res. 2200(XXI), 993 U.N.T. S. 3. Nicaragua ratified the ICESCR on 12 March 1980.

35. International Convention on the Elimination of All Forms of Racial Discrimination [hereinafter CERD], 21 December 1965, G. A. Res. 2106 A(XX), 660 U.N.T. S. 195. Nicaragua ratified the CERD on 15 February 1978.

36. Convention on the Rights of the Child [hereinafter CRC], U.N. General Assembly Doc. A/RES/44/25, 28 November 1989, 28 ILM 1448 (1989). Nicaragua ratified the CRC on October 5, 1990.

37. Universal Declaration of Human Rights [hereinafter Universal Declaration], G. A. Res. 217 A(III), 10 December 1948, Article 3; American Declaration on the Rights and Duties of Man [hereinafter American Declaration], adopted by the Ninth International Conference of American States (March 30–May 2, 1948), O.A.S. Res. 30, O.A.S. Doc. OEA/Ser.L/V/I.4, rev. (1965), Article 1; American Convention, supra note 4, at Article 4; ICCPR, supra note 33, at Article 6; ICESCR, supra note 34, at Article 6; CRC, supra note 36, at Article 6.

38. Universal Declaration, supra note 37, at Article 7; American Declaration, supra note 37, at Article 2; American Convention, supra note 4, at Article 24; ICCPR, supra note 33, at Articles 3 and 26; ICESCR, supra note 34, at Article 3; CERD, supra note 35, at Article 3.

39. Universal Declaration, supra note 37, at Article 8; American Convention, supra note 4, at Article 25; ICCPR, supra note 33, at Article 2.3.

40. Universal Declaration, supra note 37, at Article 13; American Declaration, supra note 37, at Article 8; American Convention, supra note 4, at Article 22; ICCPR, supra note 33, at Article 12.1; CERD, supra note 35, at Article 5.d.i.

41. Universal Declaration, supra note 37, at Article 17; American Declaration, supra note 37, at Article 23; American Convention, supra note 4, at Article 21; CERD, supra note 35, at Article 5.d.v.

42. Universal Declaration, supra note 37, at Article 18; American Declaration, supra note 37, at Article 3; American Convention, supra note 4, at Article 12; ICCPR, supra note 33, at Article 18.1; CERD, supra note 35, at Article 5.d.vii; CRC, supra note 36, at Article 14.1.

43. Universal Declaration, supra note 37, at Article 27; American Declaration, supra note 37, at Article 13; ICESCR, supra note 34, at Articles 15.1 and 15.2.

44. ICCPR, supra note 33, at Articles 1, 2, and 3; ICESCR, supra note 34, at Article 1.

45. Universal Declaration, supra note 37, at Articles 1 and 2; ICCPR, supra note 33, at Articles 2.1 and 26; ICESCR, supra note 34, at Article 2; CERD, supra note 35, at Article 1.

46. ICESCR, supra note 34, at Article 12.1; CRC, supra note 36, at Article 24.

47. ICESCR, supra note 34, at Article 12.1.b.

48. American Declaration, supra note 37, at Article 9; American Convention, supra note 4, at Article 11; ICCPR, supra note 33, at Article 17; CRC, supra note 36, at Article 16.

49. ICCPR, supra note 33, at Article 27; CRC, supra note 36, at Article 30.

50. CRC, supra note 36, at Article 8.

51. Inter-American Court on Human Rights, Proposed Amendments to the Naturalization Provisions of the Constitution of Costa Rica, Advisory Opinion OC-4/84 of January 19, 1984 (Ser. A.) No. 4 (1984), paras. 2, 3, and 6.

52. See section III.i. of this amicus brief.

53. The first international instruments that recognized collective rights in the case of indigenous peoples were ILO Conventions 107 and 169.

54. The Rio Summit Agreements enshrine the following collective rights: (a) internal decision making, (b) representation in national decision making, (c) collective right to land, and (d) collective right to control of development.

55. For a framework of the advances of indigenous peoples' collective rights in international law, see Russel Lawrence Barsh, *Indigenous Peoples in the 1990s: From Object to Subject of International Law*, in 7 Harv. Hum. Rts. J. 33.

56. Report on the Situation of Human Rights in Ecuador, chapter IX, Human Rights Issues of Special Relevance to the Indigenous Inhabitants of the Country, O.A.S. Country Report.

57. Commission on Human Rights, Sub-Commission on Prevention of Discrimination and Protection of Minorities, Indigenous Peoples and Their Relationship to Land, preliminary working paper prepared by Mrs. Erica-Irene Daes, Special Rapporteur, at para. 13, E/CN.4/Sub.2/1997/17.

58. Amicus Curiae presented by Nicaraguan Indigenous Organizations, Communities, and Representatives in the case of Mayagna (Sumo) Community of Awas Tingni before the Inter-American Court on Human Rights, at 4 and 5.

59. See U.N. General Assembly, Res. 37/189A, of 1982. See also U.N. Commission on Human Rights, Res. 1982/7 of 1982, and Res. 1983/43 of 1983.

60. B. G. Ramcharan, *The Right to Life*, 30 Netherlands International Law Review (1983), 301.

61. A. A. Cancado Trindade, *The Parallel Evolutions of International Human Rights Protection and of Environmental Protection and the Absence of Restrictions upon*

the Exercise of Recognized Human Rights, in Revista del Instituto Interamericano de Derechos Humanos, No. 13, at 53.

62. See "Human Rights and the Environment: Final Report prepared by Mrs. Fatma Zohra Ksentini, Special Rapporteur," E/CN.4/Sub.2/1994/9, 6 July 1994, para. 77. See generally A. Durning, *Guardians of the Land: Indigenous Peoples and the Health of the Earth* (Washington, D.C.: Worldwatch, 1993).

63. See Communication No. 167/1984, Annual Report of the Human Rights Committee, U.N. GAOR, 45th Sess., Supp. No. 40, vol. 2, Annex IX, U.N. Doc. A/45/40 (1990), reprinted in Hum. Rts. L. J. 305 (1990).

64. Caroline Dommen, *Claiming Environmental Rights: Some Possibilities Offered by the United Nations' Human Rights Mechanisms,* 11 Geo. Int'l Envtl. L. Rev., 1, 24.

65. For factual information, see Report on Discrimination Against Indigenous Peoples, Investments and Operations on the Lands of Indigenous Peoples, U.N. Commission on Human Transnationals, Sub-Commission on Prevention of Discrimination and Protection of Minorities, 43d. Sess., Agenda Item 13, U.N. Doc. E/CN.4/Sub.2/1991/49 (1991). See also Inter-American Report on Ecuador: Report on the Situation of Human Rights in Ecuador [hereinafter Ecuador Report], O.A.S., Inter-American Commission on Human Rights, OEA/Ser.L/V/II.96, doc. 10, rev. 1, 24 April 1997.

66. See *Genocide in Paraguay* (Richard Arens ed., 1976), 132–71. In the epilogue to this book, Elie Wiesel, a Holocaust survivor, Nobel Peace Prize recipient, and author, concludes that the Ache situation in Paraguay included all of the elements of genocide (Ibid., at 165–71). The last chapter, "A Lawyer's Summation," is law professor Aren's closing argument that the government of Paraguay committed genocide against the Ache (Ibid., at 132–64).

67. Cited in J. G. C. Van Aggelen, *Le rôle des organisations internationales dans la protection du droit à la vie,* Bruxelles Story-Scientia (1986), 32.

68. Cited in Th. Desch, *The Concept and Dimensions of the Right to Life (as Defined in International Standards and in International and Comparative Jurisprudence),* 36 Osterreichische Zeitschrift fur Offenrliches Recht und Volkerrecht (1985), 101.

69. For example, see U.N. Environment Programme Conference of Plenipotentiaries on the Global Convention on the Control of Transboundary Movements of Hazardous Wastes: Final Acts and Texts of the Basel Convention, 22 March 1989, 28 ILM 649, 657. Additional Protocol I and II to the Geneva Conventions, concluded at Geneva, 10 June 1977, and entered into force December 7, 1978 (relating to the Protection of Victims of International Armed Conflicts), 16 ILM 1391 (1978).

70. See ICESCR, supra note 34.

71. See O.A.S. Additional Protocol to the American Convention on Human Rights in the Areas of Economic, Social and Cultural Rights, "Protocol of San Salvador," 28 ILM 156, 161 (1988). The Protocol has been signed by Nicaragua but is not still in force.

72. Hague Declaration on the Environment, 11 March 1989, 28 ILM 1308

(1989), cited in P. Sands, *The Environment, Community and International Law,* 30 HILJ 393 (1989).

73. See Fatma Zohra Ksentini, Human Rights and the Environment, Final Report of the Special Rapporteur [hereinafter Ksentini Report], U.N. Doc. E/CN.4/Sub.2/1994/9, 6 July 1994, at 8.

74. See Proposal for a Basic Law on Environmental Protection and the Promotion of Sustainable Development, Document Series on Environmental Law No. 1, UNEP, UNEP Regional Office for Latin America and the Caribbean, Mexico, D.F., 1st. Ed., Title 1, Article 2, para. 9, 1993.

75. See Ksentini Report, supra note 73, at Part II, para. 9, Annex I. See also supra note 71, at Article 11. A regional international instrument, the 1988 Additional Protocol to the American Convention on Human Rights ("San Salvador Protocol") also includes the right to a healthy environment.

76. IUCN Commission on Environmental Law, Draft International Covenant on Environment and Development, Article 12(1) (1995).

77. Ibid., at Article 12(2).

78. For specific examples, see Ksentini Report, supra note 73, at Annex I.

79. Cancado Trindade, op. cit.; see supra note 61, at 66.

80. A. Ch. Kiss, "Le droit à la qualité de l'environnement: un droit de l'homme?" in *Le droit à la qualité de l'environnement: un droit en devenir, un droit à définir* (N. Duplé ed., Vieux-Montréal, Ed. Quebec/Amérique 1988), 69–70.

81. See Daniel W. Bromley, *Environment and Economy: Property Rights and Public Policy* (1991), 60–61.

82. Ismail Serageldin, Sustainability and the Wealth of Nations: First Steps in an Ongoing Journey, paper prepared for the Third Annual World Bank Conference on Environmentally Sustainable Development (1995). See also Robert Goodland and Herman Daly, "Environmental Sustainability: Universal and Non-Negotiable," in *Ecological Adaptations* 6(4) (1996); reprinted in Hunter, Salzman, and Zaelke, *International Environmental Law and Policy* 136 (1998).

83. Theodore Panayotou, Economic Instruments for Environmental Management and Sustainable Development, 17 (UNEP, 1994).

84. See David Pearce et al, Blueprint for a Green Economy, 154–57 (1989). See also Bromley, supra note 81, at 84–95.

85. See Sheldon Davis and Katrinka Ebbe, eds., *Traditional Knowledge and Sustainable Development: Proceedings of a Conference* (Washington, D.C.: World Bank Environmentally Sustainable Development Proceedings, 1993); Darrell A. Posey, "Indigenous Knowledge in the Conservation and Use of the World Forests," in *World Forests for the Future: Their Use and Conservation,* Kilaparti Ramakrishna and George M. Woodwell, eds. (Yale University Press, 1993).

86. Sir Ghillean Prance (Director of the Royal Botanical Gardens, Kew, United Kingdom), in *From the Ashes: Reflections on Chico Mendez and the Future of the Rainforest* (Washington, D.C.: National Wildlife Federation and Environmental Defense Fund, 1998), 12.

87. Declaration of the Principles of International Cultural Cooperation, Resolutions, Gen. Conf. of UNESCO, 4 November 1966 (Sess. 14).

88. American Declaration, supra note 37, at Article 8.

89. Universal Declaration, supra note 37, at Article 27; ICESCR, supra note 34, at Article 15, para. 1(a).

90. ICCPR, supra note 33, at Article 27.

91. See Convention (No. 169) Concerning Indigenous and Tribal Peoples in Indigenous Countries [hereinafter Convention 169], 27 June 1989, 28 ILM 1382 (1989). Even though Nicaragua has not yet ratified Convention 169, the elements referring to territorial rights in the Convention are considered the new emergent customary law. See S. J. Anaya, *Indigenous Peoples in International Law* (Oxford), 49–58. In addition, the ILO's founding charter obliges all ILO members to comply with ILO conventions, whether or not they are a signatory. See also Torres and Raidza, *The Rights of Indigenous Peoples: The Emergent International Norm,* 16 Yale J. Int'l. L. 127 (1991), 160–61.

92. Article 13 of the International Convention on Indigenous Peoples No. 169 provides that "government shall respect the special importance for the cultures and spiritual values of the peoples concerned with their relationship with the land or territories . . . in particular the collective aspects of this relationship."

93. Convention 169, supra note 91, at Article 2, para. 1(b).

94. See O.A.S. Additional Protocol to the American Convention on Human Rights in the Areas of Economic, Social and Cultural Rights, "Protocol of San Salvador," 28 ILM 156, 161 (1988).

95. Inter-American Commission on Human Rights Draft, Inter-American Declaration on the Rights of Indigenous Peoples, O.A.S. Doc. OEA/Ser/L/V/II.90, doc. 9, rev. 1 (1995) [hereinafter IADRIP].

96. IADRIP, supra note 95, at Article 7, para. 2.

97. "The Rights of the Indigenous Peoples," document prepared by a Committee of Experts, indigenous and non-indigenous, IIHR, San José, Costa Rica. Revista IIDH 26, 1998, at 65.

98. See Jose R. Martinez Cobo, Study of the Problem of Discrimination against Indigenous Populations, at 26, U.N. Doc. E/CN.4/Sub.2/1986/7/Add.4, 1987.

99. See *Omniyak, Chief of the Lubicon Lake Band v. Canada,* Communication No. 267/1984, U.N. Doc. A/45/40, Annex 9(A) (1990). See also petition by "The Mayagna Indian Community of Awas Tingni and Jaime Castillo Felipe against Nicaragua," Inter-American Human Rights Commission, 2 October 1995, at 20.

100. Ecuador Report, supra note 65.

101. CONFENIAE, "La Nacionalidad Huaorani y la Defensa de su Territorio," 1989, at 3 (filed as Annex 3 to the petition filed on behalf of the Huaorani on June 1, 1990).

102. General Comment No. 23: The Rights of Minorities, U.N. CCPR Human Rights Committee, 50th Sess., 1314th Mtg., U.N. Doc. CCPR/C/21/Rev. 1/Add. 5 (1994), http://www.austlii.edu.au/ahric/hrcomm/gencomm/index.html

103. See Communication No. 167/1984, Annual Report of the Human

Rights Committee, U.N. GAOR, 45th Sess., Supp. No. 40, vol. 2, Annex IX, U.N. Doc. A/45/40 (1990); reprinted in Hum. Rts. L. J. 305 (1990).

104. Caroline Dommen, *Claiming Environmental Rights: Some Possibilities Offered by the United Nations' Human Rights Mechanisms,* 11 Geo. Int'l Envtl. L. Rev. 1, 24.

105. Agenda 21, U.N. Conference on Environment and Development, Rio de Janeiro, 13 June 1992, U.N. Doc. A/Conf.151/26.

106. United Nations Convention to Combat Desertification in those Countries Experiencing Serious Drought and/or Desertification, particularly in Africa [hereinafter Desertification Convention], UN G.A.D. A/AC.241/15/Rev. 7, 33 ILM 1328 (1994).

107. Beijing Declaration, A/Conf.177/L.5/Add.15, 14 September 1995.

108. Declaration on the Right to Development [hereinafter DRD], G. A. Res. 41/128, 4 December 1986, preamble; reprinted in *Human Rights. A Compilation of International Instruments,* Vol. I, Part 2 (Universal Instruments, United Nations, New York, Geneva 1994), 548.

109. DRD, supra note 108, at Article 1.

110. See *Our Common Future, The World Commission on Environment and Development* (Oxford University Press 1987), 65.

111. Ibid., at 12, 115–16. ("[The] . . . traditional rights . . . [of indigenous people] . . . should be recognized and they should be given a decisive voice in formulating policies about resource development in their areas.")

112. Ibid., at 328. ("In many countries, governments need to recognize and extend NGOs' right to know and have access to information on the environment and natural resources; their right to be consulted and to participate in decision making on activities likely to have a significant effect on their environment; and their right to legal remedies and redress when their health or environment has or may be seriously affected.")

113. Shelton, in *Human Rights, Environmental Rights and the Right to Environment*, 28 Stan. Envtl. L. J. 103 (1991), writes that even with regard to "well established rights, such as public participation, the [Rio] Declaration avoids using rights terminology." See also the Rio Declaration on Environment and Development, U.N. Conference on Environment and Development [hereinafter Rio Declaration], Rio de Janeiro, 13 June 1992, U.N. Doc. A/Conf.151/26, principle 10, which advocates public participation in the context of "efficiency" rather than as a right. Agenda 21 also fails to refer to participation as a right.

114. Rio Declaration, supra note 113, at Principle 27.

115. Ibid., at preamble.

116. Ibid.

117. See, e.g., M. Bothe, "The Subsidiarity Principle," in *Fair Principles for Sustainable Development* (E. Dommen ed., 1993).

118. *Calder v. The Queen* (1973), 34 DLR (3d) 145.

119. See *Guerin v. The Queen* (1984), 2 SCR 335; *R. v. Sparrow* (1990), 1 SCR 1075.

120. See, e.g., Donna Craig and Diana Ponce Nova, *Indigenous Peoples and Environmental Law,* No. 8 (Macquary University, Sydney 1994), 115, 138.

121. See *The Nisga'a Settlement,* 4 (17) Indigenous Law Bulletin 2, http://www.ntc.bc.ca/

122. Mick Dodson, Indigenous Social Justice. Vol. I—Strategies and Recommendations, Submission to the Parliament of Australia on the Social Justice Package, 1995, Sydney Office of the Aboriginal and Torres Strait Islander Social Justice Commissioner, 21–24.

123. *Delgamuukw v. British Columbia* (1997), 153 D. L. R. (4th), 193.

124. Richard H. Bartlett, *The Content Of Aboriginal Title And Equality Before The Law,* 61 Sask. L. Rev. 377, 384 (1999).

125. *Delgamuukw,* supra note 123, at 4.

126. *Delgamuukw,* supra note 123, at 4.

127. *Delgamuukw,* supra note 123, at 6.

128. *Mabo v. Queensland* (No. 2) (1992), 175 CLR 1.

129. Ibid., 175 CLR 88.

130. Prior to *Mabo* (2), the Aboriginal Land Rights (Northern Territory) Act 1976 offered a form of freehold title for indigenous communities and—until 1997—even demanded indigenous consent in mining (No. 191 of 1976).

131. See *Cape York Peninsular Heads of Agreement,* 1 (3) Australian Indigenous Law Reporter (1996), 446–48.

132. See, e.g., Gary D. Meyers and Simone C. Mueller, "An Overview of Indigenous Land (and Resource) Use Agreements," in The National Native Title Tribunal, The Way Forward: Collaboration and Cooperation 'In Country,' Proceedings of the Indigenous Land Use Agreements Conference (26–29 September 1995, Darwin, NT, Australia), Gary D. Meyers (ed.), 2d edition, Perth, 1996.

133. Mick Dodson, supra note 122, at 19.

134. Indigenous Peoples Rights Act, Philippine Republic Act No. 8371.

135. Ibid., at Section 4.

136. Ibid., at Section 3(a).

137. Ibid., at Sections 7 and 17.

138. Ibid., at Section 16.

Selected Paragraphs of the Judgment of the Inter-American Court of Human Rights in the case of

THE MAYAGNA (SUMO) INDIGENOUS COMMUNITY OF AWAS TINGNI

v.

THE REPUBLIC OF NICARAGUA

Issued 31 August 2001

(Editors' note: As Linking Human Rights and the Environment *went to press, the Inter-American Court on Human Rights passed judgment on the Awas Tingni Case, in favor of the Awas Tingni Community, a landmark decision for indigenous rights, collective property rights, as well as specific human rights centered on environmental concerns. We have included excerpts from the sentence, translated unofficially by the Indian Law Resource Center.)*

Reasoning of the Court,

106. Article 25 of the Convention states:

> 1. Everyone has the right to simple and prompt recourse, or any other effective recourse, to a competent court or tribunal for protection against acts that violate his fundamental rights recognized by the constitution or laws of the state concerned or by this Convention, even though such violation may have been committed by persons acting in the course of their official duties.
> 2. The States Parties undertake:
>
>   a. to ensure that any person claiming such remedy shall have his rights determined by the competent authority provided for by the legal system of the state;
>   b. to develop the possibilities of judicial remedy; and
>   c. to ensure that the competent authorities shall enforce such remedies when granted.

107. Article 1(1) of the Convention establishes that:

> The States Parties to this Convention undertake to respect the rights and freedoms recognized herein and to ensure to all persons subject to their jurisdiction the free and full exercise of those rights and freedoms, without any discrimination for reasons of race, color, sex, language, religion, political or other opinion, national or social origin, economic status, birth, or any other social condition.

108. In turn, article 2 of the Convention determines that:

> Where the exercise of any of the rights or freedoms referred to in Article 1 is not already ensured by legislative or other provisions, the States Parties un-

dertake to adopt, in accordance with their constitutional processes and the provisions of this Convention, such legislative or other measures as may be necessary to give effect to those rights or freedoms.

109. The Commission alleges, as a fundamental point, the lack of recognition by Nicaragua of the rights of the Awas Tingni Community, and more concretely, the inefficiency of the procedures established in the legislation to make those rights of indigenous communities effective as well as the lack of demarcation of the lands in the Community's possession. The Commission adds that, despite the Community's numerous efforts, it still has not obtained State recognition of its communal property and, moreover, has been detrimentally affected by the logging concession granted to a company named SOLCARSA on the lands it occupies.

110. In turn, the State alleges, basically, that the Community's intentions are disproportionate, given that the lands it possesses are not its ancestral lands, that it aspires to receive title to lands which are also claimed by other indigenous communities of the Nicaraguan Atlantic Coast, and that it has never formally requested title before the competent authorities. Also, Nicaragua asserts that a legal regime exists to regulate the titling procedure of indigenous communities under the competence of the Nicaraguan Agrarian Reform Institute (INRA). In respect of the logging concession granted to SOLCARSA, the State asserts that Awas Tingni suffered no harm because the concession was not implemented and was declared unconstitutional.

111. The Court has indicated that article 25 of the Convention has established in broad terms:

> the obligation of the States to offer, to all persons subject to their jurisdiction, an effective judicial remedy against acts which violate their fundamental rights. Additionally, the Court stipulates that the guarantee of an effective judicial remedy as set forth in the State's law must apply not only with respect to those rights contained in the Convention, but also to those recognized by that State's Constitution or law.

112. Likewise, the Court has reiterated that the right of all persons to a simple and rapid remedy or to whatever other effective remedy before the competent judges and tribunals which protect that person against acts which violate their fundamental rights "constitutes one of the basic pillars, not only of the American Convention, but also of the Rule of Law in a democratic society as intended by the Convention."

113. The Court has also indicated that:

> the inexistence of an effective remedy against violations of the rights recognized by the Convention constitutes a transgression of the Convention by the State Party in which the violation would be capable of repetition. Thus, it should be emphasized that, in order for a remedy to exist, it is not enough that it be provided for in the Constitution, the law, or that it be formally allowable, it must also be the ideal remedy to establish whether a human rights violation has been suffered and provide what is necessary to remedy that violation.

114. This Tribunal has affirmed, likewise, that in order for a State to comply with that provided for in the article cited above it is not enough that remedies exist formally, they must also be effective.

115. In this case, the analysis of article 25 of the Convention should be made from two perspectives. First, whether there exists a procedure for titling of lands with all the necessary characteristics mentioned above should be analyzed, and secondly, it should be established whether those actions for redress of a constitutional right, or *amparo* actions, brought by members of the Community were resolved in accordance with article 25.

a) Existence of a procedure for the titling and demarcation of indigenous lands:

116. Article 5 of the Political Constitution of Nicaragua establishes that:

> Liberty, justice, respect for the dignity of the human being, political, social and ethnic pluralism, recognition of the distinct forms of property, free international cooperation and respect for free self-determination are principles of the Nicaraguan nation.
>
> The State recognizes the existence of indigenous peoples, that they enjoy rights, responsibilities and guarantees enshrined in the Constitution, especially those regarding the right to maintain, develop their identity and culture, have their own forms of social organization and administer their local issues, as well as maintain communal forms of ownership of their lands and enjoy the use of and benefit from them, all in accordance with the law. For the communities of the Atlantic Coast, the Autonomous regime is established in the [. . .] Constitution.
>
> The different forms of property: public, private, associative, cooperative and communitarian must be guaranteed and stimulated without discrimination in order to produce wealth, and all those within their free functioning must perform a social function.

117. In addition, article 89 of that Constitution declares that:

> The Communities of the Atlantic Coast are an indivisible part of the Nicaraguan people and as such enjoy the same rights and have the same obligations.
>
> The Communities of the Atlantic Coast have the right to preserve and develop their cultural identity in the national unity; conduct themselves under their own forms of social organization and administer their local issues in accordance with their traditions.
>
> The State recognizes the communal forms of property of the territories of the Atlantic Coast Community. It likewise recognizes their use and enjoyment of the waters and forests of their communal lands.

118. In turn, article 180 of the mentioned Constitution indicates that:

> The Communities of the Atlantic Coast have the right to live and develop under the forms of social organization inherent to their historical and cultural traditions.

> The State guarantees these communities the possession of their natural resources, the effectiveness of their communal forms of property and the free election of their authorities and representatives.
>
> Likewise, the State guarantees the preservation of their cultures and languages, religions and customs.

119. Law No. 28, published October 30, 1987 in the The Gazette No. 238, Official Daily of the Republic of Nicaragua, incorporates the Statute of Autonomy of the Regions of the Nicaraguan Atlantic Coast. With respect to that incorporation, it establishes that:

> *Art. 4.* The Regions which the Communities of the Atlantic Coast inhabit, enjoy, within the unity of the Nicaraguan State, a Regime of Autonomy which guarantees them the effective exercise of their historic and other rights, enshrined in the Political Constitution.
>
> *Art. 9.* In the rational exploitation of mining, forest, fishing and other natural resources of the Autonomous Regions, the property rights over communal lands will be recognized, and inhabitants of the region should benefit from it in just proportion through agreements between the regional and central governments.

120. Decree No. 16–96 of August 23, 1996, referring to the creation of the National Commission for the Demarcation of Indigenous Community Lands of the Atlantic Coast determines that "the State recognizes the communal forms of property of the lands of the Communities in the Atlantic Coast," and that "it is necessary to establish an appropriate administrative authority to initiate the demarcation process of the traditional lands of the indigenous communities." To that end, the decree assigns to that national commission, among other functions, that of identifying the lands that the different indigenous communities have traditionally occupied; developing a process of geographic analysis which determines the communal and State areas; and, create a demarcation project and arrange for the financing of that project.

121. In addition, Law No. 14 published on January 13, 1986, in The Gazette No. 8, Official Daily of the Republic of Nicaragua, called "Reform of the Law of Agrarian Reform," establishes in article 31 that:

> The State will arrange for the necessary lands of the Miskito, Sumo, Rama, and other ethnic communities of the Atlantic coast region of Nicaragua, with the objective of raising their standard of living and contributing to the social and economic development of the [N]ation.

122. Based on the above, the Court considers it evident that regulations recognizing and protecting communal indigenous property exist in Nicaragua.

123. However, it would seem that the procedure for titling of lands occupied by indigenous groups is not clearly incorporated into Nicaraguan legislation. According to the State, the legal framework leading to the process of titling of the in-

digenous communities in the country is that established in Law No. 14, "Reform of the Law of Agrarian Reform," and that such requests should be brought before the Nicaraguan Agrarian Reform Institute (INRA). Law No. 14 establishes the procedures for guaranteeing land ownership to all who work the land productively and efficiently, after stipulating that the following classifications of lands can be "affected" by the agrarian reform: abandoned, idle, deficiently exploited, rented or ceded in any other way; lands not being worked directly by their owners but instead by sharecroppers, settlers, revocable bailees, or other forms of peasant exploitation; and, the lands being worked by cooperatives or peasants organized under whatever other form of association. Nonetheless, the Court finds that Law No. 14 does not establish a specific procedure for the demarcation and titling of the lands occupied by indigenous communities, taking into account their particular characteristics.

124. Also emerging from the remaining evidence in this case is the fact that the State has no specific procedure for the titling of indigenous communal land. Various witnesses and experts (Marco Antonio Centeno Caffarena, Galio Claudio Enrique Gurdián Gurdián, Brooklyn Rivera Bryan, Charles Rice Hale, Lottie Marie Cunningham de Aguirre, Roque de Jesús Roldán Ortega) that appeared before the Court in the public hearing on the merits of this case, showed that in Nicaragua there is a general lack of knowledge about the issue, an uncertainty of what should be done, and to whom a request for demarcation and title should be addressed.

125. Additionally, the document of March 1998, entitled "General Diagnostic Study on Land Tenure in Atlantic Coast Indigenous Communities," performed by the *Central American and Caribbean Research Council*, and introduced by the State in this case, recognizes "[. . .] the lack of any legislation that assigns to the INRA the specific authority to title indigenous communal lands" and the document points out the possibility that "legal ambiguities may have [. . .] contributed to the marked slowness of INRA's response to indigenous requests for communal title." That diagnostic study adds that:

> [. . .] there is an incompatibility between the specific Agrarian Reform laws with respect to indigenous land and the country's legal infrastructure. That problem implies legal and conceptual confusion, and contributes to the political inefficiency of the institutions charged with resolving this issue.
> [. . .] in Nicaragua the problem is that there are no laws permitting the concretization of constitutional principles, or [that] when the laws do exist (as in the Law of Autonomy) there has not been sufficient political will to achieve their implementation.
> [. . .] beyond the relationship between national and communal land, the very concept of indigenous communal land lacks a clear definition.

126. Further, it is proved that since 1990 no lands have been titled for indigenous communities.

127. For the reasons stated, this Court holds that in Nicaragua there is no effective procedure to delimit, demarcate and title its indigenous communal lands.

.

.

.

131. With respect to a regime of simple, rapid, and effective remedies as contemplated in article 25 of the Convention, this Court has held that the procedural mechanism of the *amparo* unites the characteristics necessary for the effective protection of fundamental rights, that is, it is simple and brief. In the Nicaraguan context, in accordance with the procedure established for *amparo* actions in Law No. 49 published in The Gazette No. 241 of 1988, called "Law of *Amparo*," this action should be resolved within 45 days.

132. In the instant case, the first *amparo* action was brought before the Matagalpa Appeals Tribunal on September 11, 1995, and ruled on by judicial decision on September 19, 1995, eight days later. Because the processing of that action was denied, the Community's representative brought another action under the *de facto* procedure on September 21, 1995, before the Supreme Court of Justice, as stipulated by article 25 of the Law of *Amparo*. On February 27, 1996, the Supreme Court of Justice dismissed that action. The Inter-American Court makes the observation that the first of the judicial orders mentioned was issued in a timely manner. However, in the processing of the action brought under the *de facto* procedure, one year five months and ten days passed before this latter action was ruled on by the Supreme Court of Justice.

133. The second *amparo* action was brought before the Civil Division of the Appeals Tribunal of the Sixth Region of Matagalpa on November 7, 1997, admitted by the tribunal on November 12, 1997, and the Constitutional Division of the Supreme Court of Justice issued its ruling on October 14, 1997. Eleven months and seven days passed before the ruling on that action.

134. Because of this Court's established criteria in this area of the law and in consideration of the impact of timeliness in judicial proceedings, this Court deems that the *amparo* proceedings brought before the various tribunals in this case did not observe the timeliness principle as set forth in the American Convention. According to the standards of this Tribunal, *amparo* actions are illusory and ineffective if a ruling is subject to unjustifiable delay.

135. Also, the Court has already stated that article 24 of the Convention is intimately connected with the general obligation of article 1(1) of the Convention, which attributes functions of protection to the domestic law of the States Parties, from which it can be inferred that the State has a responsibility both to design and normatively set forth an efficient remedy, as well as to assure the due application of that remedy by its judicial authorities.

136. To that end, this Tribunal has expressed that:

the general duty of article 2 of the American Convention implies the adoption of measures in two respects. First, the suppression of whatever norms and practices that bring about a violation of the guarantees envisioned in the Convention. Second, the promotion of norms and the development of practices that lead to the effective observance of those guarantees.

137. As has been indicated, in this case Nicaragua has not adopted adequate measures in its domestic law permitting the delimitation, demarcation, and titling of the lands of indigenous communities and did not rule in a timely manner on the *amparo* actions brought by members of the Awas Tingni Community.

138. The Court holds that it is necessary to render effective the rights recognized in the Political Constitution and Nicaraguan legislation, in accordance with the American Convention. Consequently, the State must adopt in its domestic law, in accordance with article 2 of the American Convention, the legislative, administrative and, whatever other measures necessary to create an effective mechanism for delimitation, demarcation, and titling of the property of the members of the Mayagna Community of Awas Tingni, in accordance with their customary law, values, uses and customs.

139. For these reasons, the Court concludes that the State violated article 25 of the American Convention, to the detriment of the members of the Mayagna (Sumo) Community of Awas Tingni, in conjunction with articles 1(1) and 2 of the Convention.

.

.

.

Reasoning of the Court,

142. Article 21 of the American Convention establishes that:

1. Everyone has the right to the use and enjoyment of his property. The law may subordinate such use and enjoyment to the interest of society.
2. No one shall be deprived of his property except upon payment of just compensation, for reasons of public utility or social interest, and in the cases and according to the forms established by law.
3. Usury and any other form of exploitation of man by man shall be prohibited by law.

143. Article 21 of the American Convention recognizes the right to private property. In this respect it establishes:

a. that "everyone has the right to the use and enjoyment of his property";
b. that such use and enjoyment may be subordinated, by decree of law, to the "interest of society";

c. that a person may be deprived of his property for reasons of "public utility or social interest, and in the cases and according to the forms established by law"; and

d. that such deprivation of property will be permitted only upon payment of just compensation.

144. "Property" can be defined as those material goods capable of being acquired, as well as all rights that can be deemed to make up the assets of a person; this concept encompasses all movable and immovable goods, tangible and intangible goods as well as any other intangible object to which a value can be assigned.

145. During the study and deliberation of the preparatory work for the American Convention on Human Rights, the phrase "everyone has the right to *private property,* but the law may subordinate such use and enjoyment to the interest of society" was replaced by that of "everyone has the right to the *use and enjoyment* of his property. The law may subordinate such use and enjoyment to the interest of society." That is, it was deemed more appropriate to make reference to the use and enjoyment of property in place of "private property."

146. The terms of an international human rights treaty have autonomous meaning, such that they may not be limited by the meaning attributed to them under domestic law. Also, international human rights treaties are living instruments, the interpretation of which should be adapted to changes over time, and, in particular, to present-day conditions.

147. To that end, article 29(b) of the Convention establishes that no provision can be interpreted by "restricting the enjoyment or exercise of any right or freedom recognized by virtue of the laws of any State Party or by virtue of another convention to which one of the said states is a party."

148. Through an evolutional interpretation of the international instruments for the protection of human rights, taking into account the applicable norms of interpretation and, in conformity with article 29(b) of the Convention—which prohibits a restrictive interpretation of those rights—, this Court deems that article 21 of the Convention protects the right to property in the sense that it comprises, among other things, the rights of members of indigenous communities within the framework of communal possession, a form of property also recognized by Nicaragua's Political Constitution.

149. Given the characteristics of the instant case, it is necessary to understand the concept of property in indigenous communities. Among indigenous communities, there is a communitarian tradition as demonstrated by their communal form of collective ownership of their lands, in the sense that ownership is not centered in the individual but rather in the group and in the community. By virtue of the fact of their very existence, indigenous communities have the right to live freely on their own territories; the close relationship that the communities have with the land must be recognized and understood as a foundation for their cultures, spiritual life, cultural integrity and economic survival. For indigenous communities, the relationship with the land is not merely one of possession and production, but

also a material and spiritual element that they should fully enjoy, as well as a means through which to preserve their cultural heritage and pass it on to future generations.

150. In respect of this, Law number 28, published October 30, 1987 in The Gazette No. 238, Official Daily of the Republic of Nicaragua, which incorporates the Statute of Autonomy of the Regions of the Nicaraguan Atlantic Coast, declares in article 36 that:

> Communal property is comprised of the land, water, and forest which have traditionally belonged to the Communities of the Atlantic Coast, and they are subject to the following provisions:
>
> 1. Communal lands are inalienable; they cannot be gifted, sold, seized, or encumbered, and are imprescriptable.
> 2. The Communities' inhabitants have the right to work parcels on the communal property and to the usufructory rights of the resources generated by that work.

151. The customary law of indigenous peoples should especially be taken into account because of the effects that flow from it. As a product of custom, possession of land should suffice to entitle indigenous communities without title to their land to obtain official recognition and registration of their rights of ownership.

152. As already mentioned, Nicaragua recognizes communal property of indigenous peoples, but it has not established the specific procedure for putting into practice that recognition, and hence there has been no issuance of titles of this type since 1990. Additionally, in the instant case, the State has not opposed the Awas Tingni Community's proposition that it should be declared a proprietor, although there is dispute as to the size of area of that claim.

153. The Court deems that, consistent with the terms of article 5 of the Political Constitution of Nicaragua, the members of the Awas Tingni Community have a communal property right over the lands they currently inhabit, without prejudice to the rights of the neighboring indigenous communities. However, the Court emphasizes that the limits of the territory over which that property right exists have not been effectively delimited and demarcated by the State. This situation has created a climate of permanent uncertainty among the members of the Awas Tingni Community inasmuch as they do not know with certainty the geographic extension of their right of communal property, and consequently they do not know up to what point they may freely use and enjoy the corresponding resources. In this context, the Court considers that the members of the Awas Tingni Community have the right that the State,

> a. delimit, demarcate, and title the territory of the Community's property; and
> b. refrain, until this official delimitation, demarcation and titling is performed, from acts which could cause agents of the State, or third parties acting with its acquiescence or tolerance, to affect the existence, value, use, or enjoyment of the resources located in the geographic area in which the Community members live and carry out their activities.

Because of the reasons stated, and keeping in mind the criterion adopted by the Court in its application of article 29(b) of the Convention (*supra*, para. 148), the Court finds that, in light of article 21 of the Convention, the State has violated the right of the members of the Awas Tingni Mayagna Community to the use and enjoyment of their property, by not delimiting and demarcating their communal property, and by authorizing concessions to third parties for the exploitation of the land and natural resources in an area that, wholly or partially, corresponds to the lands that should be delimited, demarcated, and titled in their favor.

154. In addition, it must be remembered that, as established by this Tribunal, and grounded in article 1(1) of the American Convention, the State is obligated to respect the rights and liberties recognized in the Convention and organize its public administrative bodies to guarantee the persons under its jurisdiction the free and full exercise of their human rights. According to the rules of international State responsibility as applicable to International Human Rights Law, the act or omission of any public authority, regardless of its ranking within the hierarchy of the domestic system, constitutes an act imputable to the State, compromising its responsibility in the terms envisioned by the American Convention.

155. For the above reasons, the Court concludes that the State violated article 21 of the American Convention, to the detriment of the members of the Mayagna (Sumo) Community of Awas Tingni, in connection with articles 1(1) and 2 of the Convention.

About the Contributors

Ignacio J. Alvarez is a graduate of the Andres Bello Catholic University of Venezuela and has a masters in international law and human rights from the American University in Washington, DC. He served as Special Rapporteur on Freedom of Expression for the Inter-American Commission on Human Rights from 2006 to 2008 and worked as an attorney of the IACHR for ten years. From 2008 to 2009 Ignacio served the Public Safety Department of the Organization of American States. He presently is an independent international consultant. He has published widely on human rights and international law.

S. James Anaya is Samuel M. Fegtly Professor of Law at the University of Arizona in Tucson. James previously served as a professor of law at the University of Iowa and was lead counsel among the group of attorneys that has represented the community of Awas Tingni in the proceedings described herein. Since 2008 James Anaya has served as UN Special Rapporteur on the Situation of Human Rights and Fundamental Freedoms of Indigenous Peoples.

Caroline Dommen brings long experience in both international trade and development policy and environmental policy to this position. She comes to QUNO from the NGO 3D, where she was founder and director. Caroline holds a masters in Law and Development from London University and is a member of several professional bodies, including the International Advisory Network of the Business & Human Rights Resource Centre, the IUCN–World Conservation Union Commission on Environmental Law, and the Sustainable Development Committee of the International Law Association. Caroline will be helping to develop and shape this program in line with the changing global economic and environmental circumstances.

Alexandre Kiss (In Memory) was born in Budapest in 1925 and had been a resident of France since 1947. He was a distinguished jurist, served as Director of Research Emeritus at the French National Center for Scientific Research, and was Professor of Law at the University Robert Schuman. He specialized in international law and contributed extensively to the evolution of the human rights and environment linkage. Professor Kiss passed away in 2007 at the age of 81.

Owen Lynch is a fellow at the Rights and Resources Initiative (RRI) in Washington, DC. He served as senior attorney and managing director of the Law and Communities and Human Rights and Environment programs at the Center for International Environmental Law (CIEL) in Washington, DC, and as a Senior Associate at the World Resources Institute. Owen has been actively engaged for three decades in fostering public interest law careers in Asia, Africa, and the Pacific, with a substantive focus on environmental justice and sustainable development. His area of expertise is on community-based property rights and their legal recognition in national and international law. Owen earned a BA cum laude from St. Johns University (Minnesota) in 1975, a JD from the Catholic University of America in 1980, and Master of Laws and Doctor of Laws degrees with honors from Yale University in 1985 and 1992.

Romina Picolotti is the founder of the Center for Human Rights and Environment (CEDHA), which is based in Argentina, where she promotes access to justice for victims of environmental degradation. Romina served as Secretary of Environment of Argentina from 2006 to 2008, focusing national environmental policy on control, compliance, and normative strengthening. In 2006 she won the prestigious Sophie Prize, given for unique and innovative global contributions to sustainable development, and particularly for her work at linking human rights and the environment. As Environment Secretary she led global negotiations under the Montreal Protocol, securing an agreement to eliminating climate-contaminating HCFCs, for which she won EPA's 2008 Climate Protection Award. E-mail: rpicolotti@gmail.com.

Claudia Saladin is Senior Program Officer for the Sustainable Commerce Program at the World Wildlife Fund in Washington, DC. The views expressed in this essay are solely of the author and do not necessarily reflect those of the World Wildlife Fund.

Michael G. Shaw is a retired civil rights and environmental law attorney. Before retiring, Michael was an attorney at the Washington, DC, law firm of Terris, Pravlik & Millian, LLP, which concentrates on public interest environmental law. He is a magna cum laude graduate of American University–Washington College of Law, in Washington, DC, where he was on the staff of the *International Law Review*. After graduation, he served as a U.S. federal judicial law clerk.

Dinah Shelton is Manatt/Ahn Professor of International Law at George Washington University. She directed the doctoral program in International Human Rights Law at the University of Notre Dame and has taught at several leading academic institutions, including the University of California–Berkeley, Stanford University, the University of Paris, and the University of Strasbourg in France. She has contributed extensively to the evolution of the human rights and environment linkage and has received numerous distinctions for her academic publications on both human rights and environmental law, including the Elisabeth Haub Prize for Environmental Law in 2006. She serves as Commissioner to the Inter-American Commission on Human Rights.

Jorge Daniel Taillant is co-founder of the Center for Human Rights and Environment (CEDHA), which is based in Argentina, where he promotes access to justice for victims of environmental degradation. Daniel has worked for numerous international organizations, including the UN, World Bank, OAS, and European Union, among others. He has contributed extensively to policy promotion in the global evolution of human rights and the environment. His work focuses on the introduction of human rights and sustainability issues to corporate accountability. In 2007, because of his global advocacy to introduce human rights to sustainable development, CEDHA won the Sierra Club's distinguished international Earth Care Award.

Annecoos Wiersema specializes in international law, international environmental law, and environmental and natural resources law. Annecoos is Associate Professor at the Sturm College of Law, University of Denver. Before joining the faculty at the Sturm College of Law, Professor Wiersema was Assistant Professor at the Michael E. Moritz College of Law, Ohio State University, and worked in the Denver office of Arnold and Porter LLP as a litigation associate. She was the George W. Foley, Jr., Fellow in Environmental Law at Harvard Law School and a Visiting Scholar at the International Monetary Fund (IMF). Professor Wiersema received her LLB from the London School of Economics in 1998 and her SJD in International and Environmental Law from Harvard Law School in 2004. Her research focuses on how we can develop legal institutions both nationally and internationally that can effectively protect species and ecosystems in the face of ecological complexity and scientific uncertainty.

About the Center for Human Rights and Environment (CEDHA)

The Center for Human Rights and Environment (CEDHA), located in Córdoba, Argentina, is a non-profit organization promoting sustainable development that defends victims of environmental degradation and strives for a more harmonious relationship between the environment and people. In 2006, CEDHA's founder Romina Picolotti won the prestigious Sophie Prize given to one global advocate for unique and innovative contributions to sustainable development, precisely for CEDHA's work on linking human rights and the environment. In 2007, CEDHA won the Sierra Club's most distinguished international Earth Care Award for its promotion of greater corporate accountability linked to human rights and sustainable development.

Contact information: cedha@cedha.org.ar or www.cedha.org.ar

Index

CPSIA information can be obtained at www.ICGtesting.com
Printed in the USA
238261LV00003B/5/P